THE TRIALS OF ABU GHRAIB

THE TRIALS OF ABU GHRAIB

AN EXPERT WITNESS ACCOUNT OF SHAME AND HONOR

S. G. Mestrovic

Paradigm Publishers
Boulder • London

Copyright © 2007 by Paradigm Publishers

Published in the United States by Paradigm Publishers, 3360 Mitchell Lane, Suite E, Boulder, Colorado 80301 USA.

Paradigm Publishers is the trade name of Birkenkamp & Company, LLC, Dean Birkenkamp, President and Publisher.

Library of Congress Cataloging-in-Publication Data

Mestrovic, Stjepan Gabriel.
  The trials of Abu Ghraib : an expert witness account of shame and honor / S.G. Mestrovic.
     p. cm.
  Includes bibliographical references and index.
  ISBN-13: 978-1-59451-334-3 (hardcover : alk. paper)
  ISBN-10: 1-59451-334-1 (hardcover : alk. paper)
1. Trials (Military offenses)—United States.   2. Courts-martial and courts of inquiry—United States.   3. Abu Ghraib Prison.   4. Prisoners of war—Abuse of—Iraq.   5. Iraq War, 2003—Prisoners and prisons.   6. United States—Armed Forces—Iraq.   I. Title.
  KF7641.M47 2007
  343.73'0143--dc22

                                                                    2006030322

Printed and bound in the United States of America on acid-free paper that meets the standards of the American National Standard for Permanence of Paper for Printed Library Materials.

Designed and Typeset by Straight Creek Bookmakers.

11 10 09 08 07   1 2 3 4 5

To my daughters

CONTENTS

ABBREVIATIONS

ACLU	America Civil Liberties Union
AMA	American Medical Association
Biscuits	Behavioral Science Consultation Teams
BG	Brigadier General
CIA	Central Intelligence Agency
CID	Criminal Investigation Command
CENTCOM	United States Central Command
CJTF-7	Combined Joint Task Force 7
COL	Colonel
CPL	Corporal
CPT	Captain
FM	*Field Manual*
FOB	Forward Operating Base
Gitmo	Guantanamo Bay, Cuba
ICRC	International Committee of the Red Cross
ICRP	Theater Interrogation and Counter-Resistance Policies

IR	Internment/Resettlement
JAG	Judge Advocate General's Office
JIDC	Joint Interrogation and Detention Center
LG	Lieutenant General
LTC	Lieutenant Colonel
MAJ	Major
MG	Major General
MI	Military Intelligence
MP	Military Police
MRE	Meals Ready to Eat
NCO	Non-commissioned officer
OGA	Other Government Agencies
PFC	Private First Class
PT	Physical Training
PTSD	Posttraumatic stress disorder
PUC	Persons Under Control
SGT	Sergeant
SPC	Specialist
SSG	Staff Sergeant
UCMJ	Uniform Code of Military Justice

PREFACE AND ACKNOWLEDGMENTS

I wrote this book based on my experiences as an expert witness in sociology for the defense in the Abu Ghraib courts-martial of Javal Davis, Sabrina Harman, and Lynndie England. It quickly became obvious that these courts-martial were about more than these specific soldiers. Based on chance circumstances and my background and training in clinical psychology, I served simultaneously as an expert witness in psychology in that I was asked to give my professional opinion on the psychiatric reports and psychological factors pertaining to the abuse at Abu Ghraib. Unexpectedly, the prosecutor asked for my professional opinion on a psychiatric report while I was on the witness stand, and it turned out that I was qualified to give it—so, with the permission of the judge, I did.

Indeed, in this book I blend perspectives from sociology and psychology into something like a self-help book on public policy regarding Abu Ghraib and its consequences. As an academic, I am used to reading and writing books that merely analyze social problems but do not propose solutions. And I am used to artificial turf barriers between sociology and psychology, even though the two disciplines were practically indistinguishable at birth. It can be depressing to read such books, because one feels helpless in fixing the problems that are uncovered.

These stiff, academic barriers did not matter at all in the courtroom at Fort Hood. The judge, prosecution, and defense attorneys were invoking ideas and emotions that transcended the limits of the social sciences. Why did the soldiers obey unlawful orders? That is a question for psychologists. How did the poisoned social climate at Abu Ghraib contribute to the abuse? That is a question for sociologists. Why were officers not put on trial? Who established the unlawful policies? How could soldiers recognize an unlawful order? How can such abuse be prevented in the future?

These and other questions are for anyone who engages emotionally with the reality of what happened at Abu Ghraib.

In this book, I first analyze and then propose ways of fixing the "poisoned atmosphere" that set the stage for the abuse along the lines that a therapist would follow in trying to fix a dysfunctional relationship. It occurred to me, while sitting in the courtroom at Fort Hood, that the international, grand dimensions of the unfolding drama echoed the everyday realities of abuse in dysfunctional families. What both sorts of abuse have in common are shouting instead of talking, control instead of establishing rapport, violence instead of reasonable action, humiliation instead of respect—and, in general, a negative course that leads to unfavorable consequences instead of the desired course that leads to peace, stability, and respect.

It seems that the root causes of domestic as well as international abuse are very similar: an attitude of being above the law, arbitrary and capricious policies, chronic chaos, lack of emotional support and validation, and so on. It seems that the ways to fix dysfunctional relationships as well as groups are also similar: respect for fixed moral boundaries, consistency, stability, and empathy, among other ingredients.

Although this book deals with sensitive and emotionally disturbing matters—torture, abuse, sadism, abandonment, among others—I approach the subject matter through the lens of a social scientist, as a psychologist as well as a sociologist. This approach has several consequences. First, I regard the accused soldiers as human persons and not as caricatured "rotten apples." Like most other people, I deplore the abuse, but I try to understand the circumstances and reasons that led specific individuals to condone or commit abuse. Second, I focus on social climates, atmospheres, and environments and not the individual alone. Third, I approach laws as human constructions that are used in various ways and not as inherent absolutes. Thus, blame has been shifted onto low-ranking soldiers when, according to the doctrine of command responsibility, it could have been shifted onto high-ranking officers and civilian officials. The Geneva Conventions exist on paper and were supposed to apply in Iraq, but in practice they were not applied. Fourth, I focus on the long-term consequences of policies and behaviors for the United States and its military. From this perspective, I argue that no matter what rationalizations one uses to justify the policies that led to Abu Ghraib, the consequences have been disastrous: shame, dishonor, distrust, and a setback for democratization. Perhaps the actual, physical compound that is Abu Ghraib will be razed to the ground. But the social, symbolic consequences of the abuse at Abu Ghraib will linger, and efforts must be made to repair the damage that was done to soldiers and prisoners, as well as to the U.S. Army and other social institutions.

Let me state that I respect the military judge, COL James Pohl, even though I disagree with some of his decisions. He exhibited a sense of humor, he wanted straight answers, and he maintained an orderly courtroom despite intense emotions expressed by both sides. Similarly, I hold the prosecutor, CPT Christopher Graveline, in high esteem for his skills as a lawyer. Again, my criticisms of some of the things he said in the courtroom do not detract from this sense of respect. I share none of the snobbery that some journalists exhibited for all persons and things Texan. Similarly, my criticisms of some government policies that I believe led to the abuse at Abu Ghraib are intended to be constructive and in the spirit of free inquiry. I make it clear in this book, as I did in the courtroom, that I respect and for the most part agree with the authors of the various government reports. My main point of disagreement is the shifting of all of the blame onto low-ranking soldiers.

I am grateful to the soldiers and officers—some of whom are named in this book, and some of whom will remain anonymous—for sharing with me their versions of what happened at Abu Ghraib and at the courts-martial at Fort Hood. I believe that the honesty and sense of honor of the soldiers and officers who testified shine through my account of their testimony in chapters 4, 5, and 6. The three legal teams with whom I worked were thoroughly professional and helpful to me in my role as an expert witness. I am grateful to the U.S. Army for providing me with authenticated and unclassified documents through the various defense teams. I would also like to thank the following persons for discussions pertaining to this book: Ryan Ashley Caldwell, Joe Feagin, Keith Kerr, Ronald Lorenzo, Henry Marshall, John McDermott, Reuben May, Chris Rojek, David Rosen, Chris Rumford, Richard Russell, Hiroko Tanaka, JoAnn Wypijewski, and Adam Zagorin. I am especially grateful to Cynthia Boyd.

The most important inspiration for the template of ideas that constitute the structure for this book comes from my mentor at Harvard University, David Riesman. In this book, I am applying his idea of an inner-directed, moral "gyroscope" to the fields of public policy and international relations. His treatment of the concept of shame in his book *The Lonely Crowd* guided me as I tried to make sense of the themes of honor and shame that emerged at the trials. It is important to keep in mind that the themes of honor and shame apply to both the soldiers and the prisoners at Abu Ghraib. The U.S. government reports as well as the International Committee of the Red Cross estimate that approximately 80 percent of the prisoners at Abu Ghraib "had been arrested by mistake."[1] The army was shamed by the photographs of the abuse—but the Iraqis were shamed as well. Mark Danner quotes a young Iraqi who explained this to him:

> For Fallujans it is a *shame* to have foreigners break down their doors. It is a *shame* for them to have foreigners stop and search their women. It is a *shame* for the foreigners to put a bag over their heads, to make a man lie on the ground with your shoe on his neck. This is a great *shame*, you understand? This is a great *shame* for the whole tribe.
>
>   It is the *duty* of that man, and of that tribe, to get revenge on this soldier—to kill that man. Their *duty* is to attack them, to *wash the shame*. The shame is a stain, a dirty thing; they have to *wash* it.[1]

The overall result is that a cycle of violence is established and compulsively repeated. Shame leads to a desire for revenge—on both sides. It is imperative that a sense of honor is established for both sides and that the cycle of escalating violence is broken.   I tried to approach the accused soldiers with the open-mindedness, curiosity, and willingness to understand all sides of an issue that Riesman exhibited in daily interactions.

Note

1. Mark Danner, *Torture and Truth: America, Abu Ghraib, and the War on Terror* (New York: New York Review of Books, 2004), 3; emphasis in original.

PROLOGUE: A FEW BAD APPLES?

I had no idea of the realities I would discover when I agreed to join the defense team for SGT Javal Davis, one of the accused soldiers in the Abu Ghraib drama. His attorney, Paul Bergrin, asked me to join in the fall of 2004, when we all thought the trial would be held in Baghdad, with all its dangers. In fact, the first three of the seven "rotten apples" were court-martialed in Baghdad, amid the constant danger of mortars and roadside explosives and away from much scrutiny. When the danger from insurgents became extreme, the army finally decided to move the remaining courts-martial to Fort Hood, Texas, which is where Javal was court-martialed in February 2005. Bergrin asked me to help because of my prior experience as an expert witness in sociology at the International War Crimes Tribunal in The Hague and my publications on war crimes that were committed in the 1990s in the Balkans. With the uncertainty of where Javal's court-martial would be held, waiting for approval to testify from both the military judge and the commanding general at Fort Hood, I barely had time to prepare.

But the first court-martial exposed me to the amazing revelations in the U.S. government reports and the more amazing revelation that the facts expressed in them were mostly kept out of the trial. The government reports (along with many other reports by human rights organizations as well as newspaper articles) connect the abuse at Abu Ghraib with the abuse at Afghanistan and Guantánamo.[1] But these two words, *Afghanistan* and *Guantánamo,* seemed to be taboo in the courtroom.

One part of the government reveals facts and indicts itself—through the reports. Another part of the government conceals facts that are in the reports and prosecutes low-ranking soldiers. One part of the government established policies that led to the abuse by weakening respect for the Geneva Conventions, and another part of the government prosecuted the lowest-ranking soldiers who had committed abuse. This is a complicated story that cannot be put into a neat and tidy legal, conceptual, or emotional box.

Immediately after Javal's court-martial, CPT Patsy Takemura, one of the attorneys for SPC Sabrina Harman, asked me to join her defense team, which was led by the well-known lawyer Frank Spinner. I was shocked when Harman showed me photographs from Abu Ghraib. I also realized that photographs that the government and information media have downplayed show the full spectrum of what happened at Abu Ghraib: women and children in prison, acts of kindness by the so-called rotten apples toward Iraqis, happy Iraqi children posing with Harman, the rotten apples acting like tourists, the squalid and filthy living quarters for soldiers and prisoners alike. In fact, I learned that many of the soldiers themselves lived in jail cells at Abu Ghraib.

During Harman's court-martial, I realized that the government was limiting the script to a few carefully chosen "incidents" and carefully chosen photographs at Abu Ghraib from the fall of 2003. During her trial in May 2005, I got to say a few more sentences about the connection to Afghanistan and Guantánamo as mitigating factors, because of Spinner's skill at arguing. The judge dismissed the jury while he argued with Spinner, so when the jury returned, they listened attentively and seemed mesmerized. They had that look that seemed to say, "So that's how these rotten apples learned those nasty techniques—from techniques that had migrated from Afghanistan and Guantánamo."

Then PFC Lynndie England's attorney, CPT Jonathan Crisp, asked me to join her team. It seemed to me that the various defense teams reasoned that sociology and I were one way that they could sneak a few sentences about Afghanistan and Guantánamo into the mitigation phases of the courts-martial, and they believed that I could withstand the prosecutor's cross-examination. During this trial, I learned that the abuse at Abu Ghraib had occurred in tandem with other abuse at U.S. military bases throughout Iraq. CPT Ian Fishback was supposed to testify for the defense at England's court-martial and was purportedly going to say that he had witnessed the stacking of Iraqi prisoners into human pyramids at Forward Operating Base (FOB) Mercury. The judge denied Fishback this opportunity to testify.

I learned many other things during my participation in this saga—from soldiers over lunch and dinner and during breaks; from journalists; from family members of the accused who sat next to me in the courtroom; from interaction with the prosecution teams; and from scores of people who were involved, up to and including military guards at the courthouse. There were many pages of sworn affidavits, most of which were never mentioned in court. And I learned a lot from the government reports, which are accessible to anyone who is interested in their unclassified form. Every time Human Rights Watch and other human rights groups document the extensive, pervasive, and widespread pattern of abuse from Guantánamo to Afghanistan and Iraq, I wonder why this obvious fact is treated as a sort of "open secret" of little consequence. This fact had been revealed already in government reports, starting with the Herrington report of December 2003, and it is here to stay—at least for historians in the future. But the connection of Abu Ghraib to widespread abuse elsewhere is one of those facts that is simultaneously erased from immediate consciousness even as it is being revealed. For some reason, the widespread nature of the abuse does not seem to really register in the discourse pertaining to Abu Ghraib. One has to connect the many facts into a coherent picture because, apparently, the facts do not speak for themselves.

The related story pertaining to the alleged massacre of Iraqi civilians committed by U.S. Marines in November 2005 is similarly disconnected from both Abu Ghraib and other abuse in the public discourse. Congressman John Murtha referred publicly to Haditha as another My Lai. But My Lai was a symbol of a pattern of search-and-destroy missions in Vietnam, not an isolated event.[2] Similarly, Abu Ghraib is a symbol of a pattern of abusing prisoners, not an isolated event. Moreover, the common strand that binds the symbols My Lai, Abu Ghraib, and Haditha together is incomplete adherence to the Geneva Conventions.

The real story of what happened at Abu Ghraib can be gleaned by piecing together the pieces of an intricate puzzle that involves the government reports, the photographs, sworn affidavits by officers and soldiers that were not mentioned or used in court, and the testimony in open court, among other sources of information. Abu Ghraib cannot be understood without understanding what happened at Guantánamo Bay and in Afghanistan, because of the "migration" of unlawful "techniques." Some portions of the puzzle are like the tips of icebergs whose mass is mostly hidden and secret: The top secret portions of the reports are still classified; of the sixteen thousand photos that were taken, fewer than two hundred have been leaked to the public; and the testimony in open court did not reveal the full extent of the reality found in the sworn written statements.

The whole truth of what happened at Abu Ghraib may never be known. However, it is possible to state clearly what is *not* true about the abuse at Abu Ghraib based on the information and evidence that are available:

- It is not true that the abuse at Abu Ghraib was confined to a small cohort of rotten apples. No matter how many new apples are added to the list of rotten apples, it is still not true that they were the architects of the abuse.

- It is not true that the abuse at Abu Ghraib was limited to the incidents of abuse prosecuted by the government—scores of other incidents of abuse were not prosecuted or mentioned.

- It is not true that the abuse was confined to Abu Ghraib—it involved other military units throughout Iraq and Afghanistan.[3]

- It is not true that the abuse in Iraq was confined to Iraq—there is a clear and widespread pattern of abuse in Iraq with similar abuse at Afghanistan and Guantánamo.

- It is not true that the army and the government did not know about the abuse at Abu Ghraib prior to the initial photographs that were discovered in the spring of 2004—the International Committee of the Red Cross had already informed the army of abuse in the fall of 2003 following its visits to Abu Ghraib on September 12 and October 21, 2003. The Herrington report already disclosed some of the abuse throughout Iraq as early as December 12, 2003.

- It is not true that officers were ignorant of the abuse—testimony revealed that officers questioned some of the abusive tactics from the moment they arrived at Abu Ghraib, but they were told by their superiors that it was the way military intelligence wanted things done.

- It is not true that the abuse stemmed exclusively from an improper understanding of "interrogation techniques"—the abuse was pervasive and occurred in showers, stairwells, hallways, storage containers, vehicles, and so on. In fact, soldiers could not make out the difference between "interrogation" and "detention."

- It is not true that the so-called rotten apples had morally corrupt characters. Psychiatric tests revealed that the ones analyzed at the trials I witnessed were not sadistic in temperament or character.

- It is not true that soldiers concocted the abuse on their own and ad hoc—similar, albeit "unauthorized" and "unofficial," techniques clearly "migrated," "circulated," and were "imported" from Guantánamo and Afghanistan. In fact, one of the major causes of the abuse seems to have been the attempt to "Gitmoize" Abu Ghraib. ("Gitmo" is a popular nickname for Guantánamo.)

- It is not true that all or even most of the blame for the abuse can be shifted onto a few bad apples—the orchard is contaminated, and the orchard keepers have escaped the sort of scrutiny that was leveled at low-ranking soldiers. Gitmoization was one major, clear source of the contamination. There may have been other sources.

I do *not* mean to imply that the U.S. Army or any other component of the U.S. military is composed of abusive individuals. On the contrary, my overall impression is that the army is composed of good people who take seriously the mandates of duty, honor, and country. However, because of directives, memorandums, and orders that lessened respect for the Geneva Conventions and other moral standards in the military and because of Gitmoization, ordinary, good soldiers and officers were swept up into a vortex of conflicting standards. As such, soldiers could no longer make out clearly the difference between right and wrong, common sense versus unlawful orders; and if they could, their morally correct hunches and decisions were invalidated by the poisoned social environment in which they worked. The social system needs to be fixed from the outside, because so far, it does not seem able to self-correct.

One of my strongest suggestions in this book for fixing the problem is to reassert the Geneva Conventions as a moral standard and incorporate them into U.S. military procedures. This may seem like an obvious first step to some and debatable to others. What is clear is that the U.S. government has undermined the Geneva Conventions over the course of the past several years. The Geneva Conventions were determined *not* to apply at Guantánamo Bay and in Afghanistan. Yet some of the unlawful procedures from Guantánamo and Afghanistan were applied in Iraq, where the Geneva Conventions did and do apply. The resulting confusion, chaos, and abuse were the inevitable result of these conflicting policies.

Two Competing Scripts

If it were a movie, the prosecution's script at Fort Hood might be called *A Few Bad Apples*. This script is contradicted by the government's own reports. It is fiction that requires "magical thinking" in order to be believed. Magic is the only explanation for the prosecution's version of reality in which various rotten apples at Abu Ghraib as well as in Afghanistan and elsewhere in Iraq happened to spontaneously mimic abusive techniques from Guantánamo Bay. The script's main premises were also contradicted by testimony. The military police (MP) at Abu Ghraib were following orders from military intelligence (MI). But whose orders was MI following? The government reports suggest that MI was following the unlawful, Guantánamo model of doing things. Thus, one part of the government presents a believable version of events in the reports it issued, and another part of the government presents an unbelievable, magical version of events during the courts-martial at Fort Hood.

Ironically, the reality of Abu Ghraib and its consequences—which transcend Abu Ghraib at every point, up to and including the ever-increasing insurgency in Iraq—most resembles the actual movie *A Few Good Men.* It *is* strange that reality can resemble the main outlines of a Hollywood film. In any case, the plot in the film revolves around two marines who are court-martialed for killing a fellow marine during a hazing incident that is dubbed "Code Red." I should add that even the ambiance, rapid-fire questioning, and dizzying speed of the trials at Fort Hood all reminded me of the details in this movie. In *A Few Good Men,* the prosecutor does his best to shift all the blame onto the two lowly marine soldiers and to protect the commanding officer. There is no written record of a Code Red, and all the officers deny its existence. At the end of the film, the commanding officer, played by Jack Nicholson, finally breaks down under cross-examination and admits that he ordered a Code Red. The mystery of how and why the soldiers did what they did is resolved. They are not exempt from moral responsibility for their crime, but their humanity is redeemed, because they really were following unlawful orders, and their commander was responsible for the unlawful order. Moreover, their crimes were not the result of magical thinking, as if they were good marines one day and morally corrupt marines the next.

The Gloves Are Coming Off, Gentlemen

Is there an equivalent to a Code Red in the real Abu Ghraib story? I believe that there is, and it centers on a compelling phrase: "The gloves are coming off, gentlemen." This directive was issued to MI in the summer of 2003, and abuse followed almost immediately. Of course, it would be difficult to prove the meaning of "the gloves are coming off" any more than one can prove the meaning of "Code Red" conclusively and in a way that would satisfy everyone. It is up to the reader to decide whether it is a coincidence that the Gitmoization of Abu Ghraib began in earnest following the "gloves are coming off" order, which was e-mailed from MI at Combined Joint Task Force 7 Headquarters as an "ALCON" (to all concerned). It reads, in part:

> Provide interrogation techniques "wish list" by 17 Aug 03.
> The gloves are coming off gentlemen regarding these detainees, Col Boltz has made it clear that we want these individuals broken.

There are more connections between the film *A Few Good Men* and the government script I have titled *A Few Bad Apples.* In both cases, all the blame has been shifted onto the lowest-ranking soldiers in the drama. The legions of officers in Iraq have mostly escaped scrutiny. According to Human Rights Watch, not a single officer has been prosecuted under the military's doctrine of command responsibility, which holds that officers knew or should have known of crimes committed in their units, and that either way, the officers are responsible.

It *cannot* be the case that low-ranking soldiers dreamed up the very orders and directives that were, in fact, issued by their superiors. It *cannot* be the case that all or most of the blame for the abuse at Abu Ghraib falls on the lowest-ranking soldiers. If that were true, then what is the role of the officer in the U.S. Army? The Schlesinger report also makes is clear that officers high in the chain of command in Iraq are culpable for the abuse at Abu Ghraib. While this report concludes that officers high in the chain of command are culpable for the abuse at Abu Ghraib, it makes no specific recommendations regarding their responsibility. The important point here is that what obviously cannot be true—that low-ranking soldiers are to bear all the blame for the abuse—is presented as true. It is magical thinking to suppose that low-ranking soldiers had that much power and that high-ranking officers are that exempt from accountability.

Defense attorneys, officers, and soldiers I met at Fort Hood shook their heads in disbelief when it came to this part of the discussion: how the top brass escaped responsibility and the lowest-ranking soldiers got blamed and punished. Some soldiers and officers said the military has always done things this way, including My Lai and the USS *Pueblo.* Several officers at Fort Hood told me that they found it dishonorable and against army tradition that officers would let their soldiers "hang in the wind" and evade their responsibility.

My strategy in this book is not to pursue the issue of command responsibility beyond noting that such a doctrine really exists, even if it is not applied. Soldiers and officers told me that in the army, commanders are responsible if their soldiers are arrested for intoxication or bounce a check. According to this doctrine, commanders are responsible also for the abuse committed by soldiers at Abu Ghraib and elsewhere. It is clear that regarding abuse at Abu Ghraib, the government is divided and does not speak with one voice. Outside the closed and controlled environment of the courtroom at Fort Hood, readers can form their own opinions based on a wider spectrum of facts and evidence than what was allowed inside the courtroom. Thus, I present the broad outlines of the real story behind the government's facade to the degree that one is able to do so under present circumstances.

The Cast of Characters

The government's script, which might be called *A Few Bad Apples,* forces one to accept the cumbersome metaphors that follow: there must be an *orchard,* and there must be *orchard keepers.* This script also forces one to choose the protagonists, antagonists, and main cast of characters. This division exposes further the contradictions in the government's position. The trials were really about defending the positive image of the U.S. Army against the seven rotten apples who are depicted as having brought shame and dishonor to the army. In his closing statements, the prosecutor made it clear that the trials were about army values that the rotten apples had sullied. The theme of army *honor* emerged as the most powerful focus in the trials. The trials were *not* about the Iraqi prisoners; *not* about violations of the Geneva Conventions; *not* about policies that emanated from the White House and trickled down the chain of command; *not* about the abuse that was committed (because most of the abuse was not admitted into testimony); and *not* about Gitmoization, which seems to be the primary source of the social toxins that poisoned Abu Ghraib. To the extent that these other themes were mentioned, the prosecution consistently linked them to the powerful emotions of honor and shame. Thus, the protagonists—who sought to restore the army's honor—include the judge, prosecutors, and prosecution witnesses.

But here is the curious thing: some of the prosecution witnesses included some of the rotten apples and would-be rotten apples who testified against fellow soldiers in exchange for immunity from prosecution. Shame and honor became blurred. Did the rotten apples or their civilian and military commanders bring shame to the army? The antagonists include the defense attorneys, defense witnesses, but also the authors of government reports that would have destroyed the government's script of the few bad apples. The antagonists were trying to put the army on trial. The defense teams tried to show that the soldiers were following orders—which is a duty in the army—that stemmed from unlawful *policies.* It is a twisted and contradictory script, with the government pitted against itself.

It is helpful to describe some of the main characters so that the reader may make sense of and relate to the many different people who come up in the government's script and this book:

Rotten Apples from the Military Police

- CPL Charles Graner—testified for the defense; sentenced to ten years
- SSG Ivan Frederick—testified for the prosecution; sentenced to eight and a half years
- SPC Jeremy Sivits—testified for the prosecution; sentenced to one year
- SPC Sabrina Harman—sentenced to three months
- PFC Lynndie England—sentenced to three years
- SGT Javal Davis—sentenced to six months
- SPC Meghan Ambuhl—testified for the defense; discharged

Additional Rotten Apples from Military Intelligence

- SPC Armin Cruz—testified for the prosecution; sentenced to one year
- SPC Roman Krol—testified for the prosecution; sentenced to ten months

Additional Rotten Apples Who Were Dog Handlers

- SGT Santos Cardona—sentenced to ninety days' hard labor
- SGT Michael Smith—sentenced to six months

The dog handlers were involved in abusive incidents that also involved some of the original seven rotten apples. But those particular incidents were not used during the courts-martial of the original seven rotten apples.

Clearly, the government's initial stance, that the abuse involved only seven rotten apples, has already been changed to include eleven rotten apples. Perhaps there will be further courts-martial pertaining to Abu Ghraib in the future. In any case, for the purposes of this book, I am analyzing the army's original script of the seven rotten apples, even though this script has already been changed and may change in the future as to the number of rotten apples. The facts change and the number of rotten apples changes, but so far, the *theory* of the few rotten apples remains rigidly unchanged. The alternative theory—a contaminated apple orchard involving widespread abuse—seems to be unacceptable, even though it is documented in reports and by journalists and also emerges from testimony.

Here are some explanations about the circumstances of the courts-martial and trial process in general and pertaining to these soldiers in particular:

- In the army, a court-martialed soldier has the option of throwing him- or herself on the mercy of the judge, or pleading not guilty and demanding a full trial, or pleading guilty but having a jury decide his or her sentence instead of the judge.
- Graner, England, and Harman pleaded not guilty and had full trials with a conviction phase (guilty or not guilty) and sentencing phase (which is also called *mitigation*), in which sentences were determined by jurors, not by the judge.
- Davis pleaded guilty but still had a trial in order for the jury to decide his sentence. Thus, his trial involved only the mitigation or sentencing phase.
- Thus, there were four trials that involved juries and that were held at Fort Hood, Texas: Graner in January 2005, Davis in February 2005, Harman in May 2005, and England in September 2005. Of these, only Davis pleaded guilty but still had a trial so that jurors could sentence him. Additionally, England tried to plead guilty in August 2005, and her mitigation trial got under way, but the judge declared it a mistrial. Following the mistrial, she pleaded not guilty and had a full trial in September 2005.
- It is important for the reader to know that in a military court-martial, the jurors are allowed to ask questions of any witness.

Thus, my book covers three of the four trials held at Fort Hood (all of them except Graner's), yet covers 100 percent of the rotten apples, because all of the original seven rotten apples testified at one another's trials, either for or against the government. The "plot" in all of the courts-martial was the same on the government's side: the soldiers allegedly smeared the honor of the army. The "plot" by the defense teams was to try to get high-ranking civilian and military leaders to testify as to policies and social climates they had created. In effect, the defense teams tried to put the army on trial. For the most part, the defense teams lost—the judge did not allow orchard keepers to testify. Out of a galaxy of incidents of abuse, the army focused on two main ones in all of the courts-martial, apparently because they both involved most of the rotten apples simultaneously:

- The naked pyramid of Iraqis and the associated assault, masturbation, and simulated sex acts that occurred on November 1, 2003
- The torture of three naked Iraqi detainees on October 25, 2003

Some additional incidents were invoked but not as prominently:

- The simulated electrocution of the detainee nicknamed Gilligan, which involved Harman and Frederick
- The leash incident with the detainee nicknamed Gus, which involved England and Graner

I cannot repeat often enough that this list is small, selective, and not representative of the abuse that occurred at Abu Ghraib. More important, the prosecution's focus on *incidents* of abuse is at odds with the *climates* of abuse established from Abu Ghraib to Guantánamo.

The Iraqi prisoners did not play much of a role in this America-centric drama. The victims did not testify personally in court at Fort Hood, and what happened to them or who they were did not seem to matter. The only exception is that the judge allowed videotaped statements from three prisoners at Davis's court-martial and a few written depositions in some of the other trials. Here are some facts about the invisible victims of the abuse at Abu Ghraib:

- It is *not* true that they were mostly terrorists. The government reports state that 80 percent were definitely ordinary Iraqis who posed no threat to Americans. The remaining 20 percent may have been suspects, but the government has not released a statistic on how many, if any, were actual terrorists or a danger to Americans.
- It is *not* true that any of the Iraqis involved in the incidents that were cited in court were terrorists or dangerous to Americans. The prosecutor went out of his way to establish that 100 percent of the Iraqi victims in these incidents were ordinary Iraqis who did not pose any danger to Americans.
- The real names of the Iraqi prisoners were not used in the trials. Instead, they were referred to by the nicknames that Graner and others had given them: Gus, Gilligan, Taxi Driver, Big Bird, Shit Boy, and so forth. At other times, some prisoners were referred to by their numbers. This dehumanizing aspect of the story was never challenged during the trial but merely carried over from Abu Ghraib into the trial.
- Women and children were arrested and kept at Abu Ghraib along with the men and were used as hostages and tools of emotional blackmail. This fact came out in testimony, but the actual number of women

and children was never determined, and this issue of hostage taking was never explored during trial. It was simply mentioned, and the trial moved on. Photographs of the women and children were not used at the trials.

- The judge corrected an army special agent when he referred to the prisoners as "victims." The judge insisted that they be referred to with the euphemism "detainees."

Thus, in this strange plot, one can divide the characters into protagonists, antagonists, the anonymous choir of Muslim prisoners given nicknames (e.g., Gilligan), and the invisible choir of high-ranking American officers as follows:

The Protagonists: Defenders of the Image of the U.S. Army

- COL James Pohl, the judge
- CPT Christopher Graveline,[4] the main prosecutor
- MAJ Michael Holley and CPT Charles Neill, others on the prosecution teams
- SPC Joseph Darby, who turned in the first batch of photos in January 2004
- SSG Ivan Frederick, the rotten apple who testified against the others
- SPC Israel Rivera, who testified against the others in exchange for immunity
- SPC Jeremy Sivits, the rotten apple who testified against the others
- SPC Armin Cruz, the rotten apple who testified against the others
- SGT Hydrue Joyner, in charge of the day shift
- SPC Matthew Wisdom, who tried to report the abuse
- SGT Robert Jones, Wisdom's immediate superior
- BG Mark Kimmitt, the general whose letter was read in court, asserting that the photographs cost American soldiers their lives

The Antagonists, Group I (who testified): Putting the Army on Trial

- CPT Donald Reese, company commander at Abu Ghraib
- SGT Ken Davis, whistle-blower
- SPC Meghan Ambuhl, the rotten apple who was friends with Harman and England
- CPL Charles Graner, the rotten apple who made England pose in photos

- MAJ David DiNenna, the supply officer at Abu Ghraib who couldn't get the army to send him blankets, generators, clean water, enough food, or other essentials
- Dr. Ervin Staub, the expert witness in psychology in the Davis trial
- Dr. Xavier Amador, the expert witness in psychology in the England trial

The Antagonists, Group II (whose testimony was mentioned in part but ultimately kept out of the courtroom by the judge)

- CPT Ian Fishback, the West Point graduate and whistle-blower who was going to testify on similar abuse at FOB Mercury
- MG George Fay, the general whose report refers to the "poisoned atmosphere" created by the army at Abu Ghraib
- MG Antonio Taguba, the general whose report refers to the "perverse environment" created by the army at Abu Ghraib

The Antagonists, Group III (lawyers and other professionals who tried to puncture the government's script)

- Frank Spinner and CPT Patsy Takemura
- Paul Bergrin and CPT Scott Dunn
- CPT Jonathan Crisp and CPT Catherine Krull

The Anonymous Choir of Iraqi Prisoners

- Gus, Gilligan, "rapists," Shit Boy, Taxi Driver, Big Bird, and others

The Orchard Keepers in the Background (whose memos, orders, and commands were mentioned briefly but suppressed quickly by the judge)

- LTG Ricardo Sanchez, the general who was commander of all military units in Iraq
- MG Geoffrey Miller, the general who was commander at Guantánamo and allegedly sought to Gitmoize Abu Ghraib in the fall of 2003
- MG Barbara Fast, the general in charge of military intelligence in Iraq
- COL Thomas Pappas, one of the disputed commanders at Abu Ghraib

- LTC Steven Jordan, one of the disputed commanders at Abu Ghraib
- LTC Jerry Phillabaum, one of the disputed commanders at Abu Ghraib
- CPT Carolyn Wood, one of the intelligence officers at Abu Ghraib who came from Afghanistan
- COL (formerly a brigadier general) Janis Karpinski, in charge of all the prisons in Iraq

If these lists of incidents, protagonists, antagonists, background characters, and others do not make sense, the fault lies with the government's script, not the author. It is a disjointed, chaotic, and ultimately unsatisfactory story, because it is not the real story. The real story of Abu Ghraib will be known only when all the photographs are released, all the unnamed prisoners tell their versions, and the abuse at Guantánamo and in Afghanistan and elsewhere is finally revealed fully. I bring out as much of the real story as I can by referring to the invisible, background, sometimes unnamed characters and their trail of evidence in memorandums, testimony, and reports.

In the remainder of this prologue, I will give thumbnail sketches of the main characters in the *real* story of the trials of Abu Ghraib, a story that is continually unfolding and that may or may not come to its natural climax.

The Judge: COL James Pohl

Pohl presided over every single court-martial and hearing related to the seven rotten apples from Baghdad to Fort Hood. He consistently refused to recuse himself due to possible bias, despite such requests from various defense attorneys.

The most memorable line by the judge: "The army is not on trial here." During a pretrial hearing, he was quoted as saying, "I don't want this long discussion about White House involvement."[5]

The Prosecutor: CPT Christopher Graveline

Like the judge, Graveline was involved in the Abu Ghraib saga since its inception in Baghdad. He was always part of various prosecutorial teams, but he emerged as the chief prosecutor, even when he was not one officially. The other two prosecutors, Holley and Neill, did not have Graveline's presence in the courtroom. He was promoted to major following the Lynndie England trial.

The prosecutor's most memorable lines: "Shame on you" to the convicted soldiers; "This is our army" to the jury.

The Ringleader of the Night Shift: CPL Charles Graner

Other soldiers testified that they were scared of him, and one said that Graner was like God. But Graner was also commended for his work by his superiors and especially by MI officers. He comes across as a pawn in a much larger game but a convenient scapegoat.

Most memorable lines by Graner: "Damn, that hurt" (referring to his hand when he punched a prisoner, not the prisoner's pain). And he referred to Abu Ghraib as "Bizarro World."

The Whistle-blower Who Was Silenced: CPT Ian Fishback

Fishback was going to testify at England's trial about similar abuse at FOB Mercury, in Iraq. The judge did not allow him to testify.

Most memorable line (over the phone): "I believe in the army."

The Supply Officer: MAJ David DiNenna

DiNenna stands out because he testified for the defense in the trials of Davis, Harman, and England. Also, he was one of only two officers who testified in the trials at all. He painted a desperate picture of Abu Ghraib as lacking the most basic supplies: food, water, lights, generators, toilets. DiNenna's testimony humanized the word *chaos* that is used in the reports; it seemed, from his testimony, that both soldiers and prisoners struggled for survival at Abu Ghraib.

Most memorable line: "We were the forgotten mission."

The Nice Company Commander: CPT Donald Reese

Reese came across on the stand as the proverbial "nice guy." He was disturbed by the abuse he witnessed early on and tried to stop it, and he inquired to his superiors about the abuse. It was evident that his superiors did not validate his concerns.

Most memorable line: When he asked his superiors why naked prisoners were wearing panties on their heads, he testified that he was told, "It's an MI thing" or "a supply issue."

Another Whistle-blower Ignored: SGT Ken Davis

Davis was prepared to testify about the many incidents of abuse that he witnessed, reported, and also tried to stop. He was the model soldier who did the right things that the army accused the rotten apples of not doing (report and try to stop abuse). But he testified for the defense, not for the prosecution. And he was not allowed to tell his full story on the stand.

His most memorable line: "Did it ever occur to you that some of these guys are innocent?"

The Shy, Silent Ambassador of Goodwill: SPC Sabrina Harman

This "rotten apple" did not say much, but her fellow soldiers seemed to have nothing but good things to say about her. One of her supervisors, SGT Hydrue S. Joyner, said of her, "I think she is a very generous, good-hearted person who is incapable of doing any harm to anyone." Other soldiers said she should have been a social worker, that children chanted her name when they saw her, that she helped fellow soldiers and Iraqi prisoners alike, and, in general, that she was the proverbial "good person." She suffers from posttraumatic stress disorder (PTSD), and at the time I met her, she still had bouts of dysentery from the "Abu Bug."

Her most memorable line: "These people [the prisoners] will be our future terrorists."

The Famous Lawyer: Frank Spinner

Spinner's favorable reputation preceded him at Harman's trial. He is famous for taking on the government in defending soldiers. Spinner's skill in arguing was obvious. He comes across as a low-key, modest person—kind of like the TV character Colombo. From his mannerisms, one would not expect the devastating, logical arguments that came out of his mouth.

His most memorable lines: "Shame on the army!" This was his direct response to the prosecution's charge that Harman had shamed the army. Spinner argued that the army put soldiers like her into an impossible situation. Another memorable line by him was the question "How do you cook a frog?" He seemed to mean that you cook a frog slowly, or else it will jump out of the pot. The analogy was probably meant to illustrate how the army had established a terrible social climate at Abu Ghraib over a long period of time. By the time the soldiers (frogs) realized what was happening, it was too late.

The Soldier Who Snapped for Ten Seconds: SGT Javal Davis

Davis came across as an ordinary, nice guy who took his job seriously and was liked by the prisoners for the most part. He had a bad day and snapped for ten seconds. He came across as honest and precise in his answers to the judge and as sincerely repentant. His minister and family came to court in a strong show of emotional support.

His most memorable line: "Abu Ghraib was hell on earth."

The Defense Attorney with the Impeccable Persona: Paul Bergrin

Bergrin's skills as a lawyer are on par with Spinner's, but their styles were different. Bergrin projected the persona of a lawyer from an old-time movie.

His most memorable line: "If you treat people like animals, they will behave like animals."

The Soldier Who Did Not Seem to Know What Was Going On: PFC Lynndie England

Despite the negative ways that she was portrayed in the media, England came across as a person who had no idea of what was going on in the courtroom or in the midst of the chaos at Abu Ghraib. At Abu Ghraib, she seemed to derive her sense of security from Charles Graner. In the courtroom, she clearly could not comprehend what was happening. Experts established that she suffered from a serious cognitive deficit as well as PTSD. Sending her to prison came across as sending a disabled person to prison.

Her most memorable line: "I love my baby."

The Defense Attorney Who Was Threatened with Demotion for Arguing with the Judge: CPT Jonathan Crisp

Crisp apparently thought that demonstrating England's cognitive deficit would serve as a strong mitigating factor.

His most memorable line, to the jury: "Think of the testimony of the officers in here. Oh, right, there wasn't any."

Conclusion

In 2005, the drama among these protagonists, antagonists, other witnesses, and the invisible prisoners from Abu Ghraib unfolded in a courtroom at Fort Hood, Texas. Competing scripts emerged. The judge and the prosecutor played their roles as protectors of the army's honor and suppressors of information that would bring further shame to the army. The soldiers told the truth as they saw it: they were following orders coming from military intelligence to do "weird things" to prisoners. The soldiers described Abu Ghraib as "hell on earth" and other words and phrases to that effect. The defense teams tried, and failed, to get high-ranking officers and even the secretary of defense to testify. For the most part, the defense teams were putting the army on trial. This is the part that seems most strange about the trials: the government seemed guilty, in part, for the unlawful policies and chaos that were established at Abu Ghraib and elsewhere, yet the government was going through the rituals of justice and assigning blame onto its lowest-ranking soldiers.

The trials were a messy, chaotic, emotionally charged drama that rivals anything written by Shakespeare or other great dramatists. They invoked some of the strongest negative emotions in the human psyche: shame, fear, rage, guilt, and cruelty. But they also exposed positive traits such as honor, compassion, honesty, and commitment.

In the end, justice at the Fort Hood courthouse came across as an empty gesture. Human rights organizations report that widespread abuse continues as I write this book in 2006, long after the photos were leaked and long after the trials. Moreover, investigations are under way at the present time into several massacres of Iraqi civilians. The Abu Ghraib trials did not bring a sense of resolution but unwittingly opened many more doors to future inquiries.

Notes

1. See, for example, Douglas Jahl, "Some Abu Ghraib Abuses Are Traced to Afghanistan," *New York Times,* August 26, 2004, A11.

2. See Seymour M. Hersh, *My Lai 4: A Report on the Massacre and Its Aftermath* (New York: Vintage Books, 1970).

3. See, for example, Tim Golden and Eric Schmitt, "A Growing Prison Rivals Bleak Guantanamo," *New York Times,* February 26, 2006, regarding abuse at Bagram Air Force Base in Afghanistan.

4. Graveline was promoted to major following England's court-martial. However, I refer to him as a captain in this book because this was his rank during the courts-martial that I am analyzing.

5. Debbie Stevenson, "Judge Will Not Drop Any Charges against Reservist in Abuse Trial," *Killeen Daily Herald,* March 8, 2005.

PART ONE

METAPHORS OF THE APPLES, ORCHARD, AND ORCHARD-KEEPERS

CHAPTER ONE

THE FEW ROTTEN APPLES THEORY

JoAnn Wypijewski has already written that at the Fort Hood courts-martial, "the judge would allow none of the larger picture into the trial, a decision that consigned the court to the world of make-believe."[1] I would add that the judge allowed some, but very little, of the larger picture into the trials. I do not question the judge's legal prudence or motives in this regard. Nevertheless, the larger picture is important for understanding what happened at Abu Ghraib. The larger picture is to be found in the government reports, reports by journalists, and reports issued by human rights groups. More important, this larger picture is blurred, confusing, and contradictory. Thus, the world of make-believe exists outside the courtroom at Fort Hood.

Based on my reading of many reports from many sources, it seems to be the case that the heart of the matter regarding abuse at Abu Ghraib involves a deceptively simple contradiction and its long-lasting consequences: one part of the government depicts the abuse as the result of a few rotten apples (e.g., a handful of morally corrupt soldiers) in the face of overwhelming evidence that the abuse was and remains widespread at U.S. bases at Guantánamo Bay (Gitmo), in Afghanistan, and in Iraq other than at Abu Ghraib. This contradiction is not resolved simply by pitting the government's rotten apple theory against facts that support what might be called the government's contaminated apple orchard theory. The information media, human rights organizations, and the government itself report facts that indicate widespread abuse. The complexity lies in the fact that the government—in its own published reports—acknowledges that the abuse is widespread and exists within as well as outside Abu Ghraib *at the same time* that it insists on the theory of a few rotten apples within Abu Ghraib and beyond as the primary explanation for the abuse. The number of rotten apples seems to be growing in the government's theory, but the flawed theory is maintained. The government reports, which clearly point to a pattern of abuse throughout Iraq, Afghanistan, and Guantánamo Bay, were mostly kept out of testimony at the trials at Fort Hood.

The courts-martial at Fort Hood were a stage on which the few rotten apples became scapegoats for a policy of much wider abuse. The orchard keepers (civilians and officers high in the chain of command) have been cropped out of the picture of abuse that the government presents to the world. This obvious fact—that all the blame has been shifted onto a handful of soldiers while the culpability of the people in charge is not acknowledged seriously—was recognized privately by the journalists who had covered the trials at Fort Hood and others who had witnessed the trials. But publicly, the widespread policy for condoning widespread abuse continues to be supported by a tortured logic.

What shall one call this complex state of affairs regarding the truth concerning abuse at Abu Ghraib and elsewhere? It is not an ordinary falsehood to shift all the blame onto a handful of soldiers, because it includes truths mixed with deceit. It is true that a handful of soldiers were prosecuted for abuse that they, in fact, committed. It is not true that they concocted the abuse on their own as some sort of expression of fraternity party fun. It is not true that the abuse was confined to Abu Ghraib. Ordinarily, a falsehood, once uncovered, is retracted, and the damage to social relations caused by the falsehood is usually repaired. But regarding Abu Ghraib, the glaring inconsistency is that the abuse continued and increased at Abu Ghraib and elsewhere in Iraq following the initial exposure of the photographs that depicted the abuse and following the courts-martial that were supposed to bring the rotten apples to justice. The so-called insurgency movement has increased dramatically ever since the disclosure of the photos—and in the government's estimation, largely as a result of the disclosure of the photos. Surely multiple causes exist for the insurgency, but at the courts-martial, the photos were singled out as the primary cause. According to the short-sighted political horizons established by the government, the trials were supposed to bring closure to the matter of Abu Ghraib. In reality, the trials at Fort Hood were the equivalent of the "Mission Accomplished" banner that wrongly signaled the end of the war in Iraq. One finds disturbing long-term consequences to the evils that Abu Ghraib symbolizes: a dramatic rise in insurgency in Iraq; the very "clash of civilizations" between the United States and Islam that political scientist Samuel Huntington and others predicted; a drop in morale in the U.S. Army; and a blow to U.S. prestige in general and especially regarding the issue of human rights—among other consequences to be explored later in this book.

Several additional layers of contradiction add to the resulting confusion. First, journalists and the information media in general have documented abuse at Guantánamo Bay, in Afghanistan, and specific sites in Iraq other than Abu Ghraib, including FOB Mercury and FOB Tiger, as well as specific U.S. Army units that include the 101st Airborne Division, the 82nd Airborne Division, 3rd Special Forces, 5th Special Forces, and 7th Cavalry, among others.[2] Moreover, some of this widespread abuse involves a clear, systematic pattern, such as stacking Iraqi detainees into human pyramids at both Abu Ghraib and FOB Mercury in Iraq.

At the same time, journalists and the information media do not typically connect the dots—specifically, abuse at Guantánamo, in Afghanistan, and elsewhere in Iraq—to arrive at the logical conclusion that the abuse was not confined to a few rotten apples at Abu Ghraib and, more important, that the abuse is part of a larger, widespread pattern. Instead, for the most part, the information media dutifully report the many incidents of abuse in a disjointed way. Like the prosecution, the media tend to focus on *incidents* but not social *climates* of abuse. The result is that the many incidents of abuse across a widespread geographic area remain unconnected in the American public consciousness but seem to be connected in the Islamic public consciousness.

Second, human rights organizations such as Human Rights Watch, the American Civil Liberties Union (ACLU), and the International Committee of the Red Cross (ICRC), among others, have also documented the facts established by both the U.S. government reports and the information media regarding abuse at Abu Ghraib *as well as* widespread abuse outside Abu Ghraib. Human rights organizations point to a widespread pattern of abuse. For example, consider a Human Rights Watch Report issued in April 2006 that asserts:

> Two years ago, revelations about the abuse of detainees in U.S. custody at Abu Ghraib prison in Iraq shocked people across the world. In response, U.S. government officials condemned the conduct as illegal and assured the world that perpetrators would be held accountable. Two years later, it has become clear that the problem of torture and other abuse by U.S. personnel abroad was far more pervasive than the Abu Ghraib photos revealed—extending to numerous U.S. detention facilities in Afghanistan, Iraq, and at Guantanamo Bay, and including hundreds of incidents of abuse.[3]

But this and similar human rights reports beg several questions: How does one explain the widespread pattern of abuse? Suppose that every single *incident* of recognized abuse resulted in prison or other appropriate punishment. Would such results repair the consequences of the *climates* of abuse that were created and prevent abuse in the future?

Other perplexing contradictions are related to the issue of understanding abuse at Abu Ghraib in the context of a widespread pattern. The Bush administration insisted that Guantánamo Bay existed outside of U.S. jurisdiction and was still a part of Cuba, so that prisoners at Guantánamo Bay were not entitled to U.S. or even international protections. Therefore, the "interrogation methods" at Gitmo need not be examined as torture and abuse for the legalistic reason that Gitmo was not under U.S. jurisdiction, and the U.S. does not torture people where it holds legal jurisdiction. This argument was struck down by the U.S. Supreme Court, which ruled, in part, that the U.S. Naval Base at Guantánamo Bay does fall under U.S. jurisdiction and that no prisoners can exist in a "legal no-man's land." Despite this ruling, the status quo remains unchanged at Gitmo as of this writing. By taking this position regarding Gitmo, the government signaled to the rest of the world that it seems to operate on the principle "one law for the United States, another for everyone else." In fact, the position of the United States is that the Geneva Conventions did not and do not apply at Guantánamo and in Afghanistan, but they did and do apply legally in Iraq—even if they were not applied in Iraq in practice. The effect on U.S. relations with other nations is bound to be like the effect of the cheating spouse who operates under the rule "I'm allowed to have affairs, but my partner is not."

The euphemism *detainee* came into widespread usage to avoid the automatic assumption that prisoners are entitled to protection by the Geneva Conventions. The government, much of the information media, and even some human rights organizations continue to use the incorrect word *detainee* to refer to prisoners in Iraq. Moreover, similar "interrogation techniques" were applied and continue to be applied in Afghanistan, Iraq, and at Gitmo. Logically, the Geneva Conventions cannot apply yet not apply to similar interrogation techniques at the same time. The Geneva Conventions cannot apply yet not apply to some "detainees" but not other "detainees." But this is the perplexing logic in the government's position. One consequence of these discrepancies is the perception of a lack of consistency. Lack of consistency gradually erodes trust in relationships of any sort, up to and including international relations.

The examples cited so far suggest a twisted web of contradictions that creates conceptual chaos in trying to understand Abu Ghraib and its context. The theme of chaos is found at every step of the process used to apprehend Abu Ghraib: the government reports refer to "confusion" and to a "poisoned atmosphere" at Abu Ghraib—but the reports themselves are confusing (despite the facts that they uncover) in shifting all the blame on a few soldiers and removing all culpability from high-ranking officers. This is a striking contradiction of international as well as U.S. military doctrine. According to Human Rights Watch:

> Under the doctrine of command responsibility, a long-recognized principle of U.S. domestic and international law, commanders can be held criminally liable as principals for the criminal acts of their subordinates, if they knew or should have known about criminal activity, but did not take steps to prevent it or to punish the perpetrators.... Not a single U.S. military officer serving in Iraq, Afghanistan, or Guantanamo Bay has been criminally charged under the doctrine of command responsibility for detainee abuses committed by his or her subordinates.[4]

Fishback's Questioning of What Constitutes Lawful Treatment of Detainees

Another notable example of this frustratingly contradictory attitude by the government is the case of the handsome West Point graduate, CPT Ian Fishback, who tried to report abuse he had witnessed at FOB Mercury in Iraq—which was also documented by Human Rights Watch—but was apparently ignored by his entire chain of command until he finally won an audience with Senator John McCain. The information media reported on his meeting with McCain, and the *Washington Post* published some of Fishback's letters that he sent to his commanding officers concerning the abuse he had witnessed. However, the story abruptly disappeared from the media and from the public consciousness in September 2005, immediately following PFC Lynndie England's trial.[5] Again, Fishback's saga was not connected in the public consciousness to the glaring contradiction that the government prosecuted soldiers for failure to report abuse at the same time that it ignored or intimidated such "whistleblowers."

I have personal knowledge of and experience with Fishback's saga and its agonizing relationship to the rotten apple theory. The defense team for England requested that Fishback testify at her court-martial. He agreed to testify for the defense, and the gist of his testimony was supposed to be that he had witnessed abuse that was similar to Abu Ghraib at FOB Mercury, especially the human pyramids, so that the blame for the abuse at Abu Ghraib could not be shifted entirely onto England and her small cohort of bad apples on the night shift. During a special hearing, and at the request of the defense attorney, CPT Jonathan Crisp, the military judge, allowed me to testify as to the possible relevance of Fishback's requested testimony based on my reading of his letters to his commanding officers and to McCain, as well as a Human Rights Watch report that corroborated his claims. The prosecutor objected that the Human Rights Watch report was "hearsay" and that the similarities between the patterns of abuse at Abu Ghraib and FOB Mercury are "irrelevant." The military judge ruled that the similarities (including the stacking of detainees into human pyramids at both places) were a "coincidence," and he denied Fishback the opportunity to testify at the trial. The more far-reaching consequence of his decision was to deny Fishback the opportunity to testify to the United States and to the world about the creation of climates of abuse at places other than Abu Ghraib.

Corroboration of Fishback's Observations

In a Human Rights Watch report of September 2005, "Leadership Failure: Firsthand Accounts of Torture of Iraqi Detainees by the U.S. Army's 82nd Airborne Division,"[6] further evidence is presented that the chaotic social environment being discussed here was not restricted to Abu Ghraib but existed elsewhere in American detention facilities in Iraq. Of particular interest are the "Murderous Maniacs" (as they were called by the residents of Fallujah) of the 82nd Airborne Division at FOB Mercury, in Iraq, who "used physical and mental torture as a means of intelligence gathering and for *stress relief*" (1). The report attests that "soldiers also incorporated daily beatings of detainees in preparation for interrogations" (2). Three soldiers "expressed confusion on the proper application of the Geneva Conventions on the laws of armed conflicts in the treatment of prisoners" (2). "US troops on the battlefield were given no clear guidance on how to treat detainees. When the administration sent these soldiers to war in Afghanistan, it threw out the rules they were trained to uphold (embodied in the Geneva Conventions and the U.S. Army Field Manual on Intelligence Interrogation)" (3). The effect was such that if a prisoner was not an insurgent—and about half were released as not being insurgents—he was treated as an insurgent anyway. "If he's a good guy, you know, now he's a bad guy because of the way we treated him," one sergeant told Human Rights Watch (5). Similar to the accounts of failure to report abuse at Abu Ghraib, when a soldier raised issues of abuse with superiors at FOB Mercury, "He was consistently told to keep his mouth shut, turn a blind eye, or consider his career" (6).

Sergeant A is quoted as saying, "In retrospect what we did was wrong, but at the time we did what we had to do. Everything we did was accepted, everyone turned their heads" (8). He added, "Some days we would just get bored so we would have everyone sit in a corner and then make them get in a pyramid.... We did that for amusement" (9). This state of affairs seems familiar to the descriptions of abuse at Abu Ghraib.

In the words of Sergeant A, "We should have had MPs. We should have taken them to Abu Ghraib which was only 15 fucking minutes drive. But there was no one to talk to in the chain—it just got killed. We would talk among ourselves, say, 'This is bad.' But no one listened. We should never have been allowed to watch guys we had fought" (11). Army soldiers took out their anger and frustrations on the prisoners. Much like Ivan Frederick said to soldiers at Abu Ghraib following abuse, "You didn't see shit," Sergeant A states that, regarding an abusive sergeant at FOB Mercury, "He would always say to us, 'You didn't see anything, right? And we would always say, 'No Sergeant'" (12).

Sergeant B states that "putting guys with frustration in charge of prisoners was the worst thing to do" (14). He adds, "But we were never briefed on the Geneva Conventions" (15). An officer elaborates further: "I witnessed violations of the Geneva Conventions that I knew were violations of the Geneva Conventions when they happened but I was under the impression that that was US policy at the time" (16). This conceptually chaotic state of affairs is similar to that found at Abu Ghraib. The officer attests to further confusion with regard to the issue of treating detainees humanely: "Well, what does humane mean? We've got people with different views of what humane means and there's no Army statement that says this is the standard for humane treatment for prisoners to Army officers. Army officers are left to come up with their own definition of humane treatment" (19). This situation is similar to that found at Abu Ghraib in which soldiers and officers interpreted normative standards subjectively because fixed, normative consensus did not exist. This officer concludes, "It's unjust to hold only lower-ranking soldiers accountable for something that is so clearly, at a minimum, an officer corps problem, and probably a combination with the executive branch of government" (22).

Furthermore, this officer expressed his frustration at not being taken seriously for attempting to report the abuse he had witnessed and for asking for guidance from his chain of command. In frustration, he wrote a letter to the secretary of defense on September 16, 2005. He talked to fellow officers, his chaplain at West Point, his company commander, and his battalion commander. He received responses such as "Don't expect me to go to bat for you on this issue" and "Go talk to JAG" [Judge Advocate General's office] (17). The captain continues: "So I went to JAG and . . . he says, 'Well the Geneva Conventions are a gray area'" (17). According to Human Rights Watch, the officer

> decided to bring his concerns to the Congress since he felt they were not being adequately addressed by his chain of command. Days before this report was published his brigade commander told him to stop his inquiries; his commanding officer told him that he could not leave the base to visit with staff members of Senators McCain and Warner without approval and that approval was being denied because his commanding officer felt the officer was being naïve and would do irreparable harm to his career. (19)

In summary, the September 2005 Human Rights Watch report is one more piece of evidence that abuse at Abu Ghraib was not an isolated case and not merely the result of rogue soldiers, but that it is connected to a broader state of chaos in the U.S. Army vis-à-vis the treatment and interrogation of prisoners in Iraq. Moreover, it suggests that because attempts by an officer to report abuse at FOB Mercury were effectively ignored, it is unreasonable to expect that the low-ranking soldiers who were court-martialed at Fort Hood would have been effective in reporting or attempting to exit the abusive situation at Abu Ghraib.

Further corroboration for widespread abuse is found in numerous newspaper articles that describe various incidents of abuse throughout Iraq and Afghanistan. But it does not seem to matter. The government keeps rigidly to its few rotten apples theory as an explanation. It is a theory that is not amenable to ordinary logic.

The Framing of the Photographs

Some of the leaked photographs from Abu Ghraib were spread all over the world by the information media—especially the photograph of England holding a detainee on a leash. That particular photograph has achieved the status of a cultural icon. It is a contradiction that the photographs of the abuse at Abu Ghraib may be understood as whistle-blowing, yet soldiers were prosecuted primarily for the alleged effect these photographs had on the insurgency movement in Iraq. The prosecution's position was that those photographs caused American soldiers to die. However, had it not been for those photographs, the abuse at Abu Ghraib most likely would not have been noticed by the world as quickly as it was, and abuse would not have been suspected at other sites from Gitmo to Afghanistan. Several soldiers testified that they took the photographs in order to document the abuse, but their testimony was discounted by the prosecutor. Here is yet another instance of the government using doublespeak: it prosecuted soldiers for the crime of taking photographs and posing in photographs of abuse, which constitute a sort of whistle-blowing and documentation, at the same time that it prosecuted soldiers for not reporting the abuse.

The government has put its soldiers into a lose-lose situation: the soldier loses if he or she documents and reports abuse but also if he or she fails to report to prevent abuse. Specifically, the prosecutor read a letter from BG Mark Kimmitt at England's trial expressing his opinion that the photographs resulted in the loss of American lives. This argument was inflammatory to the jury, but it seems logical at first glance. However, a similar government argument was struck down by U.S. District Judge Alvin K. Hellerstein, who ruled that the ACLU may release even more photographs than the government had already released on the grounds that (1) there is no necessary relation between the photographs and the motives of insurgents, who may be motivated by a host of factors, and (2) the public has a right to know and see the photographs under the First Amendment.[7]

In summary, it seems to be the case that the public became aware of the abuse at Abu Ghraib primarily on the basis of photographs that, in turn, were used as primary evidence against soldiers. Abuse at other sites—even when documented through sworn affidavits and other written evidence—has not registered as powerfully in the public consciousness.

Careful Editing of the Photographs

The government edited which photographs were shown at the courts-martial. For example, a photograph of Harman smiling over the dead body of prisoner Manadel al-Jamadi was excluded from trial, even though it had circulated in the information media (she had absolutely no connection to his death). Harman was prosecuted for other crimes that involved posing in photographs (the photography was deemed "maltreatment" by the government), but not for photographs that involved this dead detainee. The government thereby avoided completely the issues pertaining to this prisoner's death. In general, extensive "editing," selection, and "framing" of issues, instances and definitions of abuse, photographs, and events occurred on the part of the government as well as the information media. The defense was not allowed to bring out the full context, extent, and range of the photographs or abuse in Afghanistan, at Gitmo, or at other sites in Iraq—most such efforts were denied by the military judge. The unwelcome result is that the government, judge, and media focused primarily on selected photographs that depicted primarily sexual and physical abuse, which in turn tarnished the image of the army as well as the United States. They did not include photographs of the defendants depicted in acts of kindness toward Iraqis, living in squalid conditions, or engaging in everyday activities. Both soldiers and prisoners were dehumanized by the particular selection of photographs that were used.

The trials excluded the criminality of forcing prisoners to be nude—which was patently obvious in many photographs—and denied the defense the opportunity to argue that this and other systemic violations of the Geneva Conventions were in place long before the accused soldiers arrived at the scene. It is as if the nudity in many of the photographs became invisible. This is a miraculous feat, sociologically speaking, and suggests that facts do not speak for themselves. The photographs that were used at the courts-martial were interpreted as showing sexual and physical abuse by a few rogue soldiers, and few questions were ever raised about why the detainees were nude.

The judge ruled that the "nudity thing" was "irrelevant"—even though it was commonplace at Abu Ghraib, permeates the government's own reports, and is documented in photographs. One needs to address the social construction of the reality that goes into arriving at as well as discarding various definitions and usages of the concept of abuse, and by whom—even when it comes to the seemingly "hard evidence" of the photograph. The government, the military judge, as well as most of the information media settled on a narrow definition of abuse as assault and sexual abuse, and they restricted these specific forms of abuse to a few specific incidents and a few specific soldiers. They chose to work with about eighty photographs out of more than fifteen thousand available photographs.

The Social Construction of the Meaning of Abuse

The terms *violent* and *sexual abuse,* as well as the incidents, photographs, and individual soldiers chosen for prosecution—along with incidents, photographs and individuals *not* chosen for prosecution—are subject to a *selective* social construction of reality. Which incidents of "abuse" were not classified as abuse, by whom, and for what reasons? Which incidents of "abuse" were chosen for prosecution, by whom, and for what reasons?

Why were insults, humiliation, and forced nudity excluded as incidents of "abuse"? Above all, how many *incidents* of abuse are required to qualify as a *climate* of abuse?

Social scientists as well as psychiatrists, human rights organizations, and the Geneva Conventions take account of a multiplicity of phenomena under the rubric of abuse, which include but are not limited to fear, intimidation, yelling, insults, devaluation, mental cruelty, the experience of suffering, humiliation, uncertainty as to one's fate, and so on. Abuse cannot be confined to specific incidents, and it carries over into long-lasting climates, experiences, relationships, and consequences of abuse. Moreover, these many forms of abuse can occur in the full spectrum of human relationships that range from the dyad, such as a boyfriend and girlfriend, through families, to prisons, mental hospitals, and other large bureaucratic institutions, including units of the U.S. Army. It is important to return to the fact that some soldiers testified at trial that they experienced fear and intimidation from each other—specifically, that fellow soldiers would harm them if they reported or tried to stop the abuse they witnessed. Some soldiers also reported fear and intimidation of the U.S. Army for whistle-blowing. For these reasons, it is useful to refer to abusive *climates,* abusive *atmospheres,* and abusive *relationships* vis-à-vis Abu Ghraib in addition to enumerating specific acts of selected abuse.

The commonplace nudity at Abu Ghraib, which is documented by photographs, reports, and testimony, suggests strongly that a poisoned social climate existed that made nudity invisible because it was so routine. The government reports offer rich texts full of facts that *do* include mention of these other forms of abuse at Abu Ghraib—including mention of a "poisoned" climate—but do *not* necessarily label or understand these climates as formal "abuse" that should be prosecuted. "Poisoned climates" are created—directly or indirectly—over a long period of time by officers high in the chain of command, and the government may have chosen to avoid this explosive issue and shift all of the blame onto low-ranking soldiers. For example, forced nudity was apparently common at Abu Ghraib but was not treated as abuse in the trials even though it is a violation of the Geneva Conventions.

What Is an Interrogation Technique?

At what point does an approved interrogation "technique" become abuse? More precisely, what is the conceptual boundary such that one can recognize where a technique *ends* and abuse *begins*? This blurring of conceptual boundaries occurred in a multiplicity of ways at Abu Ghraib, including but not limited to interrogations that were performed ad hoc in hallways and bathrooms, failure to document or supervise techniques such as sleep deprivation (soldiers said that they sometimes forgot about a prisoner who was being subjected to a technique), techniques that were implemented by MPs for the purpose of "softening up" detainees for interrogation, as well as using "techniques" for the purpose of sport and stress relief, not for any interrogation or police function. It is instructive to examine a list of authorized interrogation techniques at Abu Ghraib: direct; incentive/removal of incentive; emotional love; emotional hate; fear up harsh; fear up mild; reduced fear; pride and ego down; futility; we know all; establish your identity; repetition; file and dossier; Mutt and Jeff; rapid fire; silence; change of scenery up; change of scenery down; isolation; dietary manipulation; sleep management; yelling, loud music, and light control; sleep adjustment; presence of military working dogs; stress positions; deception.

Most of these "techniques" easily qualify as abuse in any setting other than interrogation: yelling, lying, humiliating others, controlling others, arbitrary and capricious behavior, and emotional blackmail are all common forms of abuse found in dysfunctional relationships and families. These behaviors are "techniques" to the extent that they follow the army's *Field Manual,* which admonishes that the goal is to gain the prisoner's "willing cooperation" within the framework of the Geneva Conventions. But if the techniques are out of sync with the *Field Manual,* they may become abuse or set the stage for abuse.

Other techniques were added and deleted from this list at various points of time, which led to confusion as to what was permissible. The definitions for most of these techniques are to be found in the U.S. Army's *Field Manual on Interrogation* (FM 34–52). However, in Iraq, FM 34–52 was treated as if it were obsolete at the same time that it was cited as applicable, which again led to confusion. The government reports found that unlawful "techniques" had "circulated" and "migrated" from Guantánamo Bay and Afghanistan and had coexisted with already confusing lawful techniques.

The Social Chaos at Abu Ghraib

The factual evidence for the presence of extreme social disorganization and chaos comes from the U.S. government reports pertaining to Abu

Ghraib—even though these reports never use the precise words *social disorganization* and *social chaos*—and includes, but is not limited to, the following: a systemic lack of accountability; a disorganized filing system; the fact that other government agencies (OGAs, including but not limited to Central Intelligence Agency [CIA]) operated outside established army rules and procedures; the fact that nobody was certain who was in charge of Abu Ghraib; overcrowding; a dysfunctional system for releasing prisoners; failure to screen detainees at the point that they were arrested as well as the point that they were brought to Abu Ghraib; the lack of screening for civilian contractors; the introduction of new elements (but not entire units) into the personnel structure; failure to adequately train MPs and MIs (military intelligence officers) in policing as well as interrogation procedures; the fact that MPs did not know what they or MIs were allowed to do and what they were not allowed to do; the merging of MP and MI roles; lack of military discipline; intense pressure to obtain information from a population of detainees that was mostly incapable of providing the desired information; lack of training; lack of familiarity with the Geneva Conventions; the fact that the U.S. military formally upheld the Geneva Conventions while various attorneys for the White House opined that the Geneva Conventions did not wholly apply to the treatment of prisoners; the resulting confusion stemming from the conclusion that the Geneva Conventions did not apply to prisoners at Guantánamo and in Afghanistan but did apply to prisoners in Iraq; poor paperwork procedures; confusion as to the relevance of FM 34–52 for the newly devised procedure of melding MI and MP functions; confusion as to what constituted a proper interrogation procedure vis-à-vis the FM 34–52 or the Geneva Conventions or which theater of operation; poor reporting procedures; along with a host of other facts. *Confusion* is the word that crops up most frequently as the explanation for the social chaos at Abu Ghraib. How did this extremely confused and confusing state of affairs come into existence; how did it persist; and how was its existence later denied, rationalized, and otherwise put into the background of discourse?

The sociological perspective holds that all of these findings of fact constitute evidence of egregious social disorganization and chronic, persistent social chaos that inevitably lead to abuse. Ordinarily, social systems are self-correcting and do not allow for chaos to exist for a long time.[8] The body of sociological theory and research supporting this view includes many thousands of books and published research articles. There is also some overlap between this sociological perspective and psychiatrist Robert Jay Lifton's view that both My Lai and Abu Ghraib are "atrocity-producing" situations.[9] Additionally, the sociological perspective on chronic chaos and its consequences lends itself easily to connections with recent literature in family systems theories and other psychological theories and research on dysfunctional families. The conceptual connections are the following: Contemporary therapists seem to have arrived at consensus regarding the view that a functional family is characterized by predictable, regular, and orderly habits, behavior, and emotional responses. Conversely, dysfunctional families are characterized by chronic chaos of various sorts: capricious, arbitrary, unpredictable, moody behaviors and emotional responses on the part of all the family members. When parents see a therapist to complain about a spoiled, moody, "difficult," even violent child, most therapists listen patiently to the parents but are looking for signs of how the parents have established a dysfunctional, chaotic social setting that produced the "bad" child over a long period of time. Dysfunctional families do not have regular bedtimes or chores for the children, praise and punishment are not consistent, and the child often feels that he or she is living in "prison" and not at "home." There is a lot of yelling, shouting, aggression, and humiliation in dysfunctional families; and apparently, there was a lot of yelling, shouting, aggression, and humiliation at Abu Ghraib—over the course of several months. Dysfunctional families make excuses for the abuse (e.g., the punished person deserved it), and the soldiers at Abu Ghraib made excuses for the abuse (e.g., prisoners deserved to be abused because they might have hurt or wanted to harm American soldiers). These connections enable the researcher to reconceptualize details pertaining to daily life at Abu Ghraib—for American soldiers *as well as* prisoners—in this larger context connected to family systems theory: the prisoners felt that they were at the mercy of the seemingly capricious and arbitrary moods of their American captors (parent surrogates) regarding everyday issues such as going to the bathroom, clothing, when and what they would eat, punishment, medical care, and other issues.

A skeptical reader might respond, "Of course! The detainees were in prison. Why would a prisoner expect noncapricious, let alone humane, treatment?" A rational reply is that civilized, modern nation-states pride themselves in claiming that they mete out humane and bureaucratically ordered punishment. Also, the Geneva Conventions, in tandem with other international conventions, are supposed to protect the human rights of prisoners of war, as well as civilians. Another important point is that a chronically capricious, arbitrary, and chaotic social environment will *not* yield the information that military intelligence personnel seek. On the contrary, a persistent chaotic social environment breeds fear, resentment, humiliation, defiance, and other negative emotions that preclude the "willing cooperation" that U.S. Army field manuals state is the goal of interrogation. Finally, the abusive atmosphere at Abu Ghraib led to riots, stress and fear among the soldiers, and many other negative consequences. An orderly social environment is always preferable to chaos for everyone concerned in terms of long-term consequences.

One can use metaphors to clarify these points. Living in a dysfunctional family can feel as if one were living at Abu Ghraib or in a prison, and people in dysfunctional relationships often do refer to such relationships as living in emotional prisons. Conversely, the testimonies of various soldiers at the trials suggest that the abusers at Abu Ghraib were acting out sadistic fantasies that are often found in dysfunctional families: soldiers yelled at detainees, humiliated them, tortured them verbally and emotionally, punched them for no apparent reason, and otherwise engaged in behaviors that are found in disturbed families. Soldiers testified consistently that Abu Ghraib was not a "normal prison."

In addition, the soldiers themselves were living and working in a chronically chaotic social environment at Abu Ghraib, which took its toll on them. For example, the rules of engagement changed frequently; the rules for interrogation changed at least once a month; the normal rules pertaining to Army discipline were *not* in place; OGA and CIA personnel were seen to engage in brutal behavior, while soldiers were sometimes told that the Geneva Conventions applied; soldiers were not trained in any serious way in understanding the Geneva Conventions, which were not posted anywhere at Abu Ghraib; soldiers were forced to deal with capricious changes such that their daily lives became an exercise in "on the job training." The result was stress and PTSD for many of the soldiers at Abu Ghraib but also the establishment of a chronic, poisoned climate that led to abuse. In a very real sense, both the soldiers and the detainees at Abu Ghraib were victims of long-term chaos.

The importance of this conceptual link between dysfunctional families and other dysfunctional settings is that it can lead to ways to recognize and repair dysfunction. Dysfunctional families that wish to change go into therapy, and there is no good reason why similar therapeutic principles could not be used by the army to repair the chaotic social environments that lead to abuse. Indeed, it is significant that the U.S. Army's "bible" concerning interrogation and detention, FM 34–52, aims at gaining the detainee's "willing cooperation" and emphasizes respect for the prisoner in accordance with the Geneva Conventions. Functional social systems are guided by fixed moral boundaries, such as the Geneva Conventions and the army *Field Manual.* The U.S. government reports found that FM 34–52 and the Geneva Conventions were disregarded at Abu Ghraib. A social scientist can explain the disastrous consequences of this departure by the U.S. Army from its previously institutionalized policy.

Some journalists in the information media and some organizations such as the ACLU frame the abuses at Abu Ghraib as a set of events that flowed from a general "climate" of disregard for the Geneva Conventions that was established at the highest levels of the U.S. military and political chain of command and that trickled down to the soldiers on the ground.[10] The perspective taken in the present study supposes that it is not a matter of choosing between top-down versus bottom-up explanations but integrating both perspectives and finding a middle ground between them. Specifically, personnel low in the chain of command clearly committed abuses, but personnel high in the chain of command should have known and should have taken steps to prevent the abuse. More important, officers high in the chain of command created a social climate that made abuse appear to be "normative" and that made it difficult for anyone to stop or report the abuse because unlawful behavior could not be distinguished clearly from lawful behavior in a chronically poisoned social environment.

In general, it may be the case that any objective assessment of a situation that involves war crimes in any cultural setting will most likely eschew choosing between two extreme frames of reference: that abuse was either ordered from the top *or* the spontaneous result of a few corrupt individuals. By itself, neither extreme explanation is entirely satisfactory. The most complete explanation must involve some midlevel explanation that includes elements of both the top-down *and* bottom-up explanations. According to a report prepared with MG George R. Fay as the investigating officer, an "unhealthy mystique that further poisoned the atmosphere" (53) developed at Abu Ghraib.[11] Who is responsible for creating the unhealthy mystique and the poisoned atmosphere? What effect did it have on the soldier at Abu Ghraib?

Social Psychology Perspectives: The Research by Philip Zimbardo

A midlevel explanation that combines many of the issues discussed above is offered by Philip Zimbardo's reflections on the famous Stanford Prison Experiment he conducted in 1971, which has become the staple of textbooks in sociology, psychology, and social psychology.[12] This experiment involved a group of ordinary students who were placed in an artificial prison. Half the students were transformed into sadistic guards, and half were transformed into passive, victimized prisoners. The parallel to Abu Ghraib is not exact, but it is close enough to be intriguing. Ordinary soldiers became abusive at Abu Ghraib. Were they inherently rotten apples (sadistic), or were they transformed, like Dr. Jekyll into Mr. Hyde, by the social environment at Abu Ghraib?

Another connection between Zimbardo's famous experiment and abuse is that films and lectures of his experiment were used by the U.S. Navy to train its guards in order to prevent abuse. Moreover, Zimbardo's experiment in 1971 was commissioned and funded by the U.S. Navy in order to understand abuse at its military prisons. These are all solid reasons to reexamine the relevance of Zimbardo's findings for understanding Abu Ghraib and, in particular, for examining the government's few rotten apples theory.

Let me make it clear that I am offering a new reading of Zimbardo in the context of the foregoing discussion and that Zimbardo may not agree with my interpretation. Moreover, in this book, I am not interested in a strictly academic discussion of Zimbardo's experiment. I am most interested in Zimbardo's reflections thirty years after he conducted the Stanford Prison Experiment concerning its pragmatic significance for preventing abuse. In particular, he applied his insights for understanding abuse and torture committed by police in Brazil in a book entitled *Violence Workers: Police Torturers and Murderers Reconstruct Brazilian Atrocities.*[13] In this section, I will explore the relevance of Zimbardo's theory and research for understanding the issues raised thus far concerning the abuse at Abu Ghraib: was the abuse the result of a few rotten apples or the result of a poisoned social environment or some other explanation that combines elements from these two extreme explanations? The main point is that in reflecting back on this famous research study, Zimbardo has concluded that he became a part of what might be called the poisoned climate in the famous Stanford Prison Experiment—his role was that of a prison warden in addition to that of a neutral, scientific observer.

In summary, Zimbardo found that police officers commit abuse when two conditions are met: (1) intense pressure is put on them from authorities above them in the chain of command to produce information, arrests, or other tangible results, and (2) they work in units in which some individuals have come gradually to believe themselves to work outside or above the regular normative standards that apply to their colleagues. Both of these observations resonate with findings from the U.S. government reports that establish that intense pressure was placed on the personnel at Abu Ghraib to obtain intelligence and that the general state of affairs at the prison was one of intense social disorganization and chaos.

Zimbardo relates his findings from Brazil to his Stanford Prison Experiment as follows: "Analyses of the Stanford Prison Experiment have focused on the social-psychological variables involved in transforming healthy, normal, young male research participants into pathological prisoners or guards."[14] One of the most common understandings of this study is that it shows that ordinary, healthy individuals can become abusive due to an abusive social environment. However, Zimbardo has deepened and extended his interpretation of the 1971 findings in subsequent publications. The most important aspect of his reinterpretation is his focus on international, national, and local *layers* of norms, values, sanctions, and beliefs on the individual. Thus, in the 2002 book, he relates his findings from 1971 to the study of abusive Brazilian police officers and interrogators in three ways: (1) international governments and their representatives act as the "executive producer" of a drama that unfolds on a world stage; (2) national governments act as the director and playwright by providing "the system of rewards and sanctions as well as the legal and financial structure that supports and excuses atrocity; and (3) "bystander communities, both in the perpetrator's society and in the broader world, ... watch the play unfold in silence." Zimbardo relates explicitly these three aspects that led to abuse in Brazil to his Stanford Prison Experiment:

> Science represents the international level of facilitation with its quest for objective knowledge using experimental paradigms and approved analytical tools for evaluating the validity of the obtained data. The national level of facilitation comes in the form of a local institution, in this case, Stanford University and its psychology department.... But within the context of the experiment itself, the principal investigator also played the role of prison superintendent, a tactical error that confused the dispassionate scientist-researcher with the passionate prison official who was concerned primarily with maintaining the functioning of his institution. (264)

In his famous experiment, Zimbardo randomly assigned students who were determined to be psychologically healthy into two groups: guards and prisoners. The two groups were given appropriate uniforms. and "those to be prisoners were arrested by the city police at their homes or dormitories in a series of surprise raids" (262). Zimbardo writes that "interestingly, although neither group was given instructions on how to act, each group soon began to get into their roles stereotypically" (262).

Though the experiment was designed to run for two weeks it was terminated after only six days because the "simulated prison had become too real" (262). Zimbardo elaborates:

> Within a matter of days, the guards became authoritarian and even sadistic in some cases, while the prisoners became passive and totally submissive.... The guards dehumanized prisoners in many ways through punishment and harassment.... Some of the young men began to act sadistically toward the prisoners, take apparent pleasure in their own inventive cruelty. As processes of deindividuation, dehumanization, and moral disengagement unfolded, it no longer mattered to the guards that they were just in an experiment with other college boys who had been randomly assigned to play prisoners. In the end, the guards perceived the prisoners as dangerous—so much so that they decided some needed to be kept chained or in solitary confinement for longer than the maximum allowable duration while torturing other prisoners to keep them in line or force them to obey their authority. Some guards felt they were in a real prison, albeit run by psychologists rather than by the state. The distortions of reality were so extreme that prisoners forgot they could say, "I quit this experiment." Instead, they worked within the confines of the system and only requested parole, which was denied. (262)

This experiment involved more than the creation of an artificial environment whose findings are not relevant to real-life prisons. On the contrary, Zimbardo is aware that his role as a scientist–prison superintendent, the prestige of Stanford University, and the prestige of science all played roles in convincing both sets of students to act out their roles as sadists and victims. All these factors contributed to the normalization of the abuse that occurred in the experiment. One should ask, What would have happened to Zimbardo or Stanford or the prestige of science had any of the students been seriously hurt (e.g., murdered or committed suicide) in the experiment? One reply is that lawsuits and perhaps criminal prosecution could have ensued, and Zimbardo, the president of Stanford University, and even the Palo Alto Police Department might have been found to be culpable to some extent. Zimbardo ended the experiment before serious physical or emotional injury occurred. But had injury occurred, which of these three levels of society (science, the university and the police department, Zimbardo) would have been most culpable and responsible? And proportionate to their low level of responsibility relative to these other entities that were higher in the "chain of command," what was the culpability of the students who became sadistic? One might venture the opinion that had Zimbardo's experiment gone seriously awry, the president of Stanford University as well as officers in the American Psychological Association would have been liable. The Palo Alto Police Department might also have been liable for participating in the experiment—they arrested the students, and the arrests were staged so as to appear "real."

Posed in this way, Zimbardo's experiment and its relationship to real prison abuse become relevant to the issues being discussed here vis-à-vis Abu Ghraib. The correlates to Zimbardo's three layers of social analysis would most likely correspond to events at Abu Ghraib in the following way: The international community and the Geneva Conventions represent the international level, the U.S. Army and other government organizations represent the national level, and the disputed commanders at Abu Ghraib represent Zimbardo's role. Had Abu Ghraib been an "experiment" in the way that Zimbardo's study at Stanford was an experiment, the commander at Abu Ghraib (and it was not clear to the soldiers who was in charge of Abu Ghraib) would have "called it off" when the levels of sadism and abuse became intolerable by national and international standards. But the Abu Ghraib "experiment" continued until its failure was exposed to the international community via photographs that caused outrage at and embarrassment to the United States. This analogy begs the question: Who could have stopped the Abu Ghraib "experiment" as Zimbardo did at Stanford in 1971? The answer is not obvious, and it involves complex, intricate issues of how authority and responsibility are layered in the U.S. Army.

The other relevant issue concerns the culpability and responsibility of the soldiers who were low in the chain of command and who committed abusive acts. Why couldn't they say "I quit" or in other ways refuse to participate in the abuse? This is an important question, asked in various forms by the prosecution during the courts-martial. The prosecutor asked me in my role as an expert witness why Harman did not "walk out the door" when she witnessed abuse at Abu Ghraib. My reply to him was to the effect that she could have walked out the door physically but that realistically, she could no more walk out the door at Abu Ghraib than I could have walked out through the door of the courtroom in which I was testifying. The relatively healthy norms operating in the courtroom at Fort Hood, Texas, dictated that I walk out the door only when the judge dismissed me. The mostly unhealthy norms in the poisoned atmosphere at Abu Ghraib dictated that Harman "went along" with the abuse. Harman's social situation was similar to the position of scores of people throughout the world who find themselves in abusive relationships or abusive families and who feel that they cannot "walk out the door" of the relationship until someone from the outside pulls them out of the situation or gives them "permission" to walk out the door (the role of many therapists is to give the patients permission to finally act assertively and on their own behalf). Zimbardo's reply to a similar question regarding the student guards in the Stanford Prison Experiment as well as Brazilian police is complex:

> Although the good guards [at Stanford] never openly challenged the bad guards—and never even complained to the authorities about their colleagues' violations of prison rules—these good guards also never left early or arrived late for their shift.... It becomes evident that the actions of the atrocity perpetrators in the Stanford Prison Experiment must be appreciated within the concentric contexts created, provided, and maintained by the many direct and auxiliary facilitations. The same is absolutely the case among Brazil's atrocity perpetrators, whose solitary actions were always embedded in and circumscribed by legions of facilitators operating at the multiple levels outlined previously. (265)

One may elaborate on Zimbardo's explanation. The student guards in the Stanford Prison Experiment were restrained from reporting or stopping the abuse or even quitting the situation by layers of competing social and cultural rationalizations that offset the reality of the abuse. They believed that Stanford University would not permit real abuse to occur. They assumed that the institution of science would not put a student in a position that would cause him real harm or lead him to cause real harm to others. The scientist in charge of the experiment was the authority figure who would not allow the abuse to become excessive. How would a student—who holds low status in the hierarchy of the rational-legal organization that constitutes Stanford—"report" abuse to individuals who hold high status, from the officers in the Palo Alto Police Department to Professor Zimbardo, who is conducting an experiment at Stanford funded by the U.S. Navy? Of course, the student is physically capable of reporting Zimbardo or the Palo Alto Police Department. But, more important, a student does not feel psychologically or sociologically capable of reporting them due to perceived differences in social status. The student who recognized the abuse in the experiment might have felt invalidated by the prestige of the high-status individuals who approved of the "experiment." In other words, there existed a plethora of authority figures and symbols who carried great prestige and whose approval of the experiment precluded serious questioning of the abuse that occurred during the Stanford Prison Experiment. Similarly, Zimbardo argues that the perpetrators of abuse in the Brazilian police looked up to and idealized various authority figures and symbols whose approval of the abuse was assumed.

Applying these insights to the abuses committed at Abu Ghraib, one might conclude the following: The soldier who witnessed or even participated in the abuse at Abu Ghraib looked up to and idealized the prestige of the U.S. Army and of the international community whose support was assumed in the war against Saddam Hussein's pariah regime. One assumes that the soldier at Abu Ghraib felt trust, respect, and loyalty toward his or her superiors. One assumes that the soldiers at Abu Ghraib felt that their mission was honorable. The soldier would probably have assumed that the U.S. Army would not put him or her in a position in which he or she would be harmed unnecessarily, cause unlawful harm to others, or engage in actions that would bring forth disgrace to the military unit or the U.S. Army. Fay's report shows that in many instances, soldiers who questioned the abuse that they had witnessed were ignored, ridiculed, or invalidated in other ways. The most important finding by Fay in this regard is that the ICRC's reports of abuse were initially denied and ignored for an excessive period of time. His report notes that the response by Pappas to the copy of the ICRC results was "He did not believe it" (66). "He [Pappas] recalled he might have related to the staff that 'this stuff couldn't have been happening'" (66). In general, according to Fay, the reports by the ICRC "were not believed, nor were they adequately investigated" (64). The ICRC represents the international layer of norms in Zimbardo's explanation. If the voice of the international community was silenced at Abu Ghraib, what realistic chance did a soldier have to be heard? Similarly, therapists find that denial is a common response to the initial finding of abuse in dysfunctional relationships and families.

Zimbardo reflects that out of the fifty "outsiders" who visited his makeshift "prison" in the basement of the Psychology Department at Stanford University, only one expressed moral outrage at what was occurring. That one person was later given the status of a hero of sorts by the American Psychological Association.[15] A parallel may be drawn in this regard to the Abu Ghraib situation: If Zimbardo "heard" the protest of only one other professor during the Stanford Prison Experiment, he is probably correct to have concluded that he, along with the participants, had already been contaminated by the abuse that was occurring. Similarly, the denial of and failure to investigate the ICRC's observations suggest that the normative climate at Abu Ghraib had already been contaminated to the point that the abuse was no longer perceived as abuse. The abuse had been "normalized," so that an accurate perception of reality would not be validated by others in the social system.

I draw two important conclusions from this analysis of Zimbardo's "experiment." First, the *layering* of authority and norms in any situation is a valuable insight that I will use to analyze Abu Ghraib as well as to make constructive recommendations for preventing future abuse. The international, national, and local layers of authority must be lawful and synchronized with each other. Second, since the 1970s, contemporary research and review boards have been established at most universities in order to ensure that experiments and research studies that involve humans are ethical and do not cause harm to the participants—including psychological trauma. It is doubtful that Zimbardo's 1971 experiment would be approved in contemporary times. The lesson that I draw, and apply to the Abu Ghraib scandal, is that the military might consider similar review boards before embarking on new "experiments" in interrogation and detention. The costs of the failed "experiments" at Abu Ghraib, Guantánamo, and elsewhere seem to outweigh the benefits. It appears that very little intelligence was gathered while great harm has been inflicted on the honor and prestige of the United States and its military forces, on innocent people, and on international relations for many years to come.

Conclusion

The government's few rotten apples theory is problematic but persistent. No matter how many new cases of abuse are investigated and prosecuted, with regard to Abu Ghraib and elsewhere, the government can always blame the abuse on a few corrupt individuals. This theory relies on magical thinking to explain facts that are inconsistent with it. The abuse at Abu Ghraib was part of a widespread *pattern* of abuse and climate of abuse at Guantánamo Bay, in Afghanistan, and elsewhere in Iraq. The abuse has continued and, by some reports, increased at these geographically distant locations since the discovery of abuse at Abu Ghraib. Magical thinking would have one believe that corrupt soldiers at Abu Ghraib, Guantánamo Bay, and other locations spontaneously invented remarkably similar methods of committing abuse that include forced nudity, pyramid stacking, yelling, sleep deprivation, stress positions, and so on. More magical thinking is required to explain away the observation that some of these methods bear remarkable resemblance to interrogation techniques gone awry. And still more magical thinking is required to explain the fact that officers, who bear command responsibility, and who knew or should have known of this abuse, are cut out of the picture almost entirely. At the courts-martial that I witnessed, the various defense teams requested the testimony of dozens of officers and were granted the testimony of only *two* officers. I have not exhausted the many other resorts to magical thinking that are required to maintain the theory of the few rotten apples as the explanation for the abuse at Abu Ghraib *and* elsewhere.

Notes

1. JoAnn Wypijewski, "Judgment Days," *Harper's,* February 2006, 40.
2. See, for example, Josh White, "5 Soldiers Charged with Abuse of Detainees; 3 Beaten in Iraq, Army Alleges," *Washington Post,* November 8, 2005, A12: these soldiers were "with the 75th Ranger Regiment in Iraq"; Mark Mazzetti and John Hendren, "Mock Executions of Iraqi Detainees Cited by Army," *Los Angeles Times,* May 18, 2005, A5: "Capt. Shawn L. Martin of the 3rd Armored Cavalry Regiment was convicted of aggravated assault and battery [and] sentenced to 45 days confinement and fined $12,000"; Scott Gold, "5 California Guardsmen Face Charges of Abusing Iraqis," *Los Angeles Times,* August 23, 2005, A1: they were part of the "3rd Infantry Division in Iraq"; Sarah Left, "US Abuse of Afghan Prisoners Widespread," *The Guardian,* May 20, 2005: "Seven soldiers have been charged in connection with abuse at Bagram, where the paper reports that harsh treatment by some interrogators was routine"; James Ross, "Shine Light on Dark Stain of US Prisoner Abuse," *Baltimore Sun,* October 11, 2005; Arthur Kane, "Iraqi General Beaten 2 Days before Death: Maj. Gen. Abed Mowhoush Was Severely Beaten by CIA and Special-Forces Soldiers during Questioning," *Denver Post,* April 5, 2005; Gwendolyn Driscoll and John McDonald, "Army Charges 11 'Night-Stalkers' in Abuse of Captives: Entire Company Is Restricted and Their Commander Is Suspended," *Houston Chronicle,* July 29, 2005, A26: "accused soldiers from the 184th Infantry Regiment"; Jamie Wilson, "Marines Beat US Workers in Iraq," *The Guardian,* June 9, 2005; Jamie Wilson and Ian Traynor, "East Europe Has Secret CIA Jails for al-Qaida," *The Guardian,* November 3, 2005; Robert Cornwell, "US Navy to Investigate New Images of Apparent Abuse of Hooded Detainees," *The Independent,* December 5, 2004, 18.
3. Human Rights Watch, "By the Numbers: Findings of the Detainee Abuse and Accountability Project," vol. 18, no. 2G (New York: Author, April 26, 2006), http://hrw.org/reports/2006/ct0406/ct0406web.pdf, 1.
4. Human Rights Watch, "By the Numbers," 11.
5. See, for example, Adam Zagorin, "Another Abu Ghraib?" *Time,* September 26, 2005.
6. Vol. 17, no. 3G, http://hrw.org/reports/2005/us0905. Page numbers referring to this report are cited in parentheses,
7. See "Judge Orders Release of Prisoner Abuse Photos," Associated Press,

June 9, 2006, which quotes the judge as saying, "Terrorists do not need pretexts for their barbarism."

8. This is the dominant assumption in a paradigm called *structural-func-tionalism,* which is the dominant paradigm in social theory. It is typically attributed to the Harvard sociologist Talcott Parsons, among others.

9. Richard Falk, Irene Gendzier, and Robert Jay Lifton, eds., *Crimes of War: Iraq* (New York: Nation Books, 2006), 340.

10. See American Civil Liberties Union, "The Civil Liberties and Civil Rights Record of Attorney General Nominee Alberto Gonzales" (Washington, D.C.: Author, 2005), http://www.aclu.org/FilesPDFs/gonzalesreport.pdf; U.S. Department of Justice, "Memorandum for Alberto R. Gonzales, Counsel to the President," August 1, 2002.

11. "AR 15–6 Investigation of the Abu Ghraib Detention Facility and 205th MI Brigade," August 23, 2004.

12. See Philip G. Zimbardo, "The Power and Pathology of Imprisonment," *Congressional Record,* Serial No. 15, October 25, 1971; C. Haney, W. Banks, and P. Zimbardo, "Study of Prisoners and Guards in a Simulated Prison," *Naval Research Reviews* 9 (1973): 1–17 (Washington D.C.: Office of Naval Research); C. Haney, W. Banks, and P. Zimbardo, "Interpersonal Dynamics in a Simulated Prison," *International Journal of Criminology and Penology* 1 (1973): 69–97.

13. Martha K. Huggins, Mika Haritos-Fatouros, and Philip G. Zimbardo, *Violence Workers: Police Torturers and Murderers Reconstruct Brazilian Atrocities* (Berkeley: University of California Press, 2002).

14. Huggins et al., *Violence Workers,* 261.

15. Christina Maslach, "The Stanford Prison Experiment: Still Powerful after All These Years," paper presented at the annual meeting of the American Psychological Association, August 12, 1996, Toronto.

CHAPTER TWO

THE POISONED ORCHARD

At Fort Hood, the military judge said, "The army is not on trial here." But in the government reports, it seems as if the army *is* on trial. Some of the reports are available to the public through the Internet and in book form[1] as well, but they do not seem to have had much impact on public opinion or the information media. To read and comprehend the reports is to realize what the government and the information media have left out of the story of Abu Ghraib. To be more precise: one part of the government disclosed a great deal in its reports, while another part of the government suppressed and distorted the reports.

Overall, the reports provide insights into the social and psychological context of the "orchard" at Abu Ghraib. Some of the reports are brief and relatively unknown, whereas others, such as the Taguba, Fay, and Schlesinger reports, are lengthy and better known. All the reports suggest a widespread pattern of abuse throughout Iraq, links with abuse at Guantánamo and in Afghanistan, and an abnormal social climate at Abu Ghraib.

The Herrington Report

One of the most neglected reports in the Abu Ghraib saga was issued as early as December 12, 2003, by retired colonel Stuart Herrington. The date of the report suggests that the army knew or should have known of abuse at Abu Ghraib well before the photographs were leaked. It is worth quoting at some length because of the serious problems that it uncovered:

> Approximately 6,000 detainees are interred there, both criminal and security detainees. Of these, approximately 400–500 of MI interest reside in JDIC facilities (a small tent city), while an additional 400–500 of MI interest are overflow, and live in parts of the prison proper.... The problem of

49

overpopulation at Abu Ghraib is serious, and must be resolved urgently, and that failure to resolve this problem could lead to further rioting and serious danger to U.S. personnel.... The Abu Ghraib facility is unsuitable for the exploitation of high value detainees (3–4).

Note that Herrington's investigative team found that hundreds of MI soldiers were living in the prison itself! The report goes on to cite serious problems with supplies, a fact that would be brought out during the courts-martial through the testimony of the supply officer:

We found conditions at Abu Ghraib austere, with JIDC [Joint Interrogation and Detention Center] personnel grateful for some recent improvements, but complaining of shortages of essential supplies and equipment, including computers, paper, electrical power, linguists, reports officers, vehicles to transport detainees, hand-held radios, and analyst notebook software, to name a few.... The facility is a pressure cooker where it is only a matter of time before prisoners stage an uprising (5).

The report goes on to cite a violation of the Geneva Conventions at another prison nearby, the Baghdad International Airport complex:

I personally question the wisdom and legality of keeping a senior detainee like Tarik Aziz in a 5 by 10 foot prison cell with a steel door and a pass-through (Geneva Convention, Article 44, "Officers and prisoners of equivalent status shall be treated with the regard due to their rank and age")....
If we are by policy extending Geneva Convention standards to them, Mr. Aziz and other senior Iraqi detainees should be better housed. To do so is smart from an intelligence exploitation perspective (7).

Herrington also found evidence of detainees who "showed signs of having been mistreated (beaten) by their captors" (8). He continues: "I asked the officer if he had reported this problem. He replied that 'Everyone knows about it.' I advised the officer that this was inadequate. He should document this problem in writing" (8). Herrington concludes, regarding interrogation, that "history may show that we had a 12-month opportunity to accomplish this task, and at best managed a C– in the effort" (9). He then goes on to make recommendations based on findings of fact:

- Some military units "are sweeping up large numbers of people and dumping them at the door of Abu Ghraib." Moreover, "Some detainees arrive at Abu Ghraib who were detained because the correct target of a raid was not at home, so a family member was taken in his place (either 'voluntarily' or against his will), who would then be released when the target turns himself in. This practice, if it is being done, has a 'hostage' feel to it" (9).

- "Colonel Pappas remarked that he has 3,800 detainees that he has no intention of interrogating, and whom he would release immediately if given the authority. This would defuse the potentially dangerous situation described earlier in this report. Suggest that you might consider a policy whereby a detainee must be interrogated within 21 days of arrival at the JIDC" (9).
- "Right now, at Abu Ghraib, there are approximately 350 MP personnel responsible for guarding more than 6,000 detainees, a dangerously low ratio in a facility subject to hostile action from outside, and which has already had shootouts resulting in the deaths of detainees" (10).
- "U.S. forces will not be well-placed to be co-located at this infamous and (frankly, filthy) facility [Abu Ghraib] where who-knows-what kinds of policies will be put in place by succeeding Iraqi authorities in handling their own detainees. ... Consider building a new facility and bringing in a contract prison management firm to run it" (11).
- "We should do better at conforming to the guidance in the Geneva Conventions that calls for detainees to be treated in accordance with their rank" (11).
- "Conducting sweep operations in which many persons who are detained who probably should not be detained, and who then wind up incarcerated for three to six months, is counterproductive to the Coalition's efforts to win the cooperation of the Iraqi citizenry. Similarly, mistreatment of captives as has been reported to me and our team is unacceptable, and bound to become known by the population" (12).

Herrington makes an interesting analogy to the Vietnam War in these regards:

> I do not wish to disparage our fine fighting men and women, but those of us who served in MACV in Vietnam dreaded it when USARV (U.S. line units) had to come into our districts and villages. They were often heavy-handed, reliant on massive firepower, and could undo in a few hours what we had striven to accomplish with the people for months. I am sure the same is or will be true in Iraq. (12)

It seems that none of Herrington's recommendations were followed, including the wise suggestion that the United States should not have used Abu Ghraib due to its infamous symbolism as the site of Saddam Hussein's torture, and also because it was located in the middle of a war zone. The issue of U.S. soldiers taking hostages came out briefly at the courts-martial but was not pursued. But, most important, the date of this report suggests that the government knew or had access to knowledge that serious abuse was occurring at several prisons in Iraq, including Abu Ghraib, prior to the release of the photos in January 2004. Moreover, I concur with Herrington that Iraqis would have learned of the abuse even if the photos had not been released. It was counterproductive and unwise to abuse prisoners in Iraq from the perspectives of gaining intelligence, suppressing insurgency, and building long-term trust with Iraqi citizens.

A Psychological Report on Abu Ghraib

Another important report that is not usually cited was authored by a military psychiatrist.[2] This report makes many psychological and sociological observations that explain the abuse at Abu Ghraib:

> First, soldiers were immersed in the Islamic culture, a culture that many were encountering for a first time. Clearly there are major differences in worship and beliefs, and there is the association of Muslims with terrorism. All these causes exaggerate differences and create misperceptions that can lead to a fear or devaluation of a people.
>
> Second, quality of life at Abu Ghraib was poor, and lacking most amenities present in other camps in Iraq. The population [at Abu Ghraib] was disparate, consisting of hardened Iraqi criminals watched by corrupt Iraqi prison guards, as well as varying types of detainees: males, females, juveniles, criminals, terrorists, and mentally ill.
>
> Third, all present at Abu Ghraib were truly in personal danger.
>
> Fourth, command factors were a key player.... There was not only a lack of interaction but also friction between the MP and MI command elements.... Discipline, when taken, was lenient ... thus contributing to a mentality that "I can get away with this."

The report continues: "Given this atmosphere of danger, promiscuity, and negativity, the worst human qualities and behaviors came to the fore and a perversive [*sic*] dominance came to prevail, especially at Abu Ghraib." Moreover, "the MI unit seemed to be operating in a conspiracy of silence," and "the sadistic and psychopathic behavior was appalling and shocking." Contrary to the prosecution's efforts at the courts-martial to shift all the blame onto the night shift, this report makes it clear that it was commonplace for detainees to be abused. "Detainee abuse was common knowledge among the enlisted soldiers at Abu Ghraib.... Even officers witnessed abuse on several occasions or had knowledge of abuse."

The psychiatrist notes that "everyday life was extremely stressful." He continues:

> Clearly some detainees at Abu Ghraib were totally humiliated and degraded. This is a classic example of the legal formula that "predisposition + opportunity = criminal behavior." Predisposition included the psychological factors of negativity, anger, hatred, and desire to dominate and humiliate. And, with an unsupervised workplace in which no threat of appropriate punishment would be forthcoming, there was opportunity....
>
> These detainees are male and female, young and old; they may be innocent, may have high intelligence value, or may be terrorists or criminals. No matter who they are, if they are at Abu Ghraib, they are remanded in deplorable, dangerous living conditions, as are the Soldiers. Thus, [Abu Ghraib] has both depressive and anxiety-laden elements that would grind down even the most motivated Soldier and lead to anger and possibly loss of control.

The gist of my expert testimony would be similar: the work environment at Abu Ghraib was chronically poisoned for soldiers and prisoners alike, and the abuse was inevitable. This military psychiatrist concludes, "Physicians and chaplains are needed for the body and spirit, but mental health providers are needed for the mind. A psychiatrist or psychologist should be on the lookout for significant anger/depressive/anxiety symptoms, and he/she would also provide education and support to prevent Soldiers from any negative conditioning that could impair job performance. Our Soldiers deserve no less." Physicians, psychiatrists, and psychologists have been used in dubious ways at Abu Ghraib and elsewhere to assist in activities that often deteriorated into abuse. The army seems to have overlooked the obvious fact that mental health professionals could have been used for the positive, constructive purposes of maintaining and promoting a healthy social environment for soldiers and prisoners alike.

The importance of this report is that it clearly shifts the focus away from blaming a handful of soldiers for the abuse and toward the structure of the social climate for promoting suffering and abuse for everyone at Abu Ghraib—soldiers and prisoners.

The Taguba Report

MG Antonio M. Taguba issued his report in the spring of 2004.[3] It was the first report to be issued following the disclosure of the photographs. But the Taguba report was preceded by the Ryder report, which was filed on November 5, 2003, and the Herrington report, which was filed on December 12, 2003, long before the photographs of the abuse were leaked. Of great interest is the fact that the Ryder, Herrington, and Taguba reports all found similar problems of systemic abuse and potential for more abuse even though they were written at disparate times. Taguba found that "CJTF-7 did not have authorities and procedures in place to affect a unified strategy to detain, interrogate, and report information from detainees/internees in Iraq" (6). Commenting on MG Donald J. Ryder's earlier report, Taguba writes, "Unfortunately, many of the systemic problems that surfaced during MG Ryder's Team's assessment are the very same issues that are the subject of this investigation. In fact, many of the abuses suffered by detainees occurred during, or near to, the time of that assessment" (9). This finding alone suggests a dysfunctional self-correcting mechanism in place at Abu Ghraib and the chain of command above it, in that Ryder's findings of conditions leading to abuse were not corrected adequately.

In his statements of fact, Taguba asserts that between October and December 2003, "numerous incidents of sadistic, blatant and wanton criminal abuses were inflicted on several detainees" (12). He writes, "This *systemic* and illegal abuse of detainees was intentionally perpetrated by several members of the military police guard force" (12; emphasis added). Elsewhere he implies that MPs did not concoct the abuse on their own: "Military Intelligence (MI) interrogators and other US Government Agency's (OGA) interrogators actively requested that MP guards set physical and mental conditions for favorable interrogation of witnesses" (14). In line with the other reports, Taguba found that soldiers "had received no training in detention/internee operations," adding, "I also find that very little instruction or training was provided to MP personnel on the applicable rules of the Geneva Convention Relative to the Treatment of Prisoners of War" (15). Thus, the international layer of normative structure was not sufficiently functional at Abu Ghraib.

Taguba found that "there is a general lack of knowledge, implementation, and emphasis of basic, legal, regulatory, doctrinal, and command requirements within the 800th MP Brigade and its subordinate units" (17). Furthermore, "the handling of detainees and criminal prisoners after in-processing was inconsistent from detention facility to detention facility, compound to compound, encampment to encampment, and even shift to shift throughout the 800th MP Brigade AOR" (17).

Throughout his report, Taguba found indicators of long-term social chaos without using this term. He found "lack of standardization," checks that were "regularly inaccurate," "lapses in accountability and confusion at the soldier level," "lack of discipline," accountability operations that "lacked specificity," poor accountability procedures, soldiers who were "poorly prepared and untrained," overcrowding, and that "no lessons learned seem to have been disseminated to subordinate units to enable corrective action at the lowest level" (18–19). Moreover, "neither the camp rules nor the provisions of the Geneva Conventions are posted in English or in the language of the detainees at any of the detention facilities" (21). The international layer of norms seems not to have been adequately operating at Abu Ghraib, thereby creating a closed social environment. In addition, "there was virtually a complete lack of detailed SOPs [standard operating procedures] at any of the detention facilities" (24). "Morale suffered" at Abu Ghraib (25). "The quality of life for Soldiers assigned to Abu Ghraib was extremely poor" (26). There was "friction" and "lack of effective communication" between the MI and MP brigades. There existed an "ambiguous command relationship" at Abu Ghraib (26).

Taguba writes, "In addition I find that psychological factors, such as the difference in culture, the Soldiers' quality of life, the real presence of mortal danger over an *extended time period,* and the failure of commanders to recognize these pressures contributed to the *perversive* [*sic*] *atmosphere* that existed at Abu Ghraib" (30; emphasis added). It is not clear whether Taguba meant to write "perverse atmosphere" or "pervasive atmosphere," but in either case, he seems to be describing a chronic, dysfunctional social atmosphere at Abu Ghraib along the lines of other reports.

A consistent theme in the reports is that the authors eventually link incidents of abuse to social climates, environments, and atmospheres of abuse.

The Fay Report

MG George R. Fay writes, "This investigation found that certain individuals committed offenses in violation of international and US law to include the Geneva Conventions and the UCMJ and violated Army Values. Leaders in key positions failed properly to supervise the interrogation operations at

Abu Ghraib and failed to understand the dynamics created at Abu Ghraib" (7). Note that several layers of normative structure are invoked and that Fay is treating Abu Ghraib as a social system, although he does not use this sociological term explicitly. He claims correctly that any given criminal act committed at Abu Ghraib may be conceptualized as breaking several layers of norms simultaneously—in this case, ranging from international laws to local understandings of values held by U.S. Army military units.

The general continues, "The *environment* created at Abu Ghraib contributed to the occurrence of such abuse and the fact that it remained undiscovered by higher authority for a *long period of time*. What started as nakedness and humiliation ... *carried over* into sexual and physical assaults by a small group of morally corrupt and unsupervised Soldiers and civilians" (10; emphasis added). Subsequent findings by human rights organizations dispel the premature conclusion that the abuse was limited to a small group of corrupt soldiers (rotten apples). More important, Fay seems to be claiming that the gradual tolerance of initial abuse in the form of nakedness and humiliation created a *social climate* in which abuse was normalized, and serious abuse eventually ensued. Throughout his report, he makes the correct, sociological connection between the social "environment," or what he calls elsewhere social "atmosphere," to abuse. Although he does not say it explicitly, he is clearly not writing about the environment and atmosphere as phenomena pertaining to meteorology. He is using these terms to refer to "social environment" as a system of norms, values, sanctions, and beliefs, although he does not use this sociological vocabulary explicitly.

However, it is not clear on what basis Fay concludes that the sexual and physical assault was the result of a small group of morally corrupt individuals. First, he makes it clear that the sexual and physical abuse was part of the overall "poisoned" atmosphere at Abu Ghraib. Second, he makes it clear that the sexual and physical abuse was part of an overall, long-term, and gradually progressive pattern of normative breakdown that includes other forms of abuse, including unauthorized use of dogs, the improper use of isolation, humiliating and degrading forms of treatment, nudity, and other forms of abuse. Third, he fails to explain how and why the officers at Abu Ghraib would have permitted morally corrupt individuals to commit abuse or why officers failed to properly sanction them after the initial acts of abuse. A healthy social system supposedly corrects itself at the first signs of abuse, whereas an unhealthy or dysfunctional social system is unable or unwilling to self-correct, and thereby spirals into a vortex of further abuse. Fourth, Fay does not explain his logic in singling out sexual and physical abuse as the attributes of corrupt individuals and not attributing the other forms of abuse to corrupt individuals. Finally, morally corrupt individuals (e.g., the small minority of persons who can be identified as sadists, perverts, or otherwise severely disturbed through the use of psychological testing, such as those with personality disorders) exist in all social settings, but this does not mean that they are able to impose easily their abusive fantasies and sadistic behavior onto others. Under normal conditions, a healthy social system will keep morally corrupt individuals under control through the layered system of norms, values, sanctions, and beliefs that regulates everyone, from the healthiest individuals to the most corrupt.

Thus, I do not question Fay's findings of fact. I do understand and support his sociological connection between an unhealthy social environment and resultant abuse overall. But I do not support and do not find him explaining or justifying his conclusion that the physical and sexual abuse was the result of a few morally corrupt individuals. He contradicts himself regarding this conclusion in any event: if the poisoned social climate set the stage for all the abuse, including physical and sexual abuse, then the real culprit is the poisoned social climate, not a handful of individuals. The most apt explanation is that the gradual, long-term development of an unhealthy social climate at Abu Ghraib led to the normalization of abuse, which then led to more serious abuse as well as conditions that would make it difficult if not impossible to distinguish or report the abuse.

Fay writes: "The climate created at Abu Ghraib provided the opportunity for such abuse to occur and to continue undiscovered by higher authority for a long period of time" (71). This important claim begs the question: Who or what is responsible for introducing the unlawful climate and failing to restore it to a lawful, normative state? Fay does not address this question. He then makes the critical logical leap: "What started as undressing and humiliation, stress and physical training (PT), *carried over* into sexual and physical assaults by a small group of morally corrupt and unsupervised Soldiers and civilians" (71). Note that he has added "stress" and "physical training"—which are somewhat normative in the U.S. Army in that its own soldiers are routinely exposed to stress and PT—to a list of phenomena that includes nudity and humiliation, which are not as normative. The fascinating notion of quasi-abusive and potentially abusive behavior being "carried over" into full-fledged abuse is sociologically apt. It is not sufficient to blame a morally corrupt individual as an explanation for any crime or abusive act, because the social setting that failed to set appropriate limits and boundaries must be taken into account.

How and why did the unauthorized undressing and humiliation begin in the first place? What led to the initial breach of norms, and how did these breaches "carry over" into systemic breaches of norms that resulted in chaotic abuse? This is the crux of the issue that needs to be explained yet is not addressed by the U.S. government reports.

Confusion as to Who Was in Charge

Fay notes that at Abu Ghraib, "people made up their own titles as things went along" (43). He adds that "some people thought COL Pappas was the Director; some thought LTC Jordan was the Director" (43). It seems frankly incredible that no one was certain who in the U.S. Army was in charge of and responsible for Abu Ghraib. However, other facts and testimony suggest that MI officers in general were in charge of Abu Ghraib—this is the gist of Karpinski's complaint that her role as MP commander in Iraq was usurped. She writes in her book that Taguba asked her whether she thought that her superiors were blowing her off:

> "Yes, sir," I answered, and later I elaborated. "They did not want to be bothered by me. And were they blowing me off because I was a reservist? Yes.... And for a lot of other reasons? Absolutely."
>
> After a long career spent in avoiding the caricature of an "emotional" woman, I made sure to keep my voice level throughout the session. Long before it concluded, I saw clearly that I was being set up.[4]

Karpinski was the commander at Abu Ghraib—but not really. Pappas was the commander at Abu Ghraib—but not really. Soldiers testified at the courts-martial that they were not sure who was in charge.

Confusion between Approved versus Abusive Activities

According to Fay, "Theater Interrogation and Counter-Resistance Policies (ICRP) were found to be poorly defined, and changed several times. As a result, interrogation activities sometimes crossed into abusive activity" (7). The general is referring here to various memorandums that were out of sync with established military protocol concerning interrogation and detention. Note again the fascinating yet astute observation that the confusion in policy "crossed over" into abuse in the manner previously discussed. Apparently, social chaos existed at the highest as well as the lowest levels in the chain of command.

The Gitmoization and Afghanistanization of Abu Ghraib

Fay notes that nondoctrinal approaches that were approved for use in Afghanistan and Guantánamo Bay "became confused at Abu Ghraib and were implemented without proper authorities or safeguards" and that "soldiers were not trained on non-doctrinal interrogation techniques" (8). However, nondoctrinal methods (which violated the Geneva Conventions) were "doctrinal" in Afghanistan and Guantánamo Bay, and they might have been "doctrinal" in Iraq except that the government asserted that the Geneva Conventions were supposed to apply in Iraq. Without using the word, Fay is really writing about the Gitmoization of Abu Ghraib. It is unclear whether the unlawful techniques being discussed migrated to Abu Ghraib primarily from Guantánamo Bay or in tandem with unlawful techniques from Afghanistan.

The Unauthorized Use of Dogs

One of the nondoctrinal approaches to which Fay refers is the use of dogs based on "several documents that spoke of exploiting the Arab fear of dogs" (10). He concludes that in Iraq, "the use of dogs in interrogations to 'fear up' detainees was utilized without proper authorization" (10). But the entire notion of "proper authorization" was open to social construction and was ambiguous at Abu Ghraib. It is mind-numbing to read these and other accounts of what was doctrinal versus nondoctrinal, lawful versus unlawful, allowed versus prohibited at Abu Ghraib because there is no definitive answer.

Fay writes that as of November 20, 2003, "abuse of detainees was already occurring and the addition of dogs was just one more abuse device" (83). Interrogators were influenced by several documents that "spoke of exploiting the Arab fear of dogs," and controversy arose over who "owned" the dogs and how they would be used. MG Fay writes that the use of dogs is "associated with MG G. Miller's visit" in September 2003. Fay notes that "even with all the apparent confusion over roles, responsibilities and authorities, there were early indications that MP and MI personnel knew the use of dog teams in interrogations was abusive" (84). How did they know? If some soldiers suspected that their use of dogs as weapons was abusive at the same time that they engaged in abuse because of chaos and unlawful orders, they were placed in what social scientists call a "double-bind" situation: one is damned if one does and damned if one does not engage in abuse. Following the quasi-authoritative order to use the dogs damns them into committing abuse. Refusing to follow the quasi-authoritative order damns them into possible court-martial proceedings for disobeying orders as well as the censure of their peers who were, for the most part, "going along" with the perceived abuse. Double-bind situations are common in dysfunctional families such that the child or dependent spouse is punished or rewarded for behaving or not behaving in a certain way. Prolonged periods of experiencing double-bind situations have been found to lead to some forms of mental illness. One can empathize with the extreme stress that both soldiers and prisoners experienced at Abu Ghraib as a result of double-bind situations.

Insufficient Training

Fay writes, "As pointed out clearly in the MG Taguba report, MP units and individuals at Abu Ghraib lacked sufficient training on operating a detainment/interrogation facility" and that "MI units and individuals also lacked sufficient, appropriate training to cope with the situation encountered at Abu Ghraib" (46). The lack of normative consensus was so great that Fay asserts that soldiers did not know what they were permitted to do or not do:

> Guard and interrogation personnel at Abu Ghraib were not adequately trained or experienced and were certainly not well versed in the cultural understanding of the detainees. MI personnel were *totally ignorant* of MP lanes in the road or rules of engagement. A common observation was that MI knew what MI could do and what MI couldn't do; but MI did *not know* what the MPs could or could *not* do in their activities. (46; emphasis added)

In this passage, the general seems to imply that role confusion occurred such that MI did not know the role expectations for MPs. However, in another passage, Fay suggests that this role confusion was pervasive, extending to the role expectations for MIs, MPs, and their perceptions of each other's role expectations: "Again, who was allowed to do what and how exactly they were to do it was *totally unclear*. Neither of the communities (MI and MP) knew what the other could and could not do" (70; emphasis added). The phrase "totally unclear" constitutes a very powerful description of the apparently drastic extent of social chaos at Abu Ghraib. Fay does not use milder qualifiers such as "somewhat unclear," "often unclear," or "mostly unclear"—but "*totally* unclear." According to Fay, "Most of the MPs were *never trained* in prison operations" (46; emphasis added). One could not expect even the minimal semblance of "social order" and consensus in a social milieu that relied on persons who were not trained in the normative expectations for their roles. This aspect of the social milieu at Abu Ghraib might be likened to a university whose professors were trained to be auto mechanics or a medical clinic run by personnel trained in agriculture.

Furthermore, according to Fay, "approximately 35% of the contract interrogators lacked formal military training as interrogators" (50). In addition, "proper oversight did not occur at Abu Ghraib due to a lack of training and inadequate contract management and monitoring" (52).

In the court-martial of Javal Davis, the prosecutor asserted that no one needs to be trained to know the difference between right and wrong and, more specifically, that Davis knew it was wrong to stomp on the hands and feet of detainees. But using the prosecutor's logic, one could argue that the U.S. government knew or should have known that it was wrong to run the prison at Abu Ghraib in the disorganized and chaotic way in which it was apparently run. Who in the army signed off that the soldiers were prepared for their mission at Abu Ghraib? In summary, this report makes it clear that the U.S. Army failed to train its soldiers in the many norms, values, beliefs, and sanctions that pertain to interrogation and detention techniques in accord with its own manuals as well as the Geneva Conventions.

Lack of Social Integration within the Military Units at Abu Ghraib

Fay writes, "The JIDC was created in a very short time period with parts and pieces of various units. It lacked unit integrity, and this lack was a fatal flaw" (9). The very act of conjoining interrogation and detention activities is nondoctrinal. Elsewhere, Fay elaborates that "cross-leveling" (the military name for the process of transferring individual soldiers instead of the more normative process of transferring entire military units) occurred with the "disadvantage of inserting Soldiers into units shortly before deployment who had never trained with those units" (32). In summary, "The Soldiers did not know the unit," and "the unit and the unit leadership did not know the Soldiers" (32). Pappas had at his disposal "disparate elements of units and individuals, including civilians, that had never trained together but now were going to have to fight together" (32). Later in the report, Fay emphasizes this point: "It is important to understand that the MI units at Abu Ghraib were far from complete units. They were small elements from those units. Most of the elements that came to Abu Ghraib came without their normal command structure. The unit Commanders and

Senior NCOs did not go to Abu Ghraib but stayed with the bulk of their respective units" (41). He also notes that "JIDC interrogators, analysts, and leaders were unprepared for the arrival of contract interrogators and had no training to fall back on in the management, control, and discipline of these personnel" (19). Moreover, the civilian contract interrogators were supposed to be screened yet "such screening was not occurring" (40).

In his conclusion, Fay explains:

> The JIDC was established in an ad hoc manner without proper planning, personnel, and logistical support for the missions it was intended to perform. Interrogation and analyst personnel were quickly kluged together from a half dozen units in an effort to meet personnel requirements. Even at its peak strength, interrogation and analyst manpower at the JIDC was too shorthanded to deal with the large number of detainees at hand. (113)

Lack of adequate social integration among the individuals who make up a social system has been found by sociologists to lead to many problems, ranging from divorce to suicide.[5] In a landmark study of the American military, sociologist Samuel Stouffer found that social integration correlates with high morale and that lack of social integration correlates with low morale and numerous social problems.[6] This is because soldiers who train together and fight together in the same military units develop bonds of friendship and loyalty to each other even more than they develop loyalty to the government's cause in fighting a war. Moreover, such bonds of affection act as a deterrent on abuse in ways that are similar to how an emotionally warm and integrated family unit deters abuse among its members: the individual can be corrected with a look or a mild reprimand and will comply with group norms out of a sense of affection and loyalty. On the other extreme, when soldiers do not feel emotionally attached to other members in the military unit—which may have been the case in the Vietnam War due to cross-leveling and the rapid rotation of individuals within some units—each soldier may feel that he or she is basically on his or her own, waiting for the tour of duty to expire.[7]

Similarly, soldiers at Abu Ghraib apparently did not feel emotionally connected with each other or as part of the same team or mission. Morale suffers, as Stouffer, Lifton, and others have found, but more important for the purposes of this study, morality suffers also when social integration is low. Soldiers come to *fear* each other instead of experiencing feelings of trust and affection for each other. For example, during Harman's court-martial, a soldier confessed on the witness stand that he did not try to stop the abuse he witnessed because he feared that his fellow soldiers would abuse him like they were abusing prisoners had he tried to stop them. It is important to make the connection that dysfunctional families are also dominated by negative emotions such as fear, obligation, shame, and guilt instead of positive, integrative emotions such as trust, affection, honor, and acceptance.

Rapid Changes in the Social Milieu

Fay writes, "By mid-October, interrogation policy in Iraq had changed three times in less than 30 days" (28). He also notes, "There is no formal advanced interrogation training in the U.S. Army" (17). Furthermore, "most interrogator training that occurred at Abu Ghraib was on-the-job training" (18). Rapid social change is in itself a promoter of stress and contributes to social disorganization. These findings must be conjoined with Fay's other findings that MI and MP roles were blurred (a finding confirmed in the Taguba and Schlesinger reports) so that the "on the job" training in interrogation applied to MPs as well as MIs. The state of affairs described in the Fay report constitutes yet another variety of social chaos at Abu Ghraib.

The literature in the subfield of medical sociology on the effects of rapid social change on stress is vast and convincing. From the pioneering work by Hans Selye[8] to empirical verification by subsequent researchers, social scientists have found that any change, positive or negative, leads to stress: marriage as well as divorce, promotion as well as demotion, inheriting wealth as well as losing money, holidays as well as the rat race of mundane life, and so forth, all promote change and thereby result in stress. Soldiers at Abu Ghraib were forced to undergo numerous, extreme, and rapid instances of change that go far beyond the changes in interrogation and detention techniques that Fay detected, including rapid deployment for war, separation from loved ones, sudden separation from their usual military units, sudden deployment into a new military unit at Abu Ghraib, a sudden change in job roles, constant yet unpredictable mortar attacks, sudden influx of new prisoners, and sudden and unexplained disappearance of prisoners, among other phenomena. The general rule of thumb is that mental health is maintained by stability and that it is eroded by sudden, rapid, and unpredictable change—especially if such unpredictability becomes chronic. From this perspective, it is understandable that Davis referred to Abu Ghraib as "hell on earth," Graner called it "Bizarroworld," and other soldiers described it in everyday terms that denote extreme stress. Karpinski corroborates this feeling when she writes, "Soldiers assigned to Abu Ghraib thought they might as well have been sent to hell."[9]

Intense Pressure to Obtain Intelligence

Fay writes, "As the need for actionable intelligence rose, the realization dawned that pre-war planning had not included planning for detainee operations" (24). Later in the report, he elaborates: "LTG Sanchez did not believe significant pressure was coming from outside CJTF-7, but does confirm that there was great pressure placed upon the intelligence system to produce actionable intelligence" (42). "COL Pappas perceived intense pressure for intelligence from interrogations," he adds, and this pressure was passed "to the rest of the JIDC leadership" (42). Fay elaborates that "pressure consisted in deviation from doctrinal reporting standards" and other ways (42). To repeat: Zimbardo and others have found that intense pressure on a police unit is one of the key structural components in a social group that leads to abuse.

Confusion as to Which Norms to Follow

"Soldiers on the ground are confused about how they apply the Geneva Conventions," Fay writes, "and whether they have a duty to report violations of the conventions" (19). Given the poisoned climate at Abu Ghraib, it is certainly not obvious that soldiers would automatically know that they must report violations of the Geneva Conventions or other forms of abuse—or to whom they should report these violations. The fact that soldiers were "confused" concerning this duty again suggests extreme chaos and normative breakdown at Abu Ghraib.

Further confusion is documented in the general's discussion of a chart on rules for interrogation:

> The chart was confusing, however. It was not completely accurate and could be subject to various interpretations. . . . What was particularly confusing was that nowhere on the chart did it mention a number of techniques that were in use at the time: removal of clothing, forced grooming, hooding, and yelling, loud music and light control. Given the detail otherwise noted on the aid, the failure to list some techniques left a question of whether they were authorized for use without approval. (28)

Note that "removal of clothing" is assumed to be an interrogation "technique" in this passage—albeit, an unauthorized technique—whereas it is referred to as abuse in other passages. What is "forced grooming"? In general, the conceptual boundaries for what constitutes an interrogation technique are not clear. Conceptual chaos seems to have been one of several aspects of the widespread social chaos at Abu Ghraib.

"Unhealthy Mystique"

Fay writes that "CIA detention and interrogation practices led to a loss of accountability, abuse, reduced interagency cooperation, and an unhealthy mystique that further poisoned the atmosphere at Abu Ghraib" (53). He adds that "the systemic lack of accountability for interrogator actions and detainees plagued detainee operations in Abu Ghraib" (54). A "systemic" lack of accountability suggests something more than isolated incidents of abuse attributable to corrupt soldiers. It is intriguing that the general uses words such as *unhealthy, poisoned,* and *plagued* when referring to the social milieu at Abu Ghraib.

According to Fay, several abusive incidents "were widely known within the US community (MI and MP alike) at Abu Ghraib" (54). He adds that "speculation and *resentment* grew over the lack of personal responsibility, *of some people being above the laws and regulations.* The resentment contributed to the *unhealthy environment* that existed at Abu Ghraib" (54; emphasis added).

Fay refers again to a social "atmosphere" at Abu Ghraib when he writes, "According to COL Pappas, MG G. Miller said they, GTMO, used military working dogs, and that they were effective in setting the atmosphere for interrogations" (58). Clearly, the "social atmosphere" at Abu Ghraib was out of sync with Army doctrine, FM 34-52, the Geneva Conventions, and other systems of agreed-on social norms. This dismal state of affairs was not corrected but instead became a new, albeit deviant, normative structure.

Fay implies that humiliating nudity was part of the social atmosphere at Abu Ghraib: "Many of the Soldiers who witnessed the nakedness were told that this was an accepted practice" (68). Indeed, this fact was confirmed by the testimony of soldiers at the trials at Fort Hood. More precisely, soldiers said that nudity was treated as an accepted practice by military intelligence, who imposed it on the MPs. How did forced nudity become accepted practice, and how long did the process take by which this normalization of abuse occurred? According to Fay, "MI interrogators started directing nakedness at Abu Ghraib as early as 16 September 2003 to humiliate and break down detainees" (69).

Failure of Self-Correcting Mechanisms

Fay's report is replete with instances of soldiers objecting to or reporting abuse and supervisors ignoring them, failing to take corrective action, or invalidating their morally correct observations. Fay lists over forty such incidents. Consider incident 1 as an illustration: "1LT Sutton, 320th MP BN IRF intervened to stop the abuse and was told by the MI soldiers, 'we are professionals; we know what we are doing.' They refused 1LT Sutton's lawful order to identify themselves" (71). Sutton reported the incident "to the CID [Criminal Investigation Command, originally "Division"] who determined the allegation lacked sufficient basis for prosecution" (71). Clearly, options other than prosecution were available but not pursued. In fact, "the incident was not further pursued based on limited data and the absence of additional investigative leads" (72).

Incident 19 quotes an unnamed colonel as responding to a sergeant who cited the Geneva Conventions as the basis for objecting to the abuse he witnessed as follows: "Fine, Sergeant, you do what you have to do, I am going back to bed" (80).

Space does not permit me to go over the other incidents of documented "incidents" of abuse in detail here. Taken as a whole, they suggest that a climate of abuse was prevalent at Abu Ghraib, that soldiers were not in a position to have their objections validated by superiors, and that officers high in the chain of command did not follow their role expectations to correct the abuse within the social system that was Abu Ghraib. This conclusion is corroborated by testimony at the courts-martial. The abuse that was reported was not corrected; the abuse continued and, in fact, seems to have increased; and, again, abuse became increasingly normalized. The denial of and failure to investigate ICRC reports, previously discussed, corroborate this conclusion. At Abu Ghraib, procedures were not in place for soldiers to be validated when they objected to or reported abuse.

Cultural Insensitivity

Fay writes that soldiers at Abu Ghraib were "certainly not well versed in the cultural understandings of the detainees" (46). Ample evidence supports this claim, but the problem goes far deeper than not being "well versed." A close reading of the U.S. government reports on the abuse at Abu Ghraib suggests that the U.S. Army either failed to understand and predict the impact of forced nudity on a specifically Muslim population or, conceivably, exploited this cultural trait concerning nudity much as Fay suggests that the Arab fear of dogs was exploited. Moreover, this form of abuse seems to transcend chaos at Abu Ghraib and includes other prison facilities. Fay writes, "Removal of clothing was not a technique developed at Abu Ghraib, but rather a technique which was *imported and can be traced though Afghanistan and GTMO* [Gitmo]" (87; emphasis added). Note again that both Gitmo and Afghanistan seem consistently to have been sources of the "poison" that was "imported" to Abu Ghraib.

"Removal of clothing is not a doctrinal or authorized interrogation technique but appears to have been directed and employed at various levels within MI as an 'ego down' technique" (88). This explanation seems to indicate even more confusion than Fay had already uncovered: If the authorized technique of "ego down" was used to justify unauthorized techniques, the entire distinction between authorized versus unauthorized techniques breaks down conceptually. What other forms of abuse were misinterpreted or misrepresented as variations of lawful techniques?

According to Fay, "It is apparent from this investigation that removal of clothing was employed routinely and with the belief that it was not abuse" (88). But one could use these same words to describe other forms of abuse as well. Using a dog leash, forcing prisoners to masturbate, and so on, may all be construed as humiliation or variations of the lawful "ego down" technique, and they could have been performed with the belief that these forms of abuse were not really abuse, because the abuse came to be seen as "normal."

Fay makes the interpretation that "the use of clothing as an incentive (nudity) is *significant* in that it likely *contributed to an escalating 'de-humanization'* of the detainees and *set the stage for additional and more severe abuses to occur*" (88; emphasis added). This is a sociologically and psychologically accurate assessment. Note that this observation, and other ones like it, contradicts Fay's earlier assessment that the abuse was attributable to a few corrupt individuals and supports his overall interpretation that an unhealthy, chaotic social atmosphere was established at Abu Ghraib that gradually led to abuse by slowly eroding normative standards. According to Akbar S. Ahmed, a renowned anthropologist at American University, nudity is a cardinal normative violation in Islamic culture, which puts a high premium on modesty.[10]

Fay writes, "The interrogators believed they had the authority to use clothing as an incentive, as well as stress positions, and were not attempting to hide their use.... It is probable that use of nudity was sanctioned at some level within the chain-of-command. If not, lack of leadership and oversight permitted the nudity to occur" (90). If nudity is not an approved technique in FM 34–52 and was so common that soldiers did not try to hide the use of nudity as an "incentive," then this is yet another example of how abuse came to be normalized at Abu Ghraib.

Summary

In general, the Fay report describes the following as organizational and social problems at Abu Ghraib. There was a lack of clear command and control of detainee operations at the CJTF-7 level. The JIDC was manned with personnel from numerous organizations and consequently lacked unit cohesion. Leaders failed to take steps to effectively manage pressure placed on JIDC personnel. Some capturing units failed to follow procedures, training, and directives in the capture, screening, and exploitation of detainees. The JIDC was established in an ad hoc manner without proper planning, personnel, and logistical support for the missions it was intended to perform. Interrogation training in the Laws of Land Warfare and the Geneva Conventions was ineffective. MI leaders did not receive adequate training in the conduct and management of interrogation operations. Critical records on detainees were not created or maintained properly, thereby hampering effective operations. OGA interrogation practices led to a loss of accountability at Abu Ghraib. ICRC recommendations were ignored by MI, MP, and CJTF-7 personnel. And so on.

But every one of these and other shortcomings also produced a cultural impact on a primarily Islamic population of prisoners that was interpreted—by their cultural standards—as offensive, humiliating, degrading, disrespectful, dehumanizing, devaluing, uninterested in their cultural backgrounds, and hostile to their culture. In other words, the chronic social chaos among the U.S. soldiers at Abu Ghraib promoted hostility, insurgency, rioting, and hatred among the prisoners. Overall, the American approach at Abu Ghraib was counterproductive in terms of obtaining intelligence or promoting long-term goodwill among the Iraqis.

The Schlesinger Report

In line with the other reports, the Schlesinger report[11] finds that regarding the abuses at Abu Ghraib, "there is both institutional and personal responsibility at higher levels" even though it could find "no approved procedures [that] called for or allowed the kinds of abuse that in fact occurred" (5). In line with the other reports, it analyzes "lists of techniques" that "*circulated* from Guantánamo and Afghanistan to Iraq" (9; emphasis added). In general, the Schlesinger report focuses more strongly than the other reports on the proposition that "*interrogation techniques intended only for Guantánamo came to be used in Afghanistan and Iraq*" (72; emphasis added). I cannot overemphasize these links to Gitmo and Afghanistan as the realistic explanations for what seems to pass for magical understandings of how abuse occurred at Abu Ghraib.

This is the sort of language that sociologists and anthropologists use to describe cultural diffusion, or the transmission of cultural traits from one culture to another. It usually refers to positive traits. However, in this particular case, it seems that the Schlesinger report claims that unlawful or otherwise negative traits "migrated" or "circulated" from Guantánamo, where the Geneva Conventions did *not* apply, to Iraq, in which the Geneva Conventions *did* apply in principle. Combining insights from the various reports, one could arrive at the following formulation: The "poison" from Guantánamo Bay and Afghanistan was injected into Abu Ghraib and the rest of Iraq.

For example, the Schlesinger report notes that "when Abu Ghraib opened, the first MP unit was the 72nd MP Company, based in Henderson, Nevada." It adds that "this company called into question the interrogation practices of the MI brigade regarding nakedness of detainees" (80). In addition, "the 72nd MP Company voiced and then filed written objections to these practices" (80). Note that this is yet another instance in which abuse was reported—in writing—yet the abuse continued and even increased. It is one more fact among many that supports the proposition that abuse was normalized at Abu Ghraib over a period of time and that the abuse could not be reported in a normative way such that it would be stopped or corrected. However, as the rest of the report shows, forced, prolonged nudity was not regarded as abuse at Guantánamo even though it is against the Geneva Conventions, because the Geneva Conventions did not apply to Guantánamo. The Fay report *does* list forced nudity as abuse at Abu Ghraib, even though it does not recommend prosecution for this particular form of abuse. Most important, the objections filed by the 72nd Military Police Company were not heeded because forced nudity remained commonplace, according to the Fay report, throughout 2003 and into 2004. The following is worth noting: (1) the definition of "abuse" was socially constructed and varied by context such that what was abusive at Abu Ghraib was not necessarily perceived as abusive at Guantánamo; (2) even when soldiers properly and formally lodged a complaint, their efforts were useless because of this larger contextual confusion regarding acceptable versus unlawful methods.

The Schlesinger report notes that "the problems at Abu Ghraib intensified after October 15, 2003, when the 372nd Military Police Company took over the facility" (80). A number of factors are cited in conjunction with this transition from the 72nd to the 372nd company: Miller had completed his briefings at Abu Ghraib in the summer of 2003; the MI and MP units at Abu Ghraib were supposed to work as an integrated unit for interrogation (which the Taguba report cites as a major problem); Sanchez had issued memorandums on September 14 and October 12, 2003, which effectively rendered the 1992 version of FM 34–52 obsolete; and major "leadership shortfalls" occurred between the MPs and MIs. The Schlesinger report claims that "the model Major General Miller presented for the effective working relationship between MI and MP was neither understood nor could it have been successfully implemented" (84). This is an intriguing claim! It leads to the question, What would have been the point of understanding a policy that had no practical chance of working? The next sentence leaps to the soldiers at the lowest levels of the chain of command: "Based on the Taguba and Jones/Fay investigations, 'setting favorable conditions' had some basis in fact at Abu Ghraib, but it was also used as an excuse for abusive behavior toward detainees" (84).

Whereas the Taguba and Fay reports state unequivocally that the Geneva Conventions applied in Iraq, the Schlesinger report makes a more confusing argument. It begins with the observation that "the President determined the Geneva Conventions did not apply to the U.S. conflict with Al-Qaeda, and that Taliban detainees did not qualify for prisoner of war status" (87). Moreover, "the Panel accepts the proposition that these terrorists are not combatants entitled to the protections of Geneva Convention III" (88). In line with the other reports, the Schlesinger report claims that Operation Iraqi Freedom "clearly falls within the boundaries of the Geneva Conventions and the traditional law of war" (89). Confusion stems from the fact that protection under the Geneva Conventions is not given to certain *groups* (Taliban, Al Qaeda) that were at times identified—correctly or incorrectly—as operating within Iraq.

To add to the confusion, the Schlesinger panel does not agree with the ICRC's interpretation of the application of the Geneva Conventions: "If we were to follow the ICRC's interpretations, interrogation operations would not be allowed" (91). This assertion is open to interpretation, because the 1992 version of FM 34–52 lists and discusses interrogation techniques and approaches that apparently do comply with the Geneva Conventions. The panel believes that "there clearly must be a category for those lacking in such privileges" to the protections of the Geneva Conventions (94), but again, this assertion is open to debate.

In general, the Schlesinger report seems to acknowledge that the Geneva Conventions applied to Iraq at the same time that it criticizes the limitations of the Geneva Conventions in fighting the global war on terror. Thus, the report unwittingly exposes yet another layer of confusion and contradiction, involving both the national (U.S.) and international levels of analysis, regarding the issue of whether and in what form and to what extent the Geneva Conventions apply. This high level of disagreement and ambiguity was bound to leave the soldier on the ground in Iraq confused as to what is acceptable versus unacceptable, lawful versus unlawful orders and procedures. This is because the many competing memorandums, SOPs, field manuals, and other sources of authority do not speak in one voice. This point becomes evident from an examination of the context and impact of Sanchez's memorandum of September 14, 2003, which will be analyzed in the next chapter.

Conclusion

We have seen in chapter 1 that abuse at Abu Ghraib was part of a wide-spread *pattern* of abuse at Guantánamo, Afghanistan, and other military facilities in Iraq. U.S. government reports go a step further and establish that a *climate* or atmosphere or environment of abuse existed at Abu Ghraib. Moreover, the reports establish clearly that the poisoned climate of abuse was "imported," "circulated," or "migrated" primarily from Guantánamo Bay and also from Afghanistan.

Persons high in the chain of command must have ordered or known or should have known of these poisonous, imported policies. This is the logical conclusion to be drawn from the findings of fact in the reports and the existence of the doctrine of command responsibility. However, at the courts-martial, the government protected the top brass in the military and shifted the blame onto low-ranking soldiers as the magical explanation for the abuse at Abu Ghraib.

Notes

1. See, for example, Steven Strasser, ed., *The Abu Ghraib Investigations: The Official Reports of the Independent Panel and the Pentagon on the Shocking Prisoner Abuse in Iraq* (New York: Public Affairs, 2004).

2. This report is available at http://www.aclu.org/torturefoia/released/t1.pdf.

3. "Article 15-6 Investigation of the 800th Military Police Brigade."

4. Janis Karpinski, *One Woman's Army: The Commanding General of Abu Ghraib Tells Her Story* (New York: Hyperion, 2005), 226.

5. The classic study in this regard is Emile Durkheim, *Suicide* (Glencoe, Ill.: Free Press, [1897] 1951).

6. Samuel Stouffer, *The American Soldier: Adjustment during Army Life* (Princeton, N.J.: Princeton University Press, 1949).

7. See Robert Jay Lifton, *Home from the War: Vietnam Veterans—Neither Victims nor Executioners* (New York: Simon & Schuster, 1973), in which he refers to "the extent of the numbed warrior's dissociation from events outside of his self-enclosed system" (351) and the conclusion that "the larger crisis has to do with more fundamental psychohistorical dislocation" (363).

8. Hans Selye, *The Stress of Life* (New York: McGraw-Hill, 1976).

9. Karpinski, *One Woman's Army*, 202.

10. Akbar S. Ahmed, *Postmodernism and Islam* (London: Routledge, 1992).

11. "Final Report of the Independent Panel to Review DoD Detention Operations August 2004 by the Honorable James R. Schlesinger," August 24, 2004.

CHAPTER THREE

THE ORCHARD KEEPERS

In his book *Chain of Command: The Road from 9/11 to Abu Ghraib,* Seymour Hersh[1] has already linked White House memorandums that allowed for some sort of torture regarding detainees (but not prisoners of war) to subsequent abuse at Abu Ghraib as well as Guantánamo and Afghanistan. There is no need to travel over the paths that Hersh has already covered. However, many paths have yet to be explored—and there are many roads to Abu Ghraib, not one road that can be referred to as "the road." It seems that several roads detoured through Guantánamo and Afghanistan before reaching Abu Ghraib.

Moreover, the "roads" from 9/11 to Abu Ghraib are not logically connected: 9/11 has to do with Osama bin Laden but has no real connection with Abu Ghraib because Iraq was not connected with 9/11. The connection between 9/11 and Iraq also involves magical thinking. Twisted, disconnected, and confused roads were constructed by the orchard keepers to Abu Ghraib. More precisely, the roads to Abu Ghraib are less like paved highways and more like rugged trails forged through a wilderness.

Hersh explores the stratospheric level of the orchard keepers. But precious little is known about the midlevel orchard keepers and how they interpreted directives coming from above them, and also how they gave orders to officers below them in the chain of command. It is important to understand the subtle nuances in how the orchard keepers understood what they were doing and why. For example, according to Karpinski and others, it seems that MI knew of decisions to implement tougher "techniques" but that MPs were largely left out of the loop of information.

And those in the stratosphere of power are not unambiguously clear, either. John Yoo was one of the White House lawyers who was involved with the infamous memorandums regarding torture. In a television interview aired by the Canadian Broadcasting Company on November 16,

2005, Yoo said, "I can't talk about that." Why? "Because it's classified," he said. He did explain the following, however:

> So the torture convention says you cannot engage in torture and it says you shall undertake not to engage in cruel, inhuman and degrading treatment. So clearly, the people who drafted the treaty thought they were two different things. And when the Congress, when the Senate adopted the treaty, it only made torture criminal. It did not criminalize cruel, inhumane and degrading treatment. So clearly, Congress thought they were different concepts. I think there is a broader category of things that people can do which are cruel, inhumane and degrading and only extreme versions of that constitute torture.

It is not clear or necessarily true that torture is different from cruel, inhumane, and degrading treatment. What is significant is that this policy, adopted at one of the highest levels of the chain of command, apparently set the stage for abusive behavior at the lowest level of the chain of command—at Abu Ghraib and elsewhere—yet is fundamentally ambiguous. What is "cruel, inhumane, and degrading treatment"? This issue comes up repeatedly, and there is no unambiguous answer, because the answer depends on the eye of the beholder. What seems to be cruel, inhumane, and degrading to one individual or group or portion of the military may not seem cruel, inhumane, and degrading to a different individual or group or portion of the military. Moreover, the term *cruel, inhumane, and degrading treatment* showed up in Senator McCain's amendment that bans cruel, inhumane, and degrading treatment—without defining these terms. This confusion as to the meaning of key words is yet another instance of conceptual chaos—this time, at the highest levels of the orchard keepers who reside in the stratosphere of power, and not only the lowest-ranking soldiers who tried to make sense of this chaos at the bottom of the chain at Abu Ghraib.

The Leap to Afghanistan and Guantánamo Bay

The "sliding of meanings" regarding the definitions of the terms *torture* as well as *cruel, degrading, and inhuman treatment* were coupled with other directives from the White House that pronounced that the Geneva Conventions do not apply to the treatment of prisoners in Afghanistan and Guantánamo Bay. Borrowing from Freud, it seems that before the id (unbridled aggression) can be unleashed, one has to weaken the superego, which is the seat of conscience. The Geneva Conventions represent the international superego in a list of "thou shalt not's." The word *prisoners* was replaced with the euphemisms *detainees* and *PUCs* (persons under control), because prisoners of war are automatically protected by the Geneva Conventions, while the status of detainees and PUCs is ambiguous. The extent of abuse committed by American soldiers in Afghanistan is still a mystery, although media reports indicate considerable abuse, desecration of bodies, and other violations of the Geneva Conventions (which were opined not to apply), including homicide. Similarly, the full extent of the torture at Guantánamo Bay is not known as of this writing. For the purposes of the present discussion, the important point—made in several U.S. government reports—is that cruel techniques that were seemingly "authorized" in Afghanistan and Guantánamo Bay "migrated" or "circulated" to Iraq and specifically to Abu Ghraib, where they were "unauthorized."

I do not wish to delve into the discussion of how it is possible for unauthorized techniques to be treated as if they were quasi- or fully authorized. These are mind-numbing arguments that lead to dead ends, because little is clearly defined. Pragmatically, what happened is that methods that were violations of the Geneva Conventions made their way from Afghanistan and Guantánamo, where the Geneva Conventions supposedly did not apply to the Taliban and Al Qaeda, to Iraq, where the Geneva Conventions were supposed to apply. This migration of ideas and methods occurred along *many paths* (legal, military intelligence, political, OGA, etc.). An important and neglected link in this complex chain involves LG Ricardo Sanchez, who was the commander of coalition forces in Iraq.

The Memorandum of September 14, 2003, by LG Sanchez

Let me preface this section with the observation that Sanchez has been cleared of all wrongdoing by the U.S. Army regarding Abu Ghraib, so I shall not be addressing any legal issues of any sort pertaining to him. As a sociologist, I shall focus on his memorandum dated September 14, 2003, as a document that stands regardless of who authored or approved it, and whose origins and consequences need to be analyzed in light of the findings that are discussed in the U.S. government reports.

The Schlesinger report makes the following findings of fact regarding the history and context of Sanchez's memorandum:

> Interrogators and lists of techniques *circulated* from Guantanamo and Afghanistan to Iraq.... In August 2003, MG [Major General] Geoffrey Miller ... brought to Iraq the Secretary of Defense's April 16, 2003 policy guidelines for Guantanamo—which he reportedly gave to CJTF-7 as a potential model—recommending a command-wide policy be established. He noted, however, the Geneva Conventions did apply to Iraq. In addition to these various printed sources, there was also a *store of common lore and practice* within the interrogator community *circulating* through Guantanamo, Afghanistan and elsewhere. (37; emphasis added)

The Schlesinger report is stating that in addition to formal, rational-legal interrogation techniques approved by the U.S. Army, there existed a "folk culture" of informal, charismatic, and unofficial interrogation techniques, policies, and practices not formally approved by the U.S. Army—and that variations of both formal and informal techniques "migrated" and "circulated" vis-à-vis military posts in Guantánamo, Afghanistan, and Iraq. It is as if approved as well as illicit techniques circulated in the way that, for example, legal and bootleg videos, DVDs, and CDs circulate culturally throughout the world.

However, the formal, approved, rational-legal interrogation techniques of the U.S. Army changed rapidly, and some of them mutated into illicit techniques. The Schlesinger report continues:

> At the operational level, in the absence of more specific guidance from CENTCOM, interrogators in Iraq relied on FM 34-52 *and on unauthorized techniques that had migrated from Afghanistan.* On September 14, 2003, Commander CJTF-7 signed the theater's first policy on interrogation which contained elements of the approved Guantanamo policy and elements of the SOF policy. Policies approved for use on al Qaeda and Taliban detainees who were not afforded the protection of EPW status under the Geneva Conventions now applied to detainees who did fall under the Geneva Convention protections. CENTCOM disapproved the September 14, 2003 policy resulting in another policy signed on October 12, 2003 which essentially mirrored the outdated version of the FM 34-52. The 1987 version, however, authorized interrogators to *control all aspects of the interrogation,* "to include lighting and heating, as well as food, *clothing,* and shelter given to detainees." This was specifically left out of the 1992 version, which is currently in use. *This clearly led to confusion on what practices were acceptable.* We cannot be sure how much the number and severity of abuses would have been curtailed had there been early and consistent guidance from higher levels. Nonetheless, such guidance was needed and likely would have had a limiting effect. (37–38; emphasis added)

The Schlesinger report fails to investigate how and why orchard keepers would engage in writing rules of interrogation that are "unauthorized" in the sense that they were applying policies that circumvented the Geneva Conventions in Iraq, where the Geneva Conventions apply. This move does not seem "rational" from the rational-legal perspective as it is understood in the West; that is, it is contradictory. It seems less like a process of migration and circulation of cultural products and more like the spreading of a toxic spill.

The memorandum dated September 14, 2003, is unclassified and available from the ACLU Web site. The allusions to the two versions of FM 34-52—or the *U.S. Army Field Manual on Interrogation*—can be verified. The 1987 version of FM 34-52 does indeed claim that

> the interrogator should appear to be the one who controls all aspects of the interrogation to include the lighting, heating, and configuration of the interrogation room, as well as the food, shelter, and clothing given to the source. The interrogator must always be in control, he must act quickly and firmly. However, everything that he says and does must be within the limits of the Geneva and Hague Conventions, as well as the standards of conduct outlined in the UCMJ. (chap. 3: 5)

It is questionable whether the interrogator's total control of the prisoner's clothing, food, shelter, and other aspects was ever in full compliance with the Geneva Conventions, but it is noteworthy that the *Field Manual* consistently attempts to incorporate the Geneva Conventions. It is also possible to verify the Schlesinger report's claim that the 1992 version of FM 34-52, currently in use (at least in theory, though not necessarily in practice), specifically omits this problematic reference to total control. Instead, in these regards, the 1992 version of FM 34-52 states that all interrogation approaches

- establish and maintain control over the source and interrogation
- establish and maintain rapport between the interrogator and source
- manipulate the source's emotions and weaknesses to gain his willing cooperation (3-11)

Thus, the "confusion on what practices were acceptable" cited by the Schlesinger report stems at least from (1) a disorganized, inconsistent, and contradictory cut-and-paste approach toward an outmoded 1987 *Field Manual,* a 1992 *Field Manual,* and at least two memorandum; (2)

an informal "store of common lore and practice" that was circulating and migrating among Guantánamo, Iraq, and Afghanistan; (3) the melding of both of these disorganized, chaotic, and unauthorized versions of both formal and informal authority; and (4) an ongoing discussion and debate as to which aspects of the Geneva Conventions apply and in what manner (e.g., the letter versus the "spirit" of the Geneva Conventions). These huge problems in interpretation cannot be solved by simply stating that ideally and theoretically, the Geneva Conventions applied in Iraq. In practice, both FM 34–52 and the Geneva Conventions were being rendered obsolete by Sanchez's memorandums and other directives from the Pentagon. In addition, it should be noted that both field manuals keep the duties of the MPs and MIs separate and distinct—a point that Taguba regards as cardinal. The memorandum of September 14, 2003, introduced Miller's idea of merging MI and MP roles into the Iraqi theater of war. The Schlesinger report concludes this portion as follows:

> At Abu Ghraib, the Jones/Fay investigation concluded that MI professionals at the prison level shared a "major part of the culpability" for the abuses. Some of the abuses occurred during interrogation. As these interrogation techniques exceeded parameters of FM 34–52, no training had been developed. Absent training, the interrogators used their own initiative to implement the new techniques. To what extent the same situation existed at other prisons is unclear, but the widespread nature of abuses warrants an assumption that at least the understanding of interrogation policies was inadequate. (38)

The very meaning of the term *interrogation* became problematic and contributed to the sense of conceptual chaos. It seems that everyone at Abu Ghraib was involved in interrogation and detention simultaneously, twenty-four hours per day, seven days a week. The "interrogations" were not consistently normative but sometimes unlawful, and they spilled over into daily activities because the abuse was rationalized as "softening up" detainees for interrogation. Sanchez's memorandum is an important focal point for analysis in all of these regards: far from specifying interrogation techniques, it actually imploded the normatively accepted social meaning of the term *interrogation technique*. In other words, if one looks up the definitions of various interrogation techniques in the *Field Manual,* they do *not* match the actual behaviors at Abu Ghraib, which were later labeled as abuse.

For example, Sanchez's memorandum of September 14, 2003, orders the following:

Interrogation approaches are designed to manipulate the detainee's emotions and weaknesses to gain his willing cooperation. Interrogation operations are never conducted in a vacuum; *they are conducted in close cooperation with the units detaining the individuals.* The policies established by the detaining units that pertain to searching, silencing and segregating also play a role in the interrogation of the detainee. (13; emphasis added)

Only the first sentence, above, is taken directly from the 1992 version of FM 34-52, previously cited. The rest of the paragraph posits a policy that departs from the rational-legal authority of the 1992 version of FM 34-52. Sanchez does not cite any authority in making the momentous departure from official policy to posit that interrogations "are conducted in close cooperation with the units detaining the individuals." This paragraph seems to follow directly from Miller's visit to Iraq in September 2003, mirrors the blurring of MP and MI roles at Guantánamo, sets the tone for the blurring of MI and MP roles in Iraq, and leads directly to the confusion among soldiers that is discussed at length in U.S. government reports.

Sanchez's memorandum does state that "specific implementation guidance with respect to techniques A-CC is provided in U.S. Army Field Manual 34-52" (10). However, and in contradiction with this sentence (because FM 34-52 specifies that all approaches must stay within the bounds of the Geneva Conventions), Sanchez inserts cautionary notes for five of the techniques with regard to what "other nations" interpret as the provisions of the Geneva Conventions. Consider his wording with regard to one of these techniques as illustration:

I. Pride and Ego Down: Attacking or insulting the ego of a detainee, not beyond the limits that would apply to an EPW. [*Caution*: Article 17 of the Geneva III provides, "Prisoners of war who refuse to answer may not be threatened, insulted, or exposed to any unpleasant or disadvantageous treatment of any kind" *Other nations* that believe detainees are entitled to EPW protections may consider this technique inconsistent with the provisions of Geneva]. (emphasis added)

In five of the interrogation techniques, a similar "caution" is issued to the effect that "other nations" may view the technique or its application as violations of the Geneva Conventions. It is an odd cautionary statement that signals deviance by the United States from accepted international norms. Yet all of the U.S. government reports state that the Geneva Conventions applied to Iraq. This is a blatant contradiction. If Sanchez's memorandum cautioned that some other nations might view U.S. action as a violation of the Geneva Conventions, then, in practice, the United States was not following the Geneva Conventions in Iraq. How other nations interpret the Geneva Conventions is part of the social construction of the reality of the Geneva Conventions.

How the Orchard Keepers Rationalized Their Mistakes

It is instructive to analyze Sanchez's perspective on the history, context, and impact of his memorandum. He offered his perspective, along with Miller and LG John Abizaid at the U.S. Senate Hearing on Iraq Prison Abuse on May 19, 2004. In his opening remarks, Senator Carl Levin stated:

> The inquiry is not just about the behavior of a few soldiers at a detention facility. We, of course, must do whatever we can to ensure that the perpetrators of the abuses are held accountable. But also those who are responsible for encouraging, condoning or tolerating such behavior or who established or created an atmosphere or climate for such abusive behavior must also be held accountable.

Sanchez responded, "There is no doubt that the law of war, including the Geneva Conventions, apply to our operations in Iraq. This includes interrogations." He continued:

> I have reinforced this point by way of orders and command policies. In September and October of 2003, and in May of 2004, I issued interrogation policies that reiterated the application of the Geneva Conventions and required that all interrogations be conducted in a lawful and humane manner, with command oversight.

In fact, as Sanchez's memorandum shows, he did *not* reiterate the application of the Geneva Conventions in September 2003 but cautioned that other nations may view U.S. methods as violations of the Geneva Conventions. Abizaid admitted that "abuse has happened in Afghanistan, it's happened in Iraq, it's happened at various places," but he denied that the abuse was "systemic." This raises the interesting question of how it is possible for abuse to be simultaneously chaotic *and* widespread. How much abuse must occur, over how widespread a geographic area and over what length of time, for the abuse to be regarded as "systemic"? I will leave this issue for philosophers and legal analysts to settle later. Senator John Warner interpreted this to mean that there occurred a "breakdown of the orders that General Sanchez has clearly documented." Abizaid responded that the Fay report had not yet been issued, so he could not explain this breakdown. Since his testimony, the Fay report has been issued, and these contradictions have still not been explained. How is it possible for similar patterns of abuse to be found at Guantánamo, Afghanistan, and Iraq, and yet maintain the position that the abuse is not systemic?

Levin noted that Taguba cited Sanchez's "order of November 19 [which] effectively made the military intelligence officer, rather than the MP officer, responsible for the MP units conducting detainee operations." Sanchez responded that he did not agree with Taguba's assessment.

McCain focused on Miller's recommendation that "it is essential that the guard force be actively engaged in setting the conditions for successful exploitation of the internees." The senator asked Miller whether he thought this recommendation could have been misinterpreted. Miller responded, "No, Senator, I do not." The senator persisted:

> At least according to Gen. Taguba's report, there were at least a number of guards—I mean, guards, MPs, who were under the impression or stated that they were under the impression that they were under specific directions of military intelligence personnel to, quote, "rough up, soften up, give them a bad night" etc.

The generals who testified all insisted that their orders could not have been misinterpreted, and blamed "a breakdown in leadership on how the follow-up actions may have occurred."

For example, Sanchez stated that his orders "clearly stated that MPs were involved in passive enabling of those operations and had no involvement in the conduct of interrogations." In fact, as demonstrated, this assertion by Sanchez at the hearing contradicts his written order in the September 14 memorandum, which states, *"They [interrogations] are conducted in close cooperation with the units detaining the individuals."* "Close cooperation" does not necessarily have to be interpreted as "passive enabling." In fact, the very interpretation of the terms *active* versus *passive* are problematic, in general and specifically with regard to the present discussion. Thus, Miller stated later that "the MPs did not actively participate in any forms of the interrogation itself." Elsewhere, he stated that "our doctrinal publications say that there should be cooperation between the military police and the intelligence function ... but it does say there should not [be] any active participation." In fact, at least with regard to the September 14 memorandum, the exact wording is "close cooperation."

This particular document does not prohibit active participation, nor are any of these forms of cooperation or participation defined.

Sanchez issued a memorandum, and he, Miller and Abizaid stated that this memorandum could not have been misinterpreted. This cannot be true. Let us suppose that the Supreme Court or the surgeon general or any other person or entity that is high in a social hierarchy issues a statement. A Supreme Court ruling will be subjected to a plethora of competing interpretations by various lawyers involved in a myriad of cases, and some of these interpretations might have to be returned to the Supreme Court for validation or reinterpretation. In general, persons at the bottom of a social hierarchy do not have access to the privileged information, training, education, or other social tools that would make any document immediately "accessible" to them even if it is handed to them physically. It would be like a second grader being asked to comprehend and follow instructions by a medical doctor in a medical journal. Similarly, the soldier on the ground will require training, education, testing, and practice before he or she can be said to interpret a memorandum as it was intended to be interpreted. None of the U.S. government reports cite training, education, testing, and practice with regard to the implications of Sanchez's September memorandum. On the contrary, these reports make the point that training, education, testing, and practice with regard to interrogation and detention operations in general were inadequate—even with regard to such obvious documents such as the Geneva Conventions (which were not posted) or FM 34–52.

Senator Daniel Akaka asked Abizaid, "Is the problem of detainee abuse systemic within CENTCOM?" The general replied, "No, sir, I do not believe it's systemic. There have been instances of abuse in Afghanistan and other prisons, as you know, and in Iraq as well." Note that Abizaid does not restrict the abuse to Abu Ghraib—he clearly and correctly states that the abuse occurred in Afghanistan and elsewhere in Iraq. This fact was kept out of the courts-martial at Fort Hood. Yet he denies that this widespread abuse is systemic. However, the terms *systemic* and *abuse* are open to interpretation and are not precisely defined in this exchange or in the U.S. government reports.

Perhaps the most ambiguous and unclear exchange at this Senate hearing was the one between Senator Robert Byrd and the various generals regarding responsibility for and oversight of the memorandum of September 14:

> **BYRD**: General Sanchez, you told Senator Levin that you never saw the rules of engagement presented to this committee last week. If you do not see or

set the so called rules of engagement for the interrogation of prisoners in Iraq, who does? Who does see them?

SANCHEZ: Senator, what I had stated is that I had not seen the specific slide that was referred to. I was the one that approved the interrogation rules of engagement on the 12th of September and again in the October time frame, sir.

BYRD: Does anyone in the civilian leadership of the Pentagon need to approve the rules of interrogation operation?

SANCHEZ: Senator, those rules were forwarded to Central Command in the September time frame. And based on the inputs from Central Command, resulted in the October memorandum.

BYRD: I'll ask the question again. Does anyone in the civilian leadership of the Pentagon need to approve those rules of engagement?

ABIZAID: You know, Senator, I would say we're all responsible for making sure what happens in our organization happens right. Things don't have to go all the way to the top to be approved. We know what's right and we know what's wrong.

BYRD: But the committee needs to know if you can answer this question. Does anyone in the civilian leadership of the Pentagon need to approve the rules of interrogation operations? If so, who?

ABIZAID: My answer is no, it's our responsibility.

It is not clear to whom "we" refers in Abizaid's reply that "we know what's right and we know what's wrong." It could refer to everyone in the U.S. Army or the generals in command or the Pentagon or some other combination—but his meaning is not obvious. Moreover, the replies to the senator seem to imply that the U.S. Army, which is a formal organization and a bureaucracy based on a chain of rational-legal authority and the doctrine of command responsibility, may allow some of its commanding generals to set its own policies on interrogation on its own accord.

Consider, as an analogy, a public school in the United States. A schoolteacher is *not* allowed to set his or her own policies for even the most mundane matters such as having a pizza party, allowing students to sit on their desks, or making the Pledge of Allegiance optional. These and other matters are all approved by the principal, who in turn is constrained by rules set by the state government, which in turn is constrained by a matrix of other rules emanating from national, federal, and even international sets of norms. Thus, a teacher who allowed a pizza party in the classroom under the assumption that everyone in the teaching profession knew what is right and wrong might be "chewed out" by the principal and disciplined.

In summary, the state of affairs described by Abizaid seems implausible under the assumption that the U.S. Army is a modern bureaucracy.

The senator continued:

> **BYRD**: Then you're saying that nobody in the Pentagon approves these rules?
> **ABIZAID**: No, I'm not saying that.
> **BYRD**: Then what are you saying?
> **ABIZAID**: I am saying that the rules of engagement for interrogations are a product of Army doctrine, of Army training, of practices in the field, and of commanders doing their job out there.

Entering the discussion, Miller added, "There is no requirement that the Department of Defense review or approve the methods that we used. As Generals Abizaid and Sanchez have said, they're operating in a combat environment. The commanders have the authority to approve."

The senator asked Abizaid about "the culture of abuse" at detention centers in Iraq that was uncovered by the ICRC. The general replied, "I don't believe that a culture of abuse existed in my command." While the U.S. government reports do not use the term *culture of abuse,* they do use phrases such as "poisoned atmosphere" to describe the cultural and social conditions at Abu Ghraib.

The Human Rights Watch Report of April 2005

We have seen that several U.S. government reports refer to the "migration" of illicit techniques from Guantánamo and Afghanistan, where the Geneva Conventions did not apply, into Iraq, where they should have applied. The internationally respected organization Human Rights Watch issued a report in April 2005 (vol. 17, no. 1G) entitled "Getting Away with Torture? Command Responsibility for the U.S. Abuse of Detainees." This report supplements and deepens the U.S. government reports by providing a context. It is an important, external assessment of the role of the orchard keepers in the Abu Ghraib saga.

According to Human Rights Watch, "it has become clear that torture and abuse have taken place not solely at Abu Ghraib but rather in dozens of U.S. detention facilities worldwide, that in many cases the abuse resulted in death or severe trauma, and that a good number of the victims were civilians with no connection to al-Qaeda or terrorism" (1). The report notes that "to date, the only wrongdoers being brought to justice are those at the bottom of the chain-of-command" despite the well-known principle that people at the top of the chain of command "either knew or should have known that such violations took place as a result of their actions" (1). Importantly, the report notes that "the coercive methods approved by senior U.S. officials and widely employed over the last three years include tactics that the United States has repeatedly condemned as barbarity and torture when practiced by others. Even the U.S. Army field manual condemns some of these methods as torture" (1). This last point is especially important for understanding how the breaking of normative standards set by the *Field Manual* came to be acceptable in the U.S. Army.

In addition, the Human Rights Watch report notes that "we also know that some 100–150 detainees have been 'rendered' by the United States for detention and interrogation by governments in the Middle East such as Syria and Egypt, which, according to the U.S. State Department, practice torture routinely" (2). It adds, "Such rendition is, again, a violation of U.S. and international law."

The report notes that, regarding the U.S. government knowledge of some actions that later came to be defined and prosecuted as abuse:

> Abu Ghraib was, in fact, only the tip of the iceberg. Detainees in U.S. custody in Afghanistan had experienced beatings, prolonged sleep and sensory deprivation, forced nakedness and humiliation as early as 2001. Comparable—and, indeed, more extreme—cases of torture and inhuman treatment had been extensively documented by the ICRC and by journalists at numerous locations in Iraq outside Abu Ghraib. (8)

It is very important to note that the kinds of abuse documented at Abu Ghraib were not restricted to that location. This fact contradicts the government's few rotten apples theory. These facts beg the question: Why didn't the U.S. Army stop the abuse as early as 2001, when it was discovered in Afghanistan? Additionally, "In December 2003, retired Col. Stuart A. Herrington presented a confidential report that warned of detainee abuse throughout Iraq" (45)—well before the abuse at Abu Ghraib was disclosed in the spring of 2004. Part of the answer seems to be, as noted by Human Rights Watch, that the United States "changed the paradigm" of what constitutes violations of the Geneva Conventions and U.S. Army standards for the treatment of detainees. The report cites several milestones in this "paradigm shift," starting with a memorandum by current attorney general Alberto Gonzales dated January 25, 2002, "which would preserve the U.S.'s 'flexibility' in the war against terrorism" (9). On December 2, 2002, Secretary of Defense Donald Rumsfeld approved a list of techniques for detainees at Guantánamo that "violate not only the Geneva Conventions but the laws against torture and other prohibited ill-treatment" and that "later 'migrated' to Iraq and Afghanistan where they were regularly applied to detainees" (12). The Schlesinger report confirms this finding. The important point is that instead of responding to reported abuse in Afghanistan in 2001 by reaffirming the Geneva Conventions, the United States responded by changing the "paradigm" such that some violations of the conventions became "normative."

According to the report:

> As a consequence of these policies, which were approved at least by cabinet-level officials of the U.S. government, the United States has been implicated in crimes against detainees across the world—in Afghanistan, Iraq, Guantanamo Bay, Cuba, and in secret detention centers, as well as in countries to which suspects have been rendered. (13)

Interestingly, exposure of the Abu Ghraib abuse that occurred in 2003 did not entirely deter or alter the new paradigm: "In March 2004, prior to the publication of the Abu Ghraib photos, Human Rights Watch released an extensive report documenting cases of U.S. military personnel arbitrarily detaining Afghan civilians, using excessive force during arrests of non-combatants, and mistreating detainees" (14). As late as "March 2005, *The Washington Post* uncovered another death that occurred in CIA custody, noting that the case was under investigation but that the CIA officer implicated had been promoted" (14).[2] As late as November 2004, "the International Committee of the Red Cross told the U.S. government in confidential reports that its treatment of detainees has involved psychological and physical coercion that is 'tantamount to torture'" (15). Extraordinary renditions by the CIA occurred in 2004 as well as 2005 (16). Again, the important point is that the "paradigm shift" that began in 2002 apparently did not change as a result even of the events that occurred in Abu Ghraib in 2003, well into 2005.

Confusion Concerning the "Lawful" versus the "Unlawful" Order

At the trials, the prosecution argued that the soldier should be able to distinguish between a lawful versus an unlawful order. But what of the officer who gives an unlawful order? The prosecution's guiding assumptions are called into question when one confronts a poisoned social system and, more specifically, one in which abuse has been normalized, such as at Abu Ghraib. The U.S. government reports are correct in asserting that the state of affairs at Abu Ghraib was "confusing," although this characterization begs for deeper analysis into the sources, nature, and consequences of the confusion.

As we have seen, the "confusion" stems from the fact that lawful, authoritative procedures regarding detention and interrogation had shifted, slowly and almost imperceptibly, to unlawful procedures that broke with established bases for rational-legal authority for detention and interrogation. One should note that no evidence indicates that anyone high in the chain of command gave direct orders for torture or abuse. What seems to have occurred is that lawful standards were "stretched" and reinterpreted into new "paradigms" such that unlawful acts were "normalized," over time becoming unlawful *policies* that created climates of abuse. This was the real source of the confusion for the soldier—not an unlawful order, but unlawful policies.

For example, consider Miller's report of September 13, 2003, which has been documented to have been instrumental in instituting procedures that deviated from FM 34–52. Against the established procedures—cited most strongly by Taguba in his report—in which MI and MP roles were kept distinct under the authority of FM 34–52, Miller proposed the following: "To achieve rapid exploitation of internees it is necessary to integrate detention operations, interrogation operations and collection management under one command authority" (in Danner 2004:207).[3] Elsewhere in the report, Miller is still more explicit: "It is essential that *the guard force be actively engaged in setting the conditions for successful exploitation of the internees*" (209; emphasis added). In other words, Miller had already recommended, in September 2003, that MP soldiers be actively engaged in "interrogation" procedures, a policy shift that signaled a significant departure from the traditional separation between MIs and MPs in the army.

The inevitable result was that the soldier low in the chain of command was confronted with an unlawful situation that he or she did not choose and could not control—namely, participation in unlawful collusion between MPs and MIs who were engaged in unlawful interrogation "techniques." One is now in a position to appreciate the Schlesinger report's conclusion that the "confusion" laid the groundwork for subsequent abuse. *The origins of this confusion can be traced to the orchard keepers—not the low-ranking soldiers.* The low-ranking soldiers at Abu Ghraib did not have the ability, knowledge, or motivation to originate the confusion that led to the abuse. They were responding to the chaos created by the merging of MI and MP roles, constantly changing rules, unlawful techniques, conflicting memorandums, and so on.

Climates of Abuse

The U.S. government reports as well as the prosecution seem to focus on "sexual" and "violent" acts as abuse without considering the full range of what professionals regard as abuse. If one takes the American psychiatric community as a reference group, abuse includes but is not limited to the following: threatening, coercing, beating, lying, berating, demeaning, chastising, insulting, humiliating, exploiting, ignoring (the "silent treatment"), devaluing, verbal abuse, yelling, passive aggression, controlling, acting unpredictably and capriciously, breaking agreements, disproportional rage to the slightest slight, ever-shifting codes of conduct, inducing fear, extortion, emotional blackmail, control by proxy (making a third party do one's bidding), stalking, harassing, manipulation, creating a climate of fear, intimidation, instability, and unpredictability—to name a few. These and other patterns of behavior create climates of abuse. Most of them can be found at Abu Ghraib, as evidenced by the reports as well as testimony.

An important point is that in abusive relationships, the victim of abuse often does not know that he or she is being abused without the assistance of a therapist or other representative of a moral compass. Abused victims often stay in abusive relationships for many years because they do not fully comprehend the abuse, and they do not see it because the abuser and his or her proxies have made it seem "normal." Similarly, it would have been difficult if not impossible for an average soldier at Abu Ghraib to "see" abuse when it was embedded as policy and validated by the MIs and general ambiance at Abu Ghraib as the "normal" way of doing things. Most of the behaviors I have listed seem to have been part of the daily "routine" at Abu Ghraib. In the words of Spinner, one of the defense attorneys, abuse was "business as usual" at Abu Ghraib.

The orchard keepers failed to draw conceptual boundaries between lawful "interrogation techniques" and abuse. On the contrary, the orchard keepers muddied the waters and made an already confusing situation even more chaotic by merging MP and MI roles. In such an ambiance of abuse, the soldier would not be able to distinguish abuse from normal behavior any more than a victim of abuse in an abusive relationship could escape it without the intervention of a healthy and normative reference group or reference point.

The Gloves Come Off

In tandem with the many formal memorandums issued from high in the chain of command, it seems that MI issued an internal order, disseminated through e-mail to "all concerned," that the "gloves are coming off."

In his unclassified testimony to the 9/11 Commission, made on September 26, 2002, Cofer Black, the director of the CIA's Counterterrorist Center from 1999 to May 2002 stated, "Operational flexibility: This is a highly classified area. All I want to say is that there was 'before' 9/11 and 'after' 9/11. *After 9/11 the gloves come off*" (7; emphasis added). Similarly, in mid-August 2003, according to journalist and professor Mark Danner, a captain in military intelligence at Abu Ghraib sent his colleagues an e-mail in which, responding to an earlier request from interrogators, he sought to define "unlawful combatants." Then, reminding the intelligence people to "provide [an] interrogation techniques 'wish list' by 17 Aug 03," the captain signed off by saying, "The gloves are coming off gentlemen regarding these detainees, COL Boltz has made it clear that we want these individuals broken" (Danner 2004:33).

Specialist Sabrina Harman's Behavior in the Context of the Poisoned Atmosphere at Abu Ghraib

I devote chapter 5 to an analysis of Harman's court-martial. However, in this chapter, I would like to link her reactions to the violence and abuse all around her at Abu Ghraib to the memorandums, directives, and orders given by the orchard keepers. The lawyers and other professionals who wrote the directives live in an abstract world and evade responsibility through the clever use of words and legalistic phrases. The soldier at Abu Ghraib lived and worked in a violent, abusive atmosphere and felt invalidated to do anything about it except go along with it in order to survive.

Harman wrote a letter to her partner on October 20, 2003—a date that is fairly early in the progression of abuse at Abu Ghraib. Her letter suggests a strong sense of empathy for the abuse of prisoners that she was witnessing, a realistic sense of helplessness in doing anything to prevent it, and recognition that she was acting in the role of a whistle-blower in taking some of the photos of the abuse. Harman wrote:

> Okay. I don't like that anymore. At first it was funny but these people are going too far. Ended your letter last night because it was time to wake the MI prisoners and "mess with them" but it went too far even I can't handle what's going on. I can't get it out of my head. I walk down stairs after blowing the whistle and beating on the cells with an asp to find "the taxi cab driver" handcuffed backwards to his window naked with his underwear over his head and face. He looked like Jesus Christ. At first I had to laugh so I went on and grabbed the camera and took a picture. One of the guys took my asp and started "poking" at his dick. Again I thought, okay that's funny then it hit me. That's a form of molestation. You can't do that. I took more pictures now to "record" what is going on. They started talking to this man and at first he was talking "I'm just a taxicab driver, I did nothing." He claims he'd never try to hurt US soldiers that he picked up the wrong people. Then he stopped talking. They turned the lights out and slammed the door and left him there while they went down to cell #4. This man had been so fucked that when they grabbed his foot through cell bars he began screaming and crying. After praying to Allah he moans a constant short, Ah, ah, every few seconds for the rest of the night. I don't know what they did to this guy. The first one remained handcuffed for maybe 1½–2 hours until he started yelling for Allah. So they went back in and handcuffed him to the top bunk on either side of the bed while he stood on the side. He was there for a little over an hour when he started yelling again for Allah. Not many people know this shit goes on. The only reason I want to be there is to take the pictures to prove that the U.S. is not what they think. But I don't know if I can take it mentally. What if that was me in their shoes? These people will be our future terrorist[s]. Kelly, it's awful and you know how fucked I am in the head—both sides of me think it's wrong. I thought I could handle anything. I was wrong.

The relatively uneducated Harman seems to show more insight than some White House lawyers in making the seemingly obvious connection that treating people inhumanely will cause, not prevent, future terrorists. She seems to have been shocked by the abuse, and her initial laughter may be interpreted as the nervous laughter of someone who is exposed to abuse that goes beyond the moral boundaries that they hold. She writes to her partner that she will take photos to document the abuse—but her photos were used against her at her court-martial.

Similarly, Harman reported an incident on October 23, 2003—which is again early in the dehumanization process at Abu Ghraib—in which she witnessed a prisoner handcuffed for a prolonged period of time such that his blood circulation was being cut off. While she was successful in helping this particular prisoner on this occasion, the soldier who committed the abuse was not punished but merely removed from the tier. Harman seemed to enter into a state of "learned helplessness" following these and other incidents. *Learned helplessness* is the process by which individuals resort to defensive mechanisms such as depression and emotional numbness when they realize that they cannot escape an abusive situation they witness or experience. Similarly, as the abuse at Abu Ghraib continued after October 23, 2003, Harman, in her own words, "played along" with the others—though, according to her fellow soldiers, she never yelled at, assaulted, or otherwise engaged in abuse against prisoners. On the contrary, her fellow soldiers describe her behavior toward prisoners as consistently kind and helpful.

The learned helplessness seems to have been experienced by the soldiers and prisoners alike: no one knew how to stop the abuse. The victims and victimizers at Abu Ghraib felt trapped in what seemed to be an endless cycle of abuse. As in similar cases of spouse and family abuse, the cycle was broken only through outside intervention. When the photographs of the abuse were finally leaked to the world, the army was forced to explain itself. But again, as in typical cases of family abuse, blame was shifted onto the weakest and most vulnerable persons.

I asked Harman about the photographic equipment and the social context for the photography that was taking place at Abu Ghraib. For the most part, the cameras were digital. She said that rules were posted to the effect that photos were not allowed in the tent area due to security reasons, but nothing was said or posted about photographing prisoners in the Hard Site. She added that no one in her company forbade anyone from taking photos inside the prison.

Harman told me that some of the soldiers brought their cameras with them from the United States; others bought them from the "local" at Abu Ghraib who ran a shop selling DVDs, cameras, and other equipment. The local was an Iraqi who ran the shop within the U.S. Army compound at Abu Ghraib. To the best of her knowledge, no one was reprimanded for taking photos. She estimates that approximately 70 percent of her company had cameras.

I have not been able to find any U.S. Army regulations against taking photographs or bringing them into Abu Ghraib or a war theater. I searched actively for such a memorandum or directive. This is particularly striking because General Order Number 1A, dated December 19, 2000, and signed by Gen. Tommy R. Franks, specifically prohibits a number of other activities and objects, but not cameras or photography. Thus, General Order Number 1A prohibits privately owned firearms, entrance into a mosque, the possession of any alcoholic beverage, the possession of any controlled substance or drug paraphernalia, pornography, the taking of souvenirs—among a host of other items and behaviors—but, again, nothing pertaining to photography. The orchard keepers did not consider the uses of cameras.

This is an important, albeit neglected, part of the Abu Ghraib saga. The orchard keepers were concerned with rewriting, rethinking, and reworking abstract and legal concepts pertaining to torture, cruel, and inhumane treatment. But it did not occur to them to think about something as human and basic as a camera. The camera became the Achilles' heel of the orchard keepers.

A similar oversight in General Order Number 1A pertains to the use, possession, and sharing of computers and laptops, downloading photographs, access to a modem, and e-mails. Apparently, it was common practice for some soldiers to use their own laptops and gain access to the Internet through a computer lab at Abu Ghraib that was furnished with U.S. Army computers and a modem established by the U.S. Army. While one can rationalize this discrepancy with the humane observation that the U.S. Army allowed its soldiers easy e-mail access to family and loved ones, the fact remains that it did not regulate or control e-mail communication and thereby holds some institutional accountability for the failure to regulate such communication. Moreover, it is striking that the Schlesinger, Fay, and other government reports on Abu Ghraib fail to address the issues pertaining to cameras, photography, and e-mail access at all, given that the photographs of abuse at Abu Ghraib are at the heart of the controversy and impact of the visualization of the abuse.

Conclusion

Many roads led *to* Abu Ghraib that took many detours, and these consisted mostly of written and highly abstract, very confusing memorandums issued by the orchard keepers. But it seems that the roads *out of* the closed environment of Abu Ghraib consisted of cameras, photographs, telephone calls, letters, e-mail, and other means of communication. For many more years to come, learned persons will debate the meanings of *torture* as well as *cruel and degrading treatment*. But a picture seems truly to be worth a thousand words. The photographs of the abuse at Abu Ghraib made everyone in the world sit up and take notice immediately. There is no good reason to doubt Harman's statement that she took the photographs to document the abuse. Who would have believed her or any of the other soldiers without the evidence of the photographs?

Notes

1. Seymour M. Hersh, *Chain of Command: The Road from 9/11 to Abu Ghraib* (New York: HarperCollins, 2004).

2. Dana Priest, "CIA Avoids Scrutiny of Detainee Treatment; Afghan's Death Took Two Years to Come to Light," *Washington Post,* March 3, 2005.

3. MG Geoffrey Miller, "Assessment of DoD Counterterrorism Interrogation and Detention Operations in Iraq," in Mark Danner, *Torture and Truth: America, Abu Ghraib and the War on Terror* (New York: New York Review of Books, 2004), 205-14.

PART TWO

CHAOS AT THE COURTS-MARTIAL AT FT. HOOD

CHAPTER FOUR

THE COURT-MARTIAL OF JAVAL DAVIS—THE SOLDIER WHO SNAPPED FOR TEN SECONDS

On the day that the army finally approved me to serve as an expert witness, the defense attorney, Bergrin, put the accused soldier, Davis, on the phone. Davis is an African American soldier who was born and raised in Roselle, New Jersey. He had been a track star in high school. He told me the terrible story of Abu Ghraib with intensity and passion. "It was hell on earth," he said. He and the soldiers were mortared almost every day; every night that he went to sleep he feared he would not wake up alive in the morning; they worked twelve-hour shifts without a break; the prison was overcrowded; he had no idea what was expected of him on the job because there were no standard operating procedures and everything was on-the-job training. He said that things were normal and routine during his assignments in Bosnia and Egypt because he knew what was expected of him as a combat support military policeman. But he and the others had not been trained to work as prison guards and had no idea what to expect. Above all, he did not expect or know how to deal with the MI giving orders to do "strange things" to the prisoners in order to "soften them up" for interrogation, and he said that he did not expect that MI would run the prison.

On the night in question, November 7, 2003, he said that he "lost it" and stomped on the fingers and toes of a group of prisoners who were on the floor. There had been a serious prison riot at Abu Ghraib the day before, and he took out his frustration on the small group of prisoners who were singled out as instigators of or scapegoats for the riot. He was not involved in any other incident of abuse. He is not in any of the photographs of abuse at Abu Ghraib. He said that for the most part the prisoners liked and respected him, because he treated them kindly, and he just "snapped" for ten seconds on that one day.

He also told me that he was married and had two children. His wife and four-year-old son came to his trial as a show of support, along with many other members of his family and church, including his minister. This extensive support network took up a full three rows of the tiny court chamber, and most of them read the Bible and prayed during his trial. His entire family was dressed in their Sunday best. His son was the quietest and most well-behaved child I have ever observed for a four-year-old child.

The Road to Abu Ghraib via Fort Hood

My first impression of the courthouse, the Lawrence Williams Justice Center, was that it seemed tiny in comparison with the historically big cases that were being handled there vis-à-vis Abu Ghraib. It was kind of like the feeling one has on first seeing the Alamo in San Antonio—such a small building for such a huge history. The courthouse was clearly intended to prosecute ordinary offenses by soldiers, not extraordinarily important ones. Yet it was named for General Lawrence Williams, who had played an important role in investigating the My Lai massacre in Vietnam. I thought, "How strange that My Lai and Abu Ghraib were being juxtaposed in Texas, the home of the Alamo." History was repeating itself, in a way, such that the army was again being forced to confront its war crimes. And it was repeating the strategy it used to deal with My Lai: protect the big fish of power and go after the small minnows.

Pretrial Motions

On February 1, 2005, Bergrin made a defense motion to dismiss charges because of "unlawful command influence." He wanted to have the secretary of defense and other orchard keepers testify. The judge denied these motions. In a statement to the media, Bergrin commented later on the judge's decision: "If we had been able to present all our evidence, we would have unequivocally and categorically proven that all individuals in the chain of command, up to the highest levels, knew what was going on. The commanders condoned the actions and nobody ever condemned it."[1]

On January 16, 2005, approximately two weeks prior to the start of trial, the defense was still trying to get the judge to approve a long list of approximately forty witnesses. All were denied by the judge except for two soldiers and one officer. The officers and others who were not allowed to testify include the most important orchard keepers at Abu Ghraib, as suggested by the government reports. The judge allowed the supply officer, DiNenna, to testify. He was the only officer to take the stand at the Davis court-martial and one of only two officers who were allowed to testify in all the courts-martial that I witnessed. The other two witnesses who were allowed to testify in Davis's trial were SGT Ken Davis and the medic, SPC Helga Aldape-Moreno. In summary, Bergrin requested the appearance and live testimony of *forty* officers and soldiers, and the judge approved *only three* in Davis's defense.

Regarding the one incident that lasted for ten seconds in his life, Davis was charged with dereliction of duty for failing to protect detainees, conspiracy to maltreat detainees, assaulting detainees, cruelty and maltreatment, and lying to investigators about the incident. The "conspiracy" charge stems from the fact that the other six rotten apples were all present in some form for this particular incident of abuse, although Davis left the scene and did not participate in the physical assault and sexual degradation that others committed. Perhaps this constitutes a "conspiracy" in legal terms, but it does not come across as a conspiracy in everyday, layperson's terms.

After Davis had left the scene, Frederick went on to hit a prisoner in the chest and forced others to masturbate. Graner punched a prisoner in the head and forced them into a naked pyramid. Other soldiers watched the abuse and did not report it.

Jury Selection

The two prosecuting attorneys were MAJ Michael Holley, the lead prosecutor, and CPT Christopher Graveline. Bergrin was assisted by an army lawyer appointed to the defense, CPT Scott Dunn. Dunn worked mostly behind the scenes by writing memorandums, obtaining witnesses, and preparing written material for the trial. In the courtroom, Bergrin did most of the talking for the defense.

The jury selection was a long and painstaking process. The judge, prosecution, and defense asked the usual questions about bias, whether the potential juror had watched the news, whether the potential juror had seen photos, whether the juror could keep an open mind, and so on. For the most part, the ones who were admitted to the jury panel said that they did not really follow the news and knew little or nothing about Davis from the media. Bergrin requested that the juror pool include noncommissioned officers (sergeants), and the judge complied.

In the end, the jury consisted of nine men: four were commissioned officers (two majors and two lieutenant colonels), and five were sergeants. In terms of ethnic composition, five whites, two African Americans, one Hispanic, and one Asian sat on the jury. All the officers sat in the front row; the sergeants sat in the back row. The judge told the jury that their military ranks in the army should play no role in their jury duty.

One more point about the jury selection stood out in contrast to the other courts-martial. Every time a prospective juror was called into the courtroom to be questioned, Bergrin stood behind the seated Davis, put his hands on Davis's shoulders, and said loudly, "Good morning. My name is Paul Bergrin. It is an honor and a privilege for me to represent Javal Davis in this case." There was something striking about the impeccably groomed and well-dressed attorney's bold and supportive attitude.

The Prosecution's Opening Statement

The prosecutor began by laying out what he called the facts of the case. Davis had served seven years in the Army Reserve and had worked at Black & Decker prior to his deployment. He was first sent to Bosnia and Egypt from 2001 to 2003 and then to Iraq on February 27, 2003.

The prosecutor described the confusing array of prisons within the prison that is Abu Ghraib. Camp Ganci and Camp Vigilant were two tent prisons within the compound reserved for "common criminals." The Hard Site was further subdivided as follows: Tier 1–A was for "MI holds" (prisoners to be interrogated) and the "mentally unstable." Tier 1–B was for "females and juveniles." Tiers 2 through 4 housed more "common criminals." Although the prosecution recited nearly the same configuration in each of the courts-martial, my reaction to it now is the same as the first time I heard of it: how strange that there were prisons within the prison. How strange that the government did not seem embarrassed to state in open court that it imprisoned women, children, and the mentally ill! And how strange that all these different types of prisoners were mixed with the "high-value detainees" who supposedly held intelligence information (in reality, however, over 80 percent did not know anything of value to the United States). The prosecutor was redescribing chaos by using the language of order.

The prosecutor recounted briefly the history of the Abu Ghraib saga. Davis worked the night shift from 4 p.m. to 4 a.m. daily. Reese, the company commander, had assigned Frederick (who was serving his sentence in prison at the time of Davis's court-martial) as the noncommissioned officer in charge (NCOIC) of the night shift. On January 13, 2004, Darby had turned in two CDs of "innocuous" photos as well as photos involving nudity. The prosecutor said that Darby knew that the behavior depicted in the photographs was wrong, and it had to stop. On January 14, 2004, Davis was interviewed by the Criminal Investigation Command (CID), and he allegedly lied in his sworn statement by claiming that he did not intentionally hurt prisoners and that he was not angry during the incident.

The incident in question occurred on November 7, 2003, and involved seven prisoners who were being escorted into the Hard Site after allegedly participating in a riot in one of the tent cities within the compound. The prisoners were hooded and handcuffed. Davis twice jumped on them, even though the prisoners were unarmed and restrained, and he stomped on their feet and hands. SFC Shannon Snyder, who was in charge of the tier during the night shift, told him to stop, and Davis did stop. Moreover, Davis left the tier at this point and did *not* participate in any of the assault, sexual debauchery, and humiliation that followed.

According to the prosecutor, this abuse was not authorized and was not ordered. It involved "dehumanization." It was humiliating for the Iraqi prisoners to be naked in front of others, and this condition is a serious degradation of Islamic law. Davis admitted witnessing some of the abuse but denied participating in it.

The prosecutor's opening statement was problematic in that he said that Davis had left the scene after Snyder had yelled at him to stop stomping on fingers and toes, yet he was accusing Davis of witnessing some of the abuse that occurred after he had left. The prosecutor did not establish when Davis allegedly returned to the abusive scene. He then played an audiotape of Davis's confession that lasted for approximately forty-five minutes. This taped confession was the main piece of evidence against Davis.

The Audiotaped Confession

In the taped confession, Davis could be heard saying that he had had fifteen years of formal education. He arrived at Abu Ghraib on October 1, 2003, and was assigned to the guard tower. He was not assigned to the Hard Site, so that his presence there on the night in question was due to Frederick asking him for assistance in escorting the prisoners. He first made contact with the prisoners in the hallway leading from tier 3A to tier 1A. He said he knew ahead of time that they were rioters and that a female MP got hit in the face with a brick during the riot. (In all the courts-martial where this fact was mentioned, the female MP was never identified.) The prisoners were fully clothed, wore sandbags over their heads, and were handcuffed. They were pushed onto the ground, and Davis said he "fell" on them and stepped on their toes. Frederick "punched a guy," but Davis "kept on walking." The military judge could be heard on the audiotape asking Davis, "Were you afraid of them?" "Yes, not then and there, but what they could do. I was not scared at that time. I was mad. Disturbed. I wasn't trying to hurt them, just scare them." Davis went on to say that he stepped on their fingers and toes, and they moaned. There was "a state of confusion," and "there were a lot of people" at the scene.

The judge asked him, "Why did you do that?" Davis said he had had a bad week and a bad day. There were a lot of injuries, the soldiers were getting mortared every day, and the riot "got to me." "I lost it," he said. "Did you know what you were doing?" the judge asked. "Yes." The judge said there was no justification for what Davis had done and asked him, "Were you trying to hurt or control them?" "A little bit of both," Davis answered. He elaborated that he was holding himself back from hurting them more and wanted to scare them. The judge asked him about his training as a prison guard, and Davis said he had not received any training and that his training was really "OJT" (on-the-job training).

The incident occurred after five weeks of Davis working as a guard. The judge interpreted his statements as Davis wanting to show the detainees who was boss, and he asked, "Was this reasonable?" Davis answered, "Yes, but not in that manner." The judge established that Davis weighed 220 pounds at the time of the incident.

The judge asked a series of questions in rapid succession: "Did you work with MI?" Davis said he was introduced to MI while working in the tiers. "Did you see MI?" Not that time (on the night of November 7, when this abusive incident occurred). Did anyone authorize Davis to do what he did? Not on that night. Did anyone authorize Davis implicitly, as setting the stage for interrogation? Davis answered, "Yes sir, they did." The judge said that this was not one of those occasions for softening up prisoners. On the night of November 7, Davis was supposed to escort the prisoners. Then the judge asked, "Though you didn't receive training, you knew you had a duty to report Frederick?" "Yes, sir." The judge asked Davis whether he had seen other incidents of abuse, and there was a long pause. Before Davis could answer, the judge clarified the question as pertaining only to the night of November 7. Yes, Davis came back after he had left and saw nudity and masturbation. There was a "gaggle" of prisoners on the floor. What did Davis think about what he saw? It was "disgusting." "Was Frederick being told to do it [orchestrate the sexual abuse], or was he doing it on his own?" "Both," Davis answered, adding, "At that time I did not know."

The judge asked him whether forcing detainees to be naked was normal. Davis answered that it was normal at Abu Ghraib. There was a long pause. The judge asked whether Davis had seen any other abuse, committed by MPs, MIs, and OGA? "Yes, I have" Davis said. "Who and when?" the judge asked. "Numerous times," Davis answered. The abuse involved MIs and MPs, but he didn't know their names. "Let me narrow it down" the judge said, adding, "Did you see someone commit abuse that you knew to be an MP?" "Yes, Frederick was making them masturbate." The judge asked again if there were other occasions of abuse. Again, Davis answered, "Yes." "When and where?" the judge asked. Davis said that prisoners were "roughed up routinely" during processing. The judge asked whether he saw dog handlers commit abuse. "Yes." "Did the dogs bite the detainees?" "Yes." "Did you report the dog handlers?" "No." "Did you report Frederick?" "No."

I should add that almost a year later, one of the dog handlers was court-martialed at Fort Meade, Maryland, for the incidents that Davis (and others) saw but did not report. Ironically, the defense for the dog handlers was that they were following orders and interrogation techniques approved by Pappas. Yet Davis was being charged with dereliction of duty for not reporting "approved" techniques. In fact, as both court-martials (that of Davis and the dog-handler, Smith) showed—soldiers at Abu Ghraib could not tell the difference between approved versus unauthorized abuse.

The judge asked Davis whether he saw MIs and MPs rough up prisoners. "Yes." The judge asked a key question: "Was this an interview technique or abuse?" "Both," Davis answered. "You saw MPs rough up prisoners?" "Yes." The judge established that Davis worked as a guard between October 15 and November 7, but not after November 7, although the reason for this shift in duties was not explained. "Did you have a duty to stop this?" "Yes," Davis answered. The judge repeated that detainees were beaten up during processing. Some detainees were thrown against the wall. "You knew it was wrong?" "Yes." "Did you report it?" "No. I should have reported it. But I didn't."

The judge asked whether Davis had a duty to stop Frederick making "that guy masturbate." "Yes." "You knew you had that duty." There was a pause. The judge clarified that Davis did not have the duty to stop it as a corrections officer per se but "in your head you knew you had a duty to protect them?" "Yes." Did Davis intend to hurt the detainees? "No." Did he hurt them out of anger? Davis said it was not intentional anger. Was Davis mad that day? "Yes." Why did he change his statement? The judge answered for him: "If you told the truth you'd get in trouble, so you lied to get out of trouble." Davis agreed. The audiotape ended abruptly.

The prosecution read portions of written depositions called "stipulations of fact" by several soldiers who had witnessed the incident involving Davis, The reasons for this arrangement were not clear to the outsider. Why did the prosecution have these same soldiers testify in person at the subsequent two courts-martial but not at this one? In any event, the soldiers all said pretty much the same thing: Davis was called to assist with seven "dangerous rioters." They were "filthy" and had sandbags over their heads. The prisoners were piled on the floor. Davis leaned and "fell" on them. The prisoners did not sustain any broken bones or injuries. They did not see him abuse prisoners on any other occasion.

Sivits ended his statement with a powerful emotional statement: "From what I have seen of Sgt. Davis being in his company, I consider him to be a good soldier who was mission oriented. I saw him interact with Iraqis at Al-Hillah and he was very friendly to them from what I saw. I saw him interact with both children and adults. I would trust Sgt. Davis with my life."

The government prosecutors rested their case. Almost their entire case depended on Davis's audiotaped confession of guilt.

Opening Statement by Paul Bergrin

Bergrin stood behind Davis, put his hands on Davis's shoulders, and said to the jury again, "It is my honor and privilege to represent Javal Davis at this court-martial." Bergrin's booming voice filled the courtroom, and the jury's attention was fixed on the two of them. Bergrin said that Davis admits that what he did was wrong and that he is sorry for what he did. But he had no intention to personally injure the prisoners. Out of approximately fifty to a hundred interactions with prisoners per day, he snapped this one time. He is a good soldier. Bergrin said he would show that the "atmosphere" at Abu Ghraib was stressful, chaotic, and filthy and that a psychologist would testify that, based on his psychiatric report, Davis is not sadistic. The prosecutor objected that the social psychologist who was scheduled to testify for the defense (Staub) was not qualified to make this claim. The judge sustained the objection.

Bergrin went on to talk about the role of the CIA at Abu Ghraib, but the judge cut him off, saying that "lots of people can say this, but Davis cannot." In the heated exchange between Bergrin and the judge, the judge ruled that Davis must have been able to recognize the OGA (in this context, a euphemism for the CIA) in order for this to be admitted into testimony, but Davis had already admitted he could not recognize them. (In fact, almost all the soldiers testified in other trials that they recognized the OGA precisely because they could not recognize them. Members of the OGA deliberately chose not to wear name tags in a setting where soldiers and officers were required to wear name tags.)

Ken Davis's Testimony for the Defense

It is important not to confuse the soldier who testified for the defense, SGT Ken Davis, with the accused, SGT Javal Davis. Ken Davis was one of the rare soldiers at Abu Ghraib who saw the abuse, refused to participate in it, and reported it. The judge would not allow him to describe the specific incidents of abuse that he witnessed and reported because he said they were not relevant to the particular incident that involved Javal Davis.

In talking with Ken Davis, I learned that he suffers from PTSD as a result of his experiences at Abu Ghraib. Since talking with him, I have learned that approximately 20 percent of the soldiers deployed to Iraq suffer from PTSD, and many are not treated. Soldiers told me that they are reluctant to seek treatment because anything they say about the causes of their disorder (what they experienced, from engaging in combat to participating in or witnessing abuse) can be used against them. I confirmed this by examining an army medical referral document from Camp Victory, Iraq, which does warn the soldier that "your case file may be subject to subpoena when ordered by a judge."

In any event, Ken Davis testified that he received no training as a prison guard prior to being assigned to Abu Ghraib. He was not assigned to tier 1–A. Instead, his job was to transport prisoners between Abu Ghraib and Baghdad, and he took his job very seriously. He testified that Javal Davis complained to him that MI would often walk in and take prisoners away without accounting for them or telling him and that this bothered Javal greatly. Ken Davis also told the jury that there was an "intense struggle" in the chain of command whether the treatment of prisoners was appropriate. He said that morale among soldiers at Abu Ghraib was low, and almost everyone was asking, "Can we trust the leadership?" He also said there was "intense pressure to get intelligence" from prisoners who did not possess the information the army sought. He began to cry on the witness stand as he described the general atmosphere at Abu Ghraib. He was not present for the actual incident that occurred on the night of November 7 that involved Javal Davis, so he could not give direct testimony about it. Bergrin sought to have Ken Davis describe the chaotic atmosphere at Abu Ghraib, but the judge would not allow it beyond the short testimony described here.

What did Ken Davis want to say on the stand? He conveyed the following information to me, which was not presented in testimony. Sometime in October 2003, he came upon two MI soldiers who had handcuffed two prisoners and were abusing them. Davis said that one of the MI soldiers asked him sarcastically, "Do you think we crossed the line?" Davis said he answered, "I am not sure—you are MI." Then the other MI soldier said, "We know what we are doing."

On another occasion where he witnessed abuse, Ken Davis walked up to the MI and said, "Did you all ever consider that these guys are innocent?" The MI soldier responded, "I've been doing this longer than you've been in the military." Davis also said that Graner disclosed to him that he was taking photographs to protect himself. Davis reported the incidents of abuse that he witnessed to his immediate supervisor, who told him, "They are MI, and they are in charge, so let them do their job," or words to that effect.

Between December 2003 and April 2004, Ken Davis reported these incidents of abuse to his chaplain, five officers, and, finally, the U.S. House of Representatives Armed Services Committee. He said that he concluded that his whistle-blowing did not do any good and that he felt deeply disappointed by the army.

The Supply Officer's Testimony for the Defense

DiNenna took the stand for the defense. He had been in the U.S. Army for eighteen years and was the logistics or supply officer at Abu Ghraib. He described the conditions at Abu Ghraib as "deplorable," "filthy," "trash everywhere," "over-populated," "looted," and "overflowing with feces." The latrines did not work and were not serviced or replaced so that he had to order them to be sealed for reasons of general hygiene. Soldiers and prisoners alike used the showers or whatever place they could find for toilets. He said that everyone at Abu Ghraib, soldiers and prisoners alike, came down with dysentery and that most people were sick most of the time due to the unhealthy situation. They called it the "Abu bug." The food was contaminated with rat feces and other grime until December 2003. For this reason, he was forced to switch to meals ready to eat (MREs) for soldiers and prisoners alike, but this caused a problem for the Muslim population of prisoners, who would not eat pork or pork products. And there was always a shortage of MREs at every meal, which caused discontent and danger to the soldiers from angry prisoners. In general, the major said, "there was no way to bring edible food to the prisoners." This state of affairs "caused riots." Even when prisoners were willing to eat MREs, there were shortages of food. He notified the chain of command above him concerning this situation, but the army was unresponsive.

The major said that his main concerns at Abu Ghraib were the "spreading of disease" and the "rationing of water" to soldiers and prisoners alike. There was no clothing in the winter for the prisoners, so that some soldiers gave up their clothing to the prisoners. The prisoners would steal clothing from each other, and factions developed out of desperation. "A lot of diabetics" were among the prisoners, and medical care in general "was a challenge." "Force protection was done by ourselves," the major said. He elaborated that the soldiers had to protect the prison from external threats such as daily attacks from insurgents as well as internal threats from the prisoners. The soldiers were mortared "at least a couple of times a week," and two MIs were killed from such attacks. Soldiers in the guard towers were the most vulnerable because the prison had been "designed to look in, not look out."

The major also said that it was not clear who was in charge of the prison and that the command structure at Abu Ghraib was "extremely confusing." There were about seven to eight thousand prisoners and only sixty to seventy soldiers on any given shift. There were "civilian as well as security detainees." He added that women and children as prisoners were mixed in with the other detainees.

DiNenna's description of Abu Ghraib bears an eerie resemblance to the deplorable conditions at the Civil War prison in Andersonville, Georgia, during the 1860s.[2] At Andersonville, soldiers did not have adequate food and water, were often sick and vomited because of the unsanitary conditions, did not have access to toilets, and waited for many years to be released because of politics. The prison was overcrowded, understaffed by guards, and the scene of horrific abuse and torture. More than 150 years later, the U.S. Army was still grappling with the most fundamental aspects of running a prison in a humane and human manner.

Bergrin moved to another sensitive topic—namely, Miller's infamous visit to Iraq in the summer of 2003 for the purpose of "Gitmoizing" Abu Ghraib. Bergrin asked DiNenna whether Miller had spoken with him while in Iraq, and the prosecutor objected immediately that this question was "irrelevant." The judge sustained the objection. Bergrin was stopped from moving further with this potentially explosive yet extremely important line of questioning that was intended to allow an officer to testify to a direct, explicit link between this general's orders and the climate of abuse at Abu Ghraib.

Bergrin moved back to questions about the deplorable conditions at Abu Ghraib. The major said that there were not enough radios, generators, or equipment at Abu Ghraib. There were "ghost detainees," to which the prosecutor objected, and the judge sustained the objection. (The issue of ghost detainees, or prisoners who were never registered as prisoners, is mentioned in the U.S. government reports.) I heard a journalist sigh loudly at this point.

The prosecutor cross-examined DiNenna. He had the major agree that there were many compounds within Abu Ghraib and that overall the "mission" was challenged by "logistical and support conditions." The prosecutor also had the major agree that there was *some* training for the soldiers in rules of interaction, cultural sensitivity, "do's and don'ts," respect, and so on. The prosecutor said that a certain sergeant major talked to the incoming troops. DiNenna said that no specific training for being a prison guard was provided. The prosecutor retorted quickly that there is no specific training required to know that one should not stomp on people's toes. The major pointed out that the army did not replace the sixty MPs the unit had lost. The prosecutor said that it's a misconception that MPs just guard prisoners; in reality, MPs do many jobs. He added that Camp Ganci held many prisoners, and the vast majority of MPs did their job the right way despite hard conditions.

At some point, DiNenna said that he had sent out many e-mails per day asking for help from the army regarding shortages of food and water. "Did you get help?" the prosecutor asked. "No," the major answered. DiNenna continued: Eight thousand detainees were held at Abu Ghraib, which put tremendous pressure on the MPs. DiNenna said that there were confrontations with the OGA about nude detainees, especially about stripping them in front of females. He added that the MIs were present on the tier mainly at night. (This is an important observation because the prosecution tried to frame the abuse as the result of a deviant night shift of MPs, and the major shifted the focus to what might have been night-time deviance by the MIs who exploited the MPs for their purposes—but this line of inquiry was never pursued.) The prosecutor asked the major whether he was on tier 1-A at night, and the major answered that he was not. He elaborated that he could not spend the entire shift with every soldier.

"It was difficult to convince the OGA of anything," DiNenna said. He added, "The MI ran tier 1-A." The major said that he learned about MI tactics for using MPs to "set conditions" for interrogations much later, and these tactics "would in essence override my authority." The judge intervened at this point and said this observation by the major was "not relevant." The cross-examination ended abruptly.

The jurors asked, "Do you have a copy of the rules of interaction?" There was confusion in the courtroom as both the prosecution and defense admitted that neither side had a copy of them. The jurors also asked the major, "Where were the rules of interaction posted?" He answered, "In the MP offices and the guard towers." "When did the facility open?" The major replied that Camp Vigilant was opened in July 2003, Camp Ganci in midsummer, and the Hard Site in September 2003. "How many uprisings and riots were there?" "Always," the major answered. "How many Iraqi police were at Abu Ghraib?" There were fifteen to twenty to begin with, and the number climbed to one hundred at some point, but they were still stretched thin for guards. "What other training did the soldiers receive?" The major answered that most of the training was OJT, and all the soldiers were combat support groups doing prison work for which they were not trained. "We didn't have a training day," the major said, because that would mean that "the prisoners would have to watch themselves." The judge then dismissed DiNenna from the stand.

Addendum to DiNenna's Testimony

I have indicated that the judge prevented Bergrin from soliciting direct testimony from DiNenna concerning the link between Miller and the abuse at Abu Ghraib. But apparently the army also prevented the defense from obtaining indirect testimony in the form of e-mails that would have established this link. For example, an investigator who worked for Bergrin sent the following memorandum to a CID agent on December 15, 2004:

> The Defense Team of Sgt. Davis is requesting all E-mails that were sent from or received by Major David DiNenna's S-3 320th M.P. BN SIPRINET account. Major DiNenna was based at Abu Ghraib as the S-3 officer.
>
> Major DiNenna has been granted to the defense team of Sgt. Davis as a witness for the court martial of Sgt. Javal Davis. The trial commences on

February 2, 2005. Sgt. Davis's Defense Team is seeking to retrieve ALL of the E-mails sent out and received by Major DiNenna. Major DiNenna's E-mails set the stage for the atmosphere at Abu Ghraib. They also tell of the futility that was felt by Major DiNenna as he attempted to secure the services and amenities that were needed to properly run the Abu Ghraib prison. Major DiNenna has stated to the defense team that he had sent hundreds of E-mails to higher headquarters and even the Pentagon. *Major DiNenna had also received an E-mail that had a presentation about "Gitmoizing Abu Ghraib."* Along with Major DiNenna's testimony and the E-mails, the jury panel will get a clearer picture of conditions at the Abu Ghraib Prison. The time frame of the requested E-mails that we are seeking is 20 September 2003 to 31 December 2003. Major DiNenna does consent to this request.[3] (emphasis added)

According to the defense, the army never responded to this request. The word *SIPRINET* refers to a secret army e-mail system in Iraq, but the existence and motives for this e-mail system were never admitted into testimony. Some corroboration for DiNenna's claim that an e-mail ordered the "Gitmoizing of Abu Ghraib" is to be found in Karpinski's book, in which she also claims that Miller sought to "Gitmoize" Abu Ghraib. The problem is that these and other allusions to this highly significant concept—which links directly the orchard keepers to the orchard and rotten apples at Abu Ghraib—were suppressed from open testimony in this and the other courts-martial.

The Medic's Testimony

Aldape-Moreno was called to the stand for the defense. She was one of the medics at Abu Ghraib. She testified that she was called to tier 1–A between 1 to 2 a.m. on November 8, 2003, to treat a prisoner for breathing problems. (This was the prisoner whom Frederick had punched in the chest.) Bergrin wanted to establish that she was not called for any injuries to the feet or toes of the prisoners who were eventually stacked into the naked pyramid. The medic agreed. In this way, Bergrin had shown to the jury that the actions of Davis did not result in injuries to the prisoners.

During cross-examination, the prosecutor asked her whether she had stayed for the pyramid of naked detainees. She said that she had not because she was upset and shocked. "So you don't know if they were injured?" She said that she did not know whether they were injured after she had left. "You left because this was so upsetting," the prosecutor repeated. "Yes."

The jury asked how many average calls were made for medical assistance. She answered three calls per night. Did she treat any MPs during this same time frame (i.e., on November 7)? "No."

Aldape-Moreno was the only medic who testified, and she testified only in Davis's trial, out of the three courts-martial that I witnessed. Her brief testimony, and the very fact that she testified, opens many doors to many questions: What was the role of doctors, nurses, and medics in the abuse at Abu Ghraib and elsewhere? If the government wishes to argue that soldiers have a duty to report abuse, then by that argument, doctors and medics have an even more explicit duty to report abuse. The American Medical Association as well as international medical conventions and agreements prohibit practitioners in fields related to medicine from participating in abuse. In the wide-ranging discourse pertaining to torture at Abu Ghraib and elsewhere, the medical profession is hardly mentioned. Somehow, it seems unthinkable to accuse doctors and medics of dereliction of duty for turning a blind eye and a deaf ear to abuse. Yet it seems strangely permissible to accuse military police officers of dereliction of duty for the exact same behavior. This discrepancy does not make sense logically.

In general, the medical dimension—what doctors, nurses, and medics knew about abuse—is one of the most neglected aspects of the Abu Ghraib saga. MAJ David Auch was one of the physicians at Abu Ghraib.[4] He did not testify at this or the other trials that I witnessed, although a written statement from him was read at Lynndie England's court-martial. A logbook exists that records some of the medical treatment of prisoners at Abu Ghraib, but it was not used in testimony. The defense was lucky to get a medic to testify, but her testimony opens many doors and raises many questions about medical ethics and abuse at Abu Ghraib.

Two Expert Witnesses on the Social Climate at Abu Ghraib

Bergrin decided to have two expert witnesses testify: Staub, a social psychologist from the University of Massachusetts at Amherst, and me as an expert witness in sociology. The prosecution did not have any expert witnesses to rebut the two of us. A journalist reported in the *Killeen Daily Herald*, "The day had a rough start for the defense as testimony by Dr. Staub, a key expert witness leading a study on peace and the prevention of violence at the University of Massachusetts, appeared ambushed by government prosecutors."[5]

The apparent "ambush" had to do with commenting on the psychiatric report on Davis without adequate preparation and as somewhat of a surprise given that the two experts were supposed to testify primarily about the social climate at Abu Ghraib. What did Staub say on the stand? This is something I had to glean from media accounts,[6] even though I attended the trial. The prosecution asked me to sit alone in a closed room in the courthouse building while he testified in the courtroom. He is the only witness whom the prosecution would not let me watch in all the courts-martial I attended. From the media accounts, I gathered that Staub and I said very similar things. Matthew Closta reports the following:

> Bergrin also had two expert witnesses, one an expert on the various forces and influences leading to violence, testify about what transpired at Abu Ghraib after reviewing official reports. "Iraqis showed ingratitude while American soldiers were sacrificing their lives, this devalued the lives of the Iraqi prisoners," Dr. Ervin Staub, professor of Psychology, University of Massachusetts at Amherst, said.
>
> Both experts cited a famous Stanford study from the 1970s and drew parallels between that study and how the lawlessness and horrendous conditions at Abu Ghraib set up the potential for prisoner abuse by Soldiers as the atmosphere deteriorated sociologically and psychologically.
>
> "The environment was a kind of anything goes attitude," Staub said. "Supervision is crucial in this environment. Rules don't mean very much if you don't enforce them."
>
> "There was tremendous social disorganization at Abu Ghraib," said Dr. Stjepan Mestrovic, functional sociologist, professor of Sociology, Texas A&M University. "According to the reports, MI was not sure what MPs could do and vice versa."[7]

The journalist, Debbie Stevenson, fleshes out the alleged "ambush" in the *Killeen Daily Herald*:

> With Staub on the stand for most of the morning session, the prosecution moved to debunk his theory that Davis had been adversely affected by the prison's harsh environment, causing a normally nonviolent man to lash out at the detainees after a riot in which a military policewoman was injured in the face by a brick. "In violence-generated circumstances some people we consider normal might become violent" Staub said. "I would say many soldiers would have been induced to commit some form of excessive force at Abu Ghraib." Prosecutors criticized the psychologist's decision to discard an evaluation from Walter Reed Army Medical Center that found Davis to have occupational problems and narcissistic traits.

The report was not considered because it would not have influenced his opinion, Staub said.

"Did you look at Javal Davis' history?" Captain Chris Graveline asked. "When you interviewed Sergeant Davis, did you look at his violent past?"

I do not know whether Staub was given a chance to examine the psychiatric reports and other allegations of Davis's so-called violent past. I do know that the psychiatric reports rule out a violent nature in Davis and that the two allegations leveled at him were dismissed.

My Testimony

Bergrin asked me questions about how the chain of command established the chaos that led to the abuse and specifically about the impact of Miller's visit in the summer of 2003 intended to Gitmoize Abu Ghraib. As soon as Bergin said the words "General Miller," the prosecutor said, "Objection," and the judge said, "Sustained." As soon as Bergrin asked me to comment on the drive for intelligence leading to abuse, the prosecutor yelled, "Objection," and the judge again said, "Sustained." I was not allowed to answer. As soon as Bergrin asked me to comment on how Pappas ignored the findings of abuse made by the ICRC, the now familiar echo arose: "Objection"—"Sustained." When Bergrin brought up the issue of using dogs at Abu Ghraib to exploit Arab cultural fears, I heard "Objection"—"Sustained." As soon as Bergrin asked me to comment on confusion about rules in the army chain of command, I heard "Objection"—"Sustained." The judge overruled the prosecutor's objection only once, when the prosecutor objected to my commenting on the finding in the government reports that MPs did not know the rules the MIs were following and vice versa. A common theme runs through the material that Bergrin sought to admit and that the prosecutor found objectionable: anything and everything about the orchard keepers seemed objectionable.

During cross-examination, the prosecutor wanted me to admit that Zimbardo's findings were based on "assumptions," not facts. I said that Zimbardo and other social scientists make interpretations based on facts. He asked me whether I had read the letter from the army psychiatrist who had examined Davis, and I replied that I had (albeit on very short notice). The prosecutor asserted that the letter stated that Davis had "tendencies" that would explain what he did at Abu Ghraib. I disagreed and asked him to produce the letter. He handed it to me, and I read from it. Then I said that the psychiatrist did *not* state that Davis had any sort of disorder that produced tendencies that would lead to violence. Someone in the court-room yelled, "Touché!" But the judge and the prosecutor went around and around, back and forth, seemingly trying to make me conclude something that the military psychiatrist had not concluded and that Davis's tests did not indicate—namely, a tendency toward violence.

During this whole time, Bergrin was making objections on the grounds that the prosecutor was being argumentative and leading the witness, and so on, but the judge overruled Bergrin. The judge asked me many questions about the *Diagnostic and Statistical Manual* and the American Psychiatric Association and various diagnoses. Finally, the judge asked me to explain in plain terms why Davis had stepped on the hands and toes of the prisoners. I answered that it was my professional opinion, based on his psychiatric evaluation and my interview with him, that it was most likely because he was stressed and displaced his anger—kind of like someone who had a bad day at the office coming home and kicking the cat. That explanation finally seemed to satisfy the judge. The prosecutor said there was no point in beating a dead horse. He sat down, and the judge dismissed me from the stand.

Testimony of Prisoners from Abu Ghraib via Videotape

Bergrin had requested that eleven Iraqi prisoners from Abu Ghraib testify on Davis's behalf. Moreover, he requested that the prisoners be flown in from Iraq in order to testify in person. The judge denied this request as a whole but allowed videotaped depositions of three prisoners, identi-fied by their numbers, to be shown to the jury in open court. This was a remarkable achievement by the defense.

Two things startled me during the video presentation. The first was the emaciated, depressed, and generally wretched condition of the prisoners. I asked Bergrin later whether any of them had been released, and the an-swer was that no one knew for certain. The second was the prosecutor's incessant objections to seemingly every question that Bergrin asked the prisoners during the videotaped depositions.

Detainee _____ of tier 3A testified that Davis treated prisoners well and that he is a "peaceful man." The prisoner said that he witnessed abuse from other guards, but Davis was not present during those incidents of abuse. He also said that dogs were often used to frighten detainees. He added that he was willing to travel to the United States to testify on Davis's behalf.

Detainee _____ of tier 3A also said that Davis treated prisoners well. Asked about allegations of abuse against Davis, he replied emphatically that he does not believe this. He said words to the effect, "If anyone tells you David [the nickname for Davis used by prisoners] is a bad man, he is a liar." He also said that he witnessed abuse against fellow prisoners, but never by Davis.

The third prisoner testified in much the same way. All in all, these prisoners gave a very favorable impression of Davis through their words and emotional expressions. On the other hand, the look of despair on their faces conveyed a very negative impression of how they were treated in general at Abu Ghraib.

Testimony of Davis's Minister and Family Members

Bishop Claude Campbell, the minister at Davis's church in New Jersey, testified. He said that Davis had apologized to the entire congregation for the sin he committed at Abu Ghraib and that he and the other church members forgave him. The bishop quoted from the Bible: "Let him who is without sin cast the first stone."

Six members of Davis's family testified that Javal was a good son, father, and husband. They said that he was gentle, supportive, and "a good man."

Other Testimony Admitted through Letters of Support

Bergrin's strategy was to show that others regarded Davis as a good soldier and that the atmosphere or social climate at Abu Ghraib constituted a mitigating factor that contributed to the abuse. Letters supporting Davis's character were admitted into testimony and included ones by SGT Hydrue Joyner, SGT Robert Jones, SSG William Cathcart, and SSG Robert Elliot. In general, his fellow soldiers said that Davis was dedicated to the mission, that he was a good soldier, that he was a loving father, and that they did and would trust him with their lives. For example, Joyner asserted, "I've known Sgt. Davis since I arrived in the unit back in December 1999. And since being around him for a number of years, I consider him to be a good friend of mine. As a soldier he is a good NCO. I can say for a fact that he is someone I would trust with my life in combat."

Testimony of Javal Davis

In a tearful testimony, Davis said, "I'm embarrassed to be sitting up here in front of the world. I don't know what I was thinking. I shouldn't have done that. I am deeply sorry. I am deeply apologetic to the Iraqis I stepped on. I ask for your forgiveness." He admitted that he is not a perfect soldier. I will note here that a real rotten apple would be incapable of even faking such an apology. So-called morally corrupt individuals are generally defiant to the end. They look down on judges and juries, they cannot admit they made mistakes, and they seem incapable of saying the words "I am sorry." By contrast, Davis was contrite and apologetic.

Davis also described Abu Ghraib as something like a "Mad Max" movie "come to life." He elaborated: "We were trying to help people, and they were trying to kill us." It is important to note that all seven rotten apples, as well as other witnesses, described Abu Ghraib as a crazy, bizarre, abnormal place. Davis also said that soldiers had to sleep in filthy jail cells. This is an important and overlooked fact in the discourse pertaining to Abu Ghraib.

Bergrin's Closing Statement

In an emotional closing statement, Bergrin said that Davis gave "seven years of honorable service, except for ten seconds. When you're living like an animal, it gets to you and to the prisoners." He was appealing to powerful emotions. One set of emotions has to do with judging a person's mistakes in the context of his or her past. Was the wrong action an exception to otherwise good conduct, or was it part of a pattern? It is certain that despite its efforts, the prosecution did not disprove Bergrin's characterization that Davis had snapped for ten seconds. The other set of emotions has to do with one's feelings about a work environment in which everyone—prisoners and soldiers alike—were living and working without dignity and respect (i.e., "like an animal"). Bergrin was implying what the reports had made clear: a chronic chaotic social environment leads to abuse.

Bergrin went on to say that Davis "is a father and a man who stood up and took responsibility." In other words, he pleaded guilty and expressed regret for what he had done. Bergrin added, "Sometimes you make bad decisions, bad choices." And, "There is no tomorrow for Javal Davis. We ask for justice. Weigh that ten-second transgression against the whole man's life.... Judge Sergeant Davis the same way you would want to be judged." He went on to say that any one of us could have made wrong decisions in the heat of battle. Although Davis had made a wrong decision, he never stopped thinking about his fellow soldiers and about his duty to his country. Bergrin reminded the jury that Davis humbly and sincerely apologized for his actions and begged for forgiveness. He is a "true man" and a "true soldier." Bergrin asked the jury to consider that this was only a ten-second episode in which no one was hurt. As thorough as the government was in presenting its case, it did not present "one scintilla of live testimony." Bergrin said that the government could have called squad leaders, platoon leaders, and others in the chain of command—but it did not. He asked the jury only to reprimand Davis and not to destroy his life and his career.

The Prosecution's Closing Statement

The prosecutor admitted that poor "conditions affected things" at Abu Ghraib. But, he added, "We either are or we are not responsible for our actions." He recommended that the jury impose a sentence of twelve to twenty-four months, a bad conduct discharge, and a reduction in rank to private. In a telling sign of some mercy, he asked that Davis should keep his pay while in prison so as not to punish his children.

Sentencing

On February 5, 2005, the jury began deliberations at 3:35 p.m. They reached a verdict that same day, and it was read at 9 p.m. Javal Davis was sentenced by a military jury of four officers and five enlisted soldiers to six months in a military prison, a reduction in rank to private, and a dishonorable discharge.

Postscript

Upon his release from prison, Davis "said that he is a good person who was under tremendous stress amid horrific conditions in and around the Iraqi prison."[8] He went on to say that "the open sewage, rotting body parts and constant fear of death from rockets and bombs around Abu Ghraib would drive the most docile soldier from Gomer Pyle into Full Metal

Jacket." He added: "The way I was portrayed as a soldier at Abu Ghraib is 100 percent untrue. I'm not the bad apple soldier I was portrayed as being by the military." He described Abu Ghraib as "a city of lost souls." "It's a very dark, gloomy, dirty, dank place. Words can't describe it." And "he said he and others had to deal with an alien world in which nothing was normal."

Notes

1. Joseph A. Reaves, "Courts-martial Hit Close to Huachuca," *Arizona Republic,* February 7, 2005.

2. See William Marvel, *Andersonville: The Last Depot* (Chapel Hill: University of North Carolina Press, 1994).

3. Memorandum signed and sent by Investigator Richard Russell and used here with his permission.

4. For an informative account of Auch's difficult role as a physician at Abu Ghraib, see M. Gregg Blocke and Jonathan H. Marks, "Triage at Abu Ghraib," *New York Times,* February 4, 2005, A19.

5. Debbie Stevenson, "Soldier Sentenced for Abuse at Abu Ghraib," *Killeen Daily Herald,* February 4, 2005.

6. See, for example, T.A. Badger, "Repentant Davis Asks Jury to Save Career," Associated Press, February 4, 2005: "A psychology professor testified that Davis' abuse of detainees was triggered by the violent atmosphere at the prison and a lack of military discipline among guards.... 'Rules didn't exist,' Staub said. 'There was a lawlessness that developed.' But prosecutor Capt. Chris Graveline referred to other alleged incidents involving Davis."

7. Matthew Chlosta, "Two More Soldiers Sentenced for Abu Ghraib Abuse," *Army News,* February 10, 2005.

8. These quotes are from Wayne Perry, "Javal Davis: 'I'm a Good Person,'" Associated Press, June 2, 2005.

CHAPTER FIVE

THE COURT-MARTIAL OF SABRINA HARMAN: WHY DIDN'T SMILING GIRL JUST WALK OUT THE DOOR?

It seemed difficult to prosecute Harman. According to her fellow soldiers, she had not hit anyone; she did not yell at anyone; she did not engage in any behavior that could be termed "sexual and physical abuse" at Abu Ghraib. On the contrary, she made sure prisoners had their eyeglasses and medicine; she got some of them blankets; she reported some of the abuse she saw, albeit to no avail. Journalists used the headline "Harman Called Kind to Iraqis at Sentencing" to describe her in articles. During her trial, the prosecutor argued consistently and convincingly that the prisoners were abused for sport and amusement, not for obtaining military or any other sort of intelligence. She was the gofer on tier 1–A who ran errands for the male soldiers. Her crimes consisted of posing in photographs with a huge, All-American smile on her face; taking photographs of others committing abuse; not reporting the cases of abuse the government decided to prosecute; and not walking out the door every time the abuse occurred.

It is crucial to note that she *did* walk out the door *some* of the time the abuse occurred, and she *did* report some of the abuse. The soldiers who testified against her had either condoned abuse, had themselves committed abuse, or in a few instances walked out on the abuse, but all of them had been either sentenced or threatened with prosecution unless they testified. Fear and intimidation carried over from Abu Ghraib into the courtroom at Fort Hood.

The prosecutor hammered the jury with the alleged fact that Harman's seemingly happy smile implied that she took sadistic pleasure in "maltreatment" of detainees. He claimed that her staying during some of the abuse even if she did not commit it was "dereliction of duty" as well as "conspiracy." The story of this particular "rotten apple's" court-martial is the story of the government using serious legal concepts against a seemingly harmless, young, female soldier who had the heart of a social worker and who got caught up in a poisoned environment she did not create and felt she could not escape. The prosecutor asked that she be sentenced to three years, but she served a sentence of three months. In the win-lose language of the legal world, the government lost and the defense won. In the words of the lead defense attorney, Frank Spinner, "We dodged the bullet."

This court-martial is significant because it highlights the process of gaslighting that is omnipresent in every aspect of the Abu Ghraib narrative, from the government reports to the trials themselves. *Gaslighting* is a psychological term that refers to a subtle competition between two individuals or competing groups in a dysfunctional environment for which side should be labeled as "crazy."[1] It's similar to people in a toxic relationship saying to each other, "I'm not the problem—you're the problem." Like the other "rotten apples," Harman regarded Abu Ghraib as a bizarre, weird, and crazy world and as nothing like a "normal" prison or mission in the U.S. Army. The prosecution tried to depict her as the abnormal one who refused to uphold the army's normative standards. The prosecutor put Harman on trial, but Spinner, the defense attorney, seemingly tried to put the Army on trial. The irony of her trial was that the prosecution's own witnesses depicted Abu Ghraib as an abnormal and weird place at almost every turn. Unwittingly, the army was on trial in the Harman court-martial.

Meeting Harman and Understanding Her Smile

Harman's defense attorney, CPT Patsy Takemura, drove to my home from Fort Hood in order for me to meet and get to know Harman. My first impression was that this is one of the most shy and inhibited persons I had ever met.

Harman showed me some of the photographs of her smiling at the scenes of abuse—and I was horrified. I thought, "What in the world am I doing on the defense team for such a person?" I asked her to explain the smile, but she shrugged her shoulders and said she could not explain it. She could not explain any of her actions regarding the charges against her except to state the obvious: everybody around her was doing it, and she thought it was acceptable even though she was horrified. Intuition told me that sadism did not explain her inappropriate smile in the photos—in her meeting with me, she simply did not exhibit any of the controlling, demeaning, grandiose behaviors and attitudes that sadists typically exhibit in any interaction. Sadists *smirk,* while Harman had *smiled* inappropriately. It was inappropriate to smile over a dead body and behind a pyramid of naked Iraqis—but how does one understand and explain her smile?

Takemura sought to obtain Harman's psychiatric tests. It turned out to be a protracted process with the two military psychiatrists to obtain their reports as well as the results of the psychiatric tests they had given her. They stalled for time, objected to releasing them, questioned my qualifications in reading them, and, in general, would not give up the reports or the tests easily. They interviewed and tested her in December. I met her in March, I read their reports in April, and the court-martial was in May. Takemura wrote several sharply worded letters to the psychiatrists demanding that they release this data, because they were obligated to do so by military law. They took several weeks to release the reports, in which they referred to tests—but they did not include the tests. After more letters, they finally released the rest of the information. It took about six weeks to get them to comply fully.

The prosecution never asked these or any other psychiatrists to testify against her, probably because the reports were in her favor. The reports as well as the test results showed that she was not sadistic, that she did not have a personality disorder (the personality disordered are sadistic and cruel as a long-standing character trait, but this was not Harman's problem), and that she was suffering from depression, dependency, anxiety, and PTSD. In plain English, these terms meant that Harman was an extreme follower, very scared, very sad, and very stressed—and the psychiatric tests suggested that she was all these things at Abu Ghraib.

At the time I met her and during the trial, she was not receiving any medical treatment for any of her problems, including PTSD, because the army had made it clear that anything she said to a doctor or psychiatrist could and would be used against her. My intuition had been confirmed, but, more important, I was presented the interesting challenge of explaining why she smiled during abuse even though she was not sadistic. After much research, I concluded that she was smiling because she was pretending to go along with the abuse because she felt too depressed, helpless, and fearful to do anything about it.

The most damaging photos were not used in trial, probably because they would have hurt the army's image more than they would have hurt

Harman's case. Photos that showed dog handlers torturing prisoners were not used in her trial. (Two dog handlers would be court-martialed about a year later, in the spring of 2006). Photos that showed her kind nature, as when she sewed up the wounds on the prisoners who had been bitten by the dogs, never made it to trial. There were also photographs of Harman being friendly with Iraqi children and families while she was stationed at Al-Hillah. These photos were not used at trial. The prosecution was selective in picking which photographs would be used at court-martial.

Jury Selection

The defense strategy regarding jury selection was to minimize the number of high-ranking officers and to maximize the number of minorities and lower-ranking enlisted soldiers on the jury. I knew that this was a sound strategy from published research on juries: as a general rule, high-ranking or high-status jurors tend to be unsympathetic to low-status defendants. This became immediately evident during the questions posed by the judge and the attorneys to potential jurors. The higher the rank of the officer, the less open-minded he or she seemed to the complexity of Abu Ghraib. The minority as well as low-ranking army soldiers seemed genuinely open-minded, as evidenced by their body language and comments. The prosecution seemed to follow an opposing strategy of loading up the jury with high-ranking, white, male officers, especially those who had already served in Iraq and who said that they had never seen or heard of abuse during their tours of duty. In the high-speed game of wits between the prosecution and defense as to who would strike which juror for which legal reason—or no reason at all—the defense mostly won. In the end, the jury consisted of eight men and women, more than half of whom were African American or Hispanic. The one white, male colonel was appointed as the president of the jury, and the Judge referred to him as "Mr. President."

One of the most intriguing impressions that emerged from watching the process of jury selection is that most jurors did not remember seeing photographs of Harman from the media. The judge asked them what they had seen in the newspapers and media, and most said they remembered Lynndie England, if not by name, then as the woman holding a detainee on a leash, or words to that effect. Somehow, Harman's damning photographs flew under the radar of public opinion, even public notice. Like everybody else who pays attention to the media, I had seen some of the photographs before, but for some mysterious reason, Harman did not leave an impression on me, either. Apparently, this was the case for most of the jury as well. England became an icon of the bad American female soldier, while Harman managed to stay mostly invisible. Sociologically speaking, this is amazing. Somehow, even if viewers of the photos did not know that Harman was not a sadist as proved by her psychiatric reports, her out-of-place but wholesome smile did not register with them as cruel.

Opening Statements

The trial began on May 16, 2005. The prosecutor focused on two "incidents" out of a potential galaxy of incidents of abuse in his opening statement: The infamous naked pyramid that occurred on November 7, 2003, and the incident on October 25, 2003, in which three Iraqi detainees were stripped naked and forced to crawl on their stomachs as "punishment" for allegedly raping an Iraqi boy. The prosecutor noted that the three detainees did not commit rape and were not terrorists—they were ordinary Iraqi thieves. He also established that the detainees involved in the pyramid incident were not terrorists and had no intelligence value to the United States. Thus, in the first moments of the trial, the prosecutor established the relative innocence of the detainees who were abused. The lingering, unanswered question posed by his opening statement was, Why were these detainees brought to tier 1–A in the first place since they were innocent of seeking to harm U.S. soldiers and also had no intelligence value?

The prosecutor stated that on the night of November 7, five MPs and two non-MPs were involved in the pyramid incident: Harman, Frederick, Graner, Davis, Ambuhl, England, and Sivits. This is the original cast of the seven rotten apples. Ambuhl and Harman were girlfriends in a prison that had few female soldiers (three of whom were court-martialed). Sivits, who was a mechanic, was sentenced to one year for taking photographs during the five minutes that he was present. Every soldier except for Ambuhl who was involved in the pyramid incident—even if the involvement was confined to just being there—was sentenced to prison in some other court proceeding. For the army, the naked pyramid incident seemed to symbolize the seven rotten apples and the evils that were committed at Abu Ghraib.

The prosecutor asserted that the detainees on November 7 posed no danger to the U.S. Army soldiers, that Snyder had told Davis to stop crushing their fingers and toes and that Davis stopped, that Graner had hit a detainee in the chest with such great force that a medic was called, and that Harman had written the word *rapist* (which she misspelled as *rapeist*) on the leg of one of the detainees. He claimed that the mood and atmosphere at Abu Ghraib during this incident was jovial. None of the soldiers were performing an official duty during the incident. The detainees were stripped naked, forced to climb into a pyramid, forced to masturbate, and forced to simulate fellatio. The prosecutor established further that Harman was assigned to the 372nd Military Police Brigade out of Fort Lee, which deployed in May 2003 to Al-Hillah in Iraq and on October 15, 2003, deployed at Abu Ghraib. He pointed out that Abu Ghraib consisted of three separate prisons within the prison: (1) the Hard Site consisting of tier 1-A for detainees who would be interrogated by MIs as well as tier 1-B, which consisted of women and juveniles; (2) Camp Ganci, which was basically a tent city for the "general population" of Iraqi criminals; and (3) Camp Vigilant for "high-valued" criminals. It is significant to note that there was an Abu Ghraib within Abu Ghraib (namely, tier 1-A), much like there is a Gitmo within Gitmo—in other words, there was an especially cruel zone within the overall space that came to symbolize cruelty.

Although he mentioned that women and children were kept at Abu Ghraib, the prosecutor never explained why this was the case, and no juror asked. Through my interviews with soldiers, I learned that the women and children were "swept up" along with the men in disorganized arrest raids, and in some cases they were kept as "hostages" to make the men talk during interrogations. What is of great interest is that through the prosecutor's opening statement (and on other occasions), the government conceded in open trial that it kept women and children at Abu Ghraib but never stated the reason for their detention. If the reason stated by the soldiers is that, indeed, the women and children were held as hostages, then it seems that the U.S. Army engaged in a practice it condemns in its enemies: hostage taking. The prosecutor opened the door to one of the hidden realities of Abu Ghraib, which is also documented in the reports, but did not go through the door. (The government reports also fail to investigate the reasons for detaining women and children.)

Regarding the incident of October 25, 2003, the prosecutor mentioned that it involved eight soldiers and one Iraqi translator, but singled out Harman—who, in fact, left the scene after a few minutes. He pointed out that the detainees were forced to perform a "low crawl" and "log rolls" and that the atmosphere was jovial. I already knew that the other soldiers were far more heavily involved in this incident than Harman, yet he chose to make this incident one of the centerpieces of her trial.

The prosecutor concluded by saying that the difficulty of the combat mission at Abu Ghraib is no excuse for the abuse that occurred in these incidents. He showed some poster-size photographs of Harman in these incidents. He also alluded to Darby as the brave soldier who slid some of the photographs of the abuse under the door of a CID officer at Abu Ghraib in January 2004.

It was Frank Spinner's turn to make the defense's opening argument. Spinner spoke softly. He told the jury that the army took a young woman and forced her to "experience" a failure of leadership. This story started earlier than November 7, he added. The context for the pyramid incident includes the many officers who failed her because they did not supervise tier 1-A, and he named some of them: Reese, Brinson, Pappas, Jordan, Phillabaum, and Karpinski. Spinner claimed that the prosecution was shifting all the blame onto the night shift of low-ranking soldiers, and he named some of them as well: Frederick, Graner, Davis, Ambuhl, and Harman. But they were not trained for what awaited them at Abu Ghraib. Spinner said that Abu Ghraib was "not like a normal prison." (Here he threw down the gauntlet in the competition that constitutes gaslighting.) It was overcrowded. It was chaotic. CID had its own "holds" or prisoners. (This is a fact omitted in some government reports—namely, that not only were some prisoners "MI holds" to be interrogated, but the CID, which normally investigates wrongdoing by American soldiers, had its own separate Iraqi prisoners. The reason for this has not been explored.) Spinner repeated what the prosecutor had already admitted: that Abu Ghraib held terrorists as well as women and juveniles. But, he added, this issue of women and children at Abu Ghraib is treated as the "periphery" of the story. According to Spinner, Frederick and Graner were the "primary interface with MI" and were part of ongoing intelligence activities. The detainees in the pyramid incident were not just prisoners but rioters. It was common practice for the MI to strip prisoners naked. In the span of a few minutes, Spinner had turned the tables on the prosecution specifically on the issue of what was normal versus abnormal at Abu Ghraib.

Spinner then turned to another incident, that of the prisoner nicknamed "Gilligan" who is in the infamous photograph that depicts him standing on a box, hooded, and waiting to be electrocuted. "Why is Gilligan standing on the box?" Spinner asked. Because the technique of sleep deprivation was part of the duty of interrogators trying to save lives, he answered. At this point I thought, Harman was not an interrogator, yet MI gave her the task of depriving Gilligan of sleep. From the prosecution's perspective, his standing on the box involved more than the technique of sleep deprivation; according to the prosecutor, it involved humiliation, the fear of electrocution, and other aspects of abuse. These were two diametrically opposed versions of the reality of what happened during this and other incidents at Abu Ghraib.

Spinner told the jury he would make some concessions and would contest other claims by the government. He conceded that Harman was ordered to perform duties for which she was never trained. But he would contest that Harman entered into conspiracy or agreement with intent: she was in the photo of the naked pyramid but did not enter into an agreement. (My own take on this issue is that the government can make almost any behavior seem like an "agreement" or conspiracy.)

Spinner turned to the charges of dereliction of duty for the time frame October 20, 2003, to December 1, 2003, noting that Harman was on leave between November 9 and December 1, so that she was not physically present at Abu Ghraib during some of that time period. He then made claims that surprised me: namely, that Harman had struck up a friendship with Gilligan and that they were joking while he was standing on the box, so that this incident did not constitute maltreatment. On the one hand, there is something disturbing about using the word *friendship* to refer to a relationship in which a soldier forces a frightened, hooded prisoner to stand on a box for hours at a time. On the other hand, it seems that Spinner was touching on a real issue that psychologists call the Stockholm syndrome, in which abusers and the abused do indeed form emotional attachments between each other. And there was little doubt in my mind that she would be friendly, even warm, toward someone whom she was ordered to abuse.

"Maltreatment?" Spinner asked. "That's where the fight is." The prosecution would have one believe that taking the photographs was maltreatment. Spinner said he would concede that Harman took some of the photos. But he would fight the idea that taking the photos constitutes maltreatment. The prisoners were hooded, so they did not know they were being photographed. Hence, Spinner argued, the photography does not constitute maltreatment.

Who was right? Spinner or the prosecutor? Spinner was rattling the prosecutor's notions of what constitutes dereliction of duty, conspiracy, and maltreatment. After all, those photographs could be interpreted as instruments of whistle-blowing and exposing the poisoned atmosphere at Abu Ghraib *as well as* maltreatment. Two different versions of reality emerged during the opening statements.

The Prosecution's Case

Joyner was the first witness for the prosecution—and almost everything he said supported the defense, or constituted *a* defense. Joyner said of Harman, "She was one of the extra people," a "go-get-me-something person." He explained that the officers in charge were Pappas, Brinson, Reese, and Phillabaum, but he saw Brinson only three times during his entire stay at Abu Ghraib, and then for only two or three minutes at a time. He said that the officers avoided tier 1-A. "Nudity was common practice," the sergeant said, as was "female underwear." This was "not like anything in the civilian world," he added. "Did you raise questions?" the prosecutor asked him. "Yes," but the sergeant was told "that's how they do it," the MI wants this, and "go with it."

Frederick's Testimony

SSG Ivan Frederick was brought into the courtroom with some drama because he was still serving his sentence at Fort Leavenworth and had to be unshackled in the hallway. It was noticeable that he wore an army uniform minus the usual insignia that soldiers display. All this struck me as part of the degradation ceremony of receiving a dishonorable discharge from the army and being sent to prison—one is still "in" the army yet not in the army. It came across like the Scarlet letter.

Frederick said that other Iraqis at Abu Ghraib received Iraqi food, but detainees in tier 1-A were given MREs. Such food contains pork and other items that offend Muslim religious custom. "Did you raise questions?" the prosecutor asked him. "Yes," but again, he was told to go along with it. Frederick complained about the nudity, lack of ventilation, complete darkness, and general sense of chaos at Abu Ghraib. He said that MI was "aware of stress positions" that the MPs used on detainees, adding that the Iraqi police at the prison were corrupt. Writing on detainees was commonplace, Frederick said, as a comment on Harman's writing *rapist* on a detainee. "Was Harman a strong individual?" the prosecutor asked. "No," Frederick answered.

"Did you approve of the abuse?" the prosecutor asked. "No." "Did you stop it?" "No." "You went on and did it?" "Yes." All the witnesses gave some version of the same story in this regard: they admitted that the abuse was wrong but went along with it because they felt that they could not stop it and that MI must have had good reasons for ordering it.

Frederick said that there were about four or five cameras in use on the night of November 7, but the "pictures were not hidden." He said that photography was not forbidden, and the cameras were used in an open manner. "Who were you working for?" the prosecutor asked him. Frederick answered that it was confusing, because he took orders from three different places. Shifting to the incident of October 25, Frederick said that Harman was not there! Other witnesses testified that Harman basically walked through the hallway while the abuse was occurring and did not stop. "Did you stop it?" the prosecutor asked him again. "No." "Who was in charge?" "Graner and Cruz, and other MI."

The prosecutor asked Frederick about the incident that involved sleep deprivation for Gilligan. Frederick said that Graner had given the name "Gilligan" to this prisoner. "Graner was God," Frederick said. Like God, he named the prisoners under his control, including "Houdini," "Shit Boy," "The Claw," and "Big Bird." Frederick said that the detainees accepted their names, and the names were the same on the night and day shifts. He also said that Gilligan was not guilty of harming Americans, as initially suspected, and was given privileges because "he was a model detainee." He added that Gilligan was not traumatized by the incident. Frederick said that he put the wires on Gilligan but that Harman did not. He also said that Gilligan was "a CID detainee" and that a CID agent "wanted him stressed out so he could speak with him." Frederick added that this particular CID agent had given the order "Do whatever you want with him [Gilligan]—just don't kill him." Soldiers told me that this particular CID agent also interrogated U.S. Army soldiers suspected of abuse at Abu Ghraib. This CID agent did not testify.

Frederick's testimony was in line with the government's own reports depicting widespread chaos and confusion at Abu Ghraib regarding the most basic issues, including who was in charge. Moreover, Frederick was not implicating Harman. Frederick went on to say that he gave Harman permission to make a phone call to her partner in the United States during the abuse on the night of November 7 such that she was not present for the forced masturbation. Again, Frederick was asked, "Did you draw a line in the sand?" "No." "Could you control Graner?" "No." He said he did not go up the chain of command to report abuse because he and others had tried before and learned that it was to no avail. He spoke about Wisdom complaining about abuse to Jones, and Jones had told Frederick to keep Wisdom away, "but Jones did not address the impropriety." Frederick was Harman's superior—if he could not draw a line in the sand regarding the abuse, there was little reason to think that Harman could have stopped the abuse.

Wisdom's Testimony

SPC Matthew Wisdom was the next to testify for the prosecution. He struck me as a boy despite his twenty-two years. It is significant that Wisdom was not assigned to tier 1-A and had just returned to Abu Ghraib from a fifteen-day leave of absence when he witnessed the incident of November 7. I noticed that, as a general rule, the soldiers who came onto scenes of abuse "fresh" from the world outside the walls of Abu Ghraib were more likely to be shocked by it and to report it than the soldiers who had already adopted "learned helplessness" from being enmeshed in the abuse.

Wisdom gave a graphic description of the abuse that led to the naked pyramid on November 7: detainees wore sandbags on their heads, their hands were tied behind their backs, and they were smashed against the walls by U.S. soldiers. "You have to get some of this," Frederick said to Wisdom, which Wisdom interpreted as an invitation to participate in the abuse. Wisdom saw Graner hit detainees and pose with them, and he saw Frederick punch a detainee. At that point, Wisdom left. He literally walked out the door and testified that he "told SGT Jones everything." Jones was his supervisor and told him that he would handle it and to go back to the site of the incident. When Wisdom returned, he witnessed the forced masturbation. Another supervisor said to Wisdom, regarding the forced masturbation during this incident, "Look what these animals do." Wisdom left again. Wisdom said he had not seen abuse before or after November 7, only during this incident, but he was not assigned to tier 1-A in any event. He normally worked the day shift in the general population tiers 2 through 4.

Again, what struck me as remarkable was that Wisdom did not implicate Harman and that what he described was a sadistic, dehumanizing, chaotic situation that nobody seemed to feel they could stop or correct. The lingering question left by Wisdom's testimony was, What good, if any, came from his reporting the incident to his supervisor?

Testimony of Wisdom's Supervisor

SGT Robert Jones was the next to take the stand for the prosecution. He had been in the U.S. Army for thirteen years and at the time of his testimony worked as a police officer. Jones corroborated and added to Wisdom's testimony, saying, "Wisdom came to me. I told him to go back to work." Jones tried to explain to Wisdom that this was "justified use of force" and that Wisdom was too "young" to understand. Wisdom came back to Jones a second time, and then Jones confronted Frederick about the incident. Jones said that Frederick denied what had happened. Jones would not allow Wisdom to work or visit 1–A for the duration of his stay at Abu Ghraib.

During a very short cross-examination by Takemura, she said to him that it was hard to believe that this incident was never reported up the chain of command. Jones just shrugged his shoulders. Apparently Jones was as high in the chain of command as the report would ever go. Then she asked him to describe Harman at Al-Hillah. Jones said that Harman was "better suited to be a relief worker" than an MP and that she was "exceptionally nice to Iraqis."

Again, the prosecution was showing that next to nothing happened in terms of correcting the abuse in any long-term, meaningful way even when somebody reported it. Yet, Harman was being prosecuted, in part, for failing to stop the abuse. The prosecution witnesses were consistently depicting Harman as a nice person who was weak but not malevolent.

The Whistle-blower's Testimony

SPC Joseph Darby took the stand. He is the soldier who turned in the photographs of the abuse. Despite the historical importance of what he did as a whistle-blower, his testimony was relatively short, and both sides seemed anxious to get him off the stand fairly quickly. His testimony was that he was on leave between November 4 and November 25, 2003, so that he did not witness these incidents but that Graner had given him a CD full of photos of abuse. He looked at the photos in early December and deliberated whether he should turn them in. "They were my friends," Darby said, so he was reluctant to betray them. In a very short cross-examination, Spinner got Darby to admit that he feared retribution from his "friends."

More Testimony on Fear of Retribution

SPC Israel Rivera took the stand next, and he would add to the theme of fear and intimidation among the soldiers engaging in the abuse. He testified that Cruz (who was MI) asked him to join in the "punishment" of three Iraqi "rapists." (The prosecution had established that these prisoners were not rapists.) Rivera followed Cruz and witnessed the three prisoners rolling, crawling, and being verbally abused. They were cut and bleeding from abrasions caused by the concrete floor. "Who was present at this incident?" the prosecutor asked. MI soldiers Rivera, Cruz, and Krol; MP soldiers Graner, Harman, and Frederick; the Iraqi translator; and unknown 1 and unknown 2. The two unknowns in the photograph that was displayed were never identified. Rivera said he stood watching and was shocked. He said that the other MIs "were not doing MI stuff," that this was "not an interrogation." He added that Graner wore green gloves, which were his trademark, so that he would not be "contaminated" by the prisoners. Who took the photograph of the incident? Rivera said he did not know that photos were taken, but in any case, Harman was *not* in the photograph of the scene that the prosecution was using as an exhibit. (Indeed, it was clear from the photograph that Harman had already left by the time the photo was taken.) When Krol threw a Nerf football at one of the prisoners, Rivera left. Krol asked him whether he would tell anyone, and Rivera said he would not. But the next morning he told a friend about the incident, and the friend said it had been taken care of by a sergeant.

During cross-examination by Takemura, Rivera said that he felt shock and fear during the whole time of the incident. He admitted that he had lied to Krol that he would not tell anyone because he was afraid. Rivera also admitted that he never reported the incident to anyone in the chain of command. Takemura asked him whether the government had made a deal with him to drop charges against him if he testified against Harman. Yes, he answered, and rattled off the possible charges against him: conspiracy, maltreatment, and dereliction of duty. These are the same charges that were leveled at Harman. Takemura established that Harman was not in any photo taken of the abusive incident of October 25, and Rivera agreed. She then asked him what the soldiers did wrong that night, and he answered that they had a duty to protect the detainees and that they failed to protect them and made no attempt to stop the abuse. "Why?" Takemura asked Rivera. He answered, "I was afraid. They had authority and rank. It seemed foolish to say, 'What are you guys doing?'" He added that if they were willing to do this to detainees, why wouldn't they do it to him?

Rivera expressed his fear of fellow soldiers and his vulnerability had he tried to do the right thing. He had also indirectly expressed his fear and vulnerability relative to the U.S. Army, which coerced him into testifying against Harman so that he would not be prosecuted for the same crimes. His "crime" of standing by helplessly is similar to Harman's crime, though she was prosecuted and he was not. Rivera's and Harman's crimes pale in contrast with the brutality that others inflicted on prisoners. Yet, Rivera was a potential rotten apple in the eyes of the U.S. Army. By this standard, every soldier who failed to stop the many kinds of abuse that were occurring daily at Abu Ghraib was a rotten apple. A more plausible explanation is that most of the soldiers were good people, but it required nearly superhuman strength to defy the poisoned atmosphere at Abu Ghraib.

Armin Cruz Testifies: What Motivated the Abuse?

Rivera was followed on the stand by another young MI agent, SPC Armin Cruz. He had already served time for his role in the abuse. Cruz testified that another MI soldier named Krol woke him up and said, "Hey, we're punishing rapists." Cruz went to get Rivera. Cruz said that the "rules of engagement were loose so we could do what we want." He said that everyone was directly involved in the abuse except for Rivera. Cruz said he "helped out" by handcuffing the detainees. He admitted that at the time, he was still angry and confused about a mortar attack on September 20, 2003, and that he wanted revenge. (These three prisoners had nothing to do with that mortar attack.) "I'm still upset about it to this day," Cruz said, referring to the mortar attack. He said that Harman was present during the entire twenty to thirty minutes of the abuse and that she said to the detainees that Iraqis had "small dicks." (This testimony contradicts some of the other testimony concerning Harman's role in this incident.) Cruz said he "got a deal with the government," in that he pled guilty, served time, and in return promised to testify against other soldiers.

Why did he engage in the abuse? Cruz said he acted out of curiosity and a desire to punish and that he was personally angry at rapists. But the prosecutor had established that these three prisoners were not rapists or terrorists, just ordinary thieves. When asked about Harman's role, Cruz said "she yelled," but "not as loud" as the rest of the group. There were three MIs present (Cruz, Krol, and Rivera). Cruz insisted that the abuse was "nothing sexual" and involved "just PT" or "exercise." The prosecutor said that from the photos, it looked sexual because the detainees were forced to embrace. But Cruz insisted that the embrace was meant "to keep them from kicking, biting." Cruz admitted that he did not report the incident to the military intelligence chain of command (MICC).

Jeremy Sivits Testifies

The ex-mechanic, Jeremy Sivits, took the stand. He had already served a year for taking a photograph during the November 7 incident. Frederick had asked him to stay during the incident. Sivits said that Harman was checking names and wrote *rapist* on the leg of one of the detainees, "like a joke," that she was "having fun with it." He testified that Harman, Frederick, and England all took photos and that Graner later hit a detainee. "Did anyone object or try to stop Graner?" "No." The other soldiers were afraid of Graner. Sivits said that when the forced masturbation began, Harman "was disgusted by now" and left. Sivits admitted that he did not report the incident and that Frederick told him as Sivits was leaving, "You did not see shit." Apparently, this particular phrase was used commonly as a kind of code of silence.

Testimony on the Photographs and the Harmlessness of the Victims

Special Agent Brent Pack took the stand and testified in his role as an expert in computer forensics. He testified that more than 16,000 photos were taken by soldiers at Abu Ghraib, and 281 photos were deemed pertinent to the prosecution. (Obviously one wonders what is depicted in the remaining 15,700 or so photos that were not deemed pertinent by government). He testified that five different cameras were used and that the photographs were not altered. He also established, using computer technology, the time the photographs were taken within a margin of error of eight hours. During cross-examination, Spinner had Pack agree that his task for the government was unique, that no manual existed for this sort of work and that the eight-hour margin of error is somewhat arbitrary, "not scientific."

Special Agent Nora from the CID testified. He said that his job was to locate the "victims" from Abu Ghraib who were abused in these incidents. The judge corrected him immediately: "Call them detainees, not victims." Nora's testimony was brief and to the point: not one of these detainees was suspected of terrorism.

The Case for the Defense

The defense called the company commander, Reese, to the stand. The captain stated that he had been in the Army Reserve for eighteen years and prior to deployment to Iraq had worked in sales at Home Depot. As company commander at Abu Ghraib, he was in charge of approximately 180 soldiers. He said that Harman was "an average soldier" and that "the

[Iraqi] kids loved her." Reese also stated that his company was trained for combat support security, not for running a prison. He stated that his company received "no Geneva Conventions training." He explained that they did not know they would be prison guards, so they were not trained to be prison guards (his testimony is confirmed by the general thrust of government reports—namely, the MPs were not properly trained for their mission). In September 2003, their mission was changed from combat support to something he called IR (internment/resettlement), which is a euphemism for running prison camps with military police. He explained that the 72nd MP was in charge of Abu Ghraib prior to September 2003 and that he and his soldiers received about two weeks of on-the-job training from them. Reese stated that prison conditions were "less than favorable," there was debris everywhere, and no showers worked. Many of the U.S. Army soldiers lived in jail cells, which was an improvement over previous living conditions at Al-Hillah, where the soldiers lived in an abandoned date factory. He added that "some [soldiers] were happy" to be living in jail cells, "but it's pretty sad overall." The ratio of detainees to MPs was 150 to 1, which is unacceptable by army standards.

Reese expressed confusion about his own role and the roles of the other officers in charge. Regarding Jordan—one of several competing commanders—Reese said, "I'm not sure what he did." He said that "On the second day there, I saw nude people." He said he asked other soldiers, "Where's their clothes?" and was told that the nudity was an "MI tactic" or that it was a "supply issue." He said that tier 1–A held detainees with intelligence value but was also "really hodge-podge" in that it also held women, children, and ordinary detainees, CID holds, FBI holds, OGA holds, "you name it." There were no written guidelines. There was "no doctrine out there I can refer to" for working with MI. Because of this confusion, he explained that he decided to put soldiers who had civilian corrections experience (i.e., who used to work as prison guards) in charge—namely, Graner and Frederick. He added they had no IR experience, just civilian experience in corrections. He added that "Harman had no experience."

Spinner asked him whether he saw detainees with women's panties on their heads, and Reese replied, "I observed some of that." He also observed "sleep deprivation programs" that involved playing the radio loudly for hours. After about a month, he said he asked for the orders for these "techniques" in writing but never received them. "Did you discuss this with your predecessors" (from the 72nd MP)? "No." "Did you object to the chain of command?" Reese said he did object to the "nudity thing" at meetings but was told it was an "MI thing" or a supply issue. Overall,

Reese concluded, the army needed another two or three companies of soldiers to do the job right and that it was a "daily battle" with irregularities. Soldiers worked twelve-hour shifts with no days off. He said there were "ghost detainees," that the backdoor to the tier was insecure so that practically anybody could enter and leave without notice, and that some detainees disappeared in this way. "Don't let anyone talk to them" was the order given by MIs to MPs when the ghost detainees arrived, and they were never processed, numbers were never assigned to them, and, for all practical purposes, they did not exist. Reese said there were no rules, no guidance, and no guidelines for what MIs and MPs were supposed to do. His testimony is corroborated by the findings in the government reports.

Under cross-examination, the prosecutor had Reese agree that army soldiers are required to adapt to changing circumstances; that the soldiers possessed a "core competence" even if they were not specifically trained for their jobs; and that even though many soldiers lived in jail cells at Abu Ghraib, this was an improvement over the living conditions at Al-Hillah. The prosecutor asked whether the soldiers were "happy to have cells," and Reese agreed. The prosecutor also claimed that Camp Vigilant at Abu Ghraib was a "model camp." The prosecutor asked whether one needs training to understand abuse. "No," Reese replied. Did Reese ever receive army policy letters or guidance from high up in the chain of command, *in writing*? "No," Reese replied—there was "nothing in writing." The prosecutor also had Reese agree that photography in tier 1–A was off limits and that the women's panties were a "supply issue." The jurors asked Reese whether he had received any written guidance on how to treat detainees. "No," he answered. Were photos permitted at the Hard Site? The captain answered that no signs were posted prohibiting photography.

Ken Davis took the stand. In previous testimony, Davis had already emerged as a genuine hero in the Abu Ghraib saga because he had refused to participate in any of the abuse and consistently challenged the abusers when he confronted abuse. One important reason for this is that his job was to "escort detainees to Baghdad," and it was not his job to be a guard within the prison. He did not get enmeshed in the poisoned climate at Abu Ghraib. He said he knew Harman, but they were not friends. His testimony consisted of establishing that on the night of October 25, 2003, Harman was present for one to two minutes of the abuse, and then she left. He said that she did not get involved in the abuse.

During cross-examination, the prosecutor asked Davis whether he said anything to the abusers that night. Davis answered that Cruz taunted him by asking him, "Have we crossed the line?" Davis said he answered him by saying, "I don't know—you're MI." The prosecutor then moved to the topic of Davis and Graner handing out Bibles and candy to Iraqis. Davis admitted that he and Graner were "passing out Bibles" about six times within a time span of eight weeks. No matter what the prosecutor intended with this line of questioning or its impact on the jury, there is something powerful about the image of a whistle-blower (Davis) and convicted soldier (Graner) both handing out Bibles.

The prosecutor then moved on to try to depict Davis as a media hound by rattling off interviews Davis had given to the *Washington Post, CNN Live* with Paula Zahn, Chris Matthews, and *ABC World News Tonight.* The prosecutor asked Davis whether he liked being "the center of attention." Davis answered crisply that he reported the incident he witnessed on October 25, 2003, the next day to an officer, and "nothing was done." This last point is important because later in the trial, the prosecution would try to show that Harman had the option of going to the media to report the abuse if her claim were true that no one at Abu Ghraib listened. But here was Davis testifying that he went to the media because nothing was done when he complained. He said he wanted to report that "MIs were doing weird things with naked detainees." Would Harman have been labeled a media hound for going to the media? Here again it seems that the government was putting soldiers into a double-bind situation: they were damned if they reported the abuse and damned if they did not report it.

I had the opportunity to speak with Ken Davis on several occasions. He suffers from PTSD, including severe nightmares, phobias, depression, and other symptoms. It was my impression that he had been traumatized severely by what he witnessed at Abu Ghraib, even though he never perpetrated any abuse.

Meghan Ambuhl took the stand next. She said that she was assigned to tier 1–B, which housed a population that consisted of females, juveniles, "crazies," ordinary criminals, and, later, MI detainees. Why was she assigned to work with Harman? Ambuhl replied because there were only a few female soldiers and there were female detainees at Abu Ghraib. Regarding Harman, Ambuhl said, "She was a runner," and worked on tiers 1–A, 1–B, and 4. "She never yelled," Ambuhl added. Ambuhl testified that Sabrina was upset about the incident of November 7 and complained about it to her. Frederick gave her permission to make a phone call, and Harman left after making the phone call. Ambuhl also said guards commonly wrote on detainees with markers. Regarding the incident with

Gilligan, Ambuhl said that there existed a "friendly demeanor between Gilligan and Sabrina."

The prosecution's cross-examination of Ambuhl was particularly intense. He displayed a chart which showed that in October 2003, Ambuhl and Harman were roommates; that in January 2004, all of the suspects (including Ambuhl) were segregated from the rest of the unit and lived together; and that in February/March 2004, the suspected rotten apples continued living in close proximity with each other. The prosecutor said that all the suspects were a close-knit group who stayed in touch with each other at least through November 2004. Spinner objected, saying the prosecution was introducing bias and an implication of coconspiracy among the accused. The judge sustained the objection. The prosecutor rephrased the question: Did the accused see each other every day? "Yes." The prosecutor tried to ascertain the precise time at which Harman left the abusive scene of November 7, but Ambuhl could not recall the exact time.

The prosecutor then introduced yet another incident, which occurred on October 23, 2003—the "handcuff incident." Harman had come across a detainee whose hand was turning blue from being handcuffed to the bars of his cell and who had been abandoned. She reported the incident to a sergeant, who took the handcuffs off the detainee. The prosecutor was trying to make the point that if Harman reported the incident of October 23, she could have and should have reported the incident of November 7. This incident came up again later in the trial. It has several meanings in addition to the prosecutor's interpretation, including: no one was reprimanded or punished for the abuse that occurred on October 23 even though Harman reported the abuse, so that she learned—like many other soldiers learned—that whistle-blowing did no good at Abu Ghraib.

In a barrage of objections, accusations, and counteraccusations raised by the two opposing attorneys, the judge asked the jury to leave the courtroom. Legal questions were raised by both sides as well as the judge regarding the propriety of asking Ambuhl about Harman's state of mind, backdoor testimony, implications of conspiracy, and other issues. The issues were not ultimately resolved, and Ambuhl was dismissed from the stand.

Harman's partner took the stand. She testified that she and Harman had met in August 2002, became best friends, and started living together in September 2002. Harman worked as an assistant manager at Papa John's Pizza until she left for basic training in the spring of 2003 and deployed for Iraq that summer. Harman's partner was allowed to read a portion of a letter Harman had sent her describing abuse and her own horrified reactions to it.

Under cross-examination, the prosecutor established that the two women corresponded regularly through letters and phone calls and that Harman had called on November 7 because that was her partner's birthday. The partner said she was surprised by Harman's visit home between November 11 and November 27. What did they talk about during the phone call on November 7? The partner answered that Harman was sad that she could not be with her for her birthday. The prosecutor would remember these remarks and use them against Harman during the final closing argument for sentencing—his interpretation was that Harman had just witnessed horrific abuse, and instead of telling her partner about it, she was talking about her partner's birthday. I thought Harman's reaction was fairly ordinary: the abuse had become so commonplace that she preferred to think and talk about happy things.

Closing Arguments

The trial ended abruptly and the two opposing sides went immediately into closing arguments. The prosecutor showed the jury large reproductions of photographs pertaining to the incidents of October 25 (punishment of the alleged rapists), November 4 (Gilligan), and November 7 (the naked pyramid). He said those photos were used later to get a laugh, that the abusers were laughing taking the photographs, and that the incidents constitute mockery. "Everything is a joke" to them, he said. He said he wanted to make sure he had everyone's attention and then to Harman said, "Shame on you for your involvement," adding that she brought shame on the army. He pointed to two photographs, one of Harman smiling with her thumb up versus Gilligan hooded and in fear of electrocution. The prosecutor said that it was a frat party atmosphere on tier 1-A. He brought up the testimony that a CID agent had ordered her to do anything to Gilligan except kill him and said this was clearly an unlawful order. The prosecutor said she had to know this was an unlawful order based on common sense. (I couldn't help thinking that common sense did not seem to operate at Abu Ghraib. If it did, common sense would have led to questions as to why women's panties were worn on men's heads.) The prosecutor reviewed each and every charge and specification leveled at Harman: she took photographs, she did not report abuse, she did not stop the photography, she wrote on the leg of a detainee, she posed in photographs, she conspired with the others, and so on. He asked the jury to find her guilty on all counts.

Spinner began his closing argument with a retort to the prosecutor's shaming of Harman by exclaiming, "Shame on the army!" The army sent an ill-equipped, ill-trained soldier to challenge leadership to do the right thing. Abu Ghraib was a stressful environment, but the stress went far beyond mere combat. People have different coping skills, and Harman coped by smiling. She could not leave, because she is in the army. The photos document the events. Nothing happened when abuse was reported, so how can one expect more of her? She was desensitized by the environment. There was a failure of leadership.

Then Spinner asked, "How do you cook a frog?" He explained that one cooks a frog by turning up the heat slowly, so that the frog is too weak to jump out of the pot by the time it realizes the danger. Harman was the frog—she tried to escape the "pot" that was Abu Ghraib, but by the time she realized what was happening, it was too late. Spinner said that the medic who was called on November 7 did not report the abuse because this was business as usual on tier 1-A. He pointed out that Rivera and Cruz did not report the incidents. As for "our friend Gilligan," Spinner said that he became friends with Harman, and there was no evidence that he was traumatized. Spinner referred to the incident with Gilligan as a creative technique in sleep deprivation. He also said that Iraqis were stripped naked in front of women. It was an abusive atmosphere. Instead of putting the army on trial, the prosecutor went to plan B and put someone else on trial—Harman. Wisdom and Rivera were repulsed by what they witnessed, and so was Harman.

Finally, Spinner said that the trial presented contradictory facts as evidence. What really happened at Abu Ghraib? Frederick testified under a grant of immunity. Others were intimidated. "What is real here?" he asked.

The prosecutor had the last word. He said that Harman did have a choice. She could have reported the abuse. He presented a chart to the jury that listed the various persons she could have contacted, ranging from the media to her congressman. (But the testimony showed that reporting the abuse up the chain of command, through the media and up to Congress did nothing to stop the abuse.) "It's not the government's position that Specialist Harman is the most evil person ever," the prosecutor said.

Neither side referred primarily to facts in their closing arguments, even though the trial exposed many facts. Instead, both sides seemed to appeal primarily to emotions. The prosecution invoked some of the most powerful and negative emotions in the human psyche: shame, mockery, honor, and loyalty to the army. The defense invoked the weaker emotion of compassion for Harman and the other soldiers who, like frogs, were metaphorically boiled in the scalding waters of Abu Ghraib. And Spinner reflected shame back on the army.

I had a sinking feeling following the closing arguments that Harman would be found guilty. Most people instinctively cringe when they experience shame, whereas empathy requires some effort. The prosecutor wanted the jury to feel ashamed for what she had done to their army, and Spinner wanted them to feel ashamed for what the army had done to her. Most persons try to rid themselves of feeling shame as quickly as possible and will take the path of least resistance. It is much easier to displace negative emotions onto a person than an institution.

The jury deliberated for less than three hours and returned a verdict of guilty on all counts except one—she did not conspire in the incident of October 25. At that point, she was facing a maximum sentence of five years in prison.

Between Trials: Tank Destroyer Boulevard

Harman was understandably devastated following the verdict. The defense team had one night to prepare for the next phase of the trial, mitigation. Spinner and Takemura exited quickly to their makeshift office to begin preparing, and I had dinner at a Chinese restaurant with some of the soldiers. The mood was somber, but the soldiers talked freely about Abu Ghraib and the impossible situation in which they found themselves. They all agreed that abuse occurred daily at Abu Ghraib and was not confined to "incidents," that nudity was common and widespread, and that they all thought that the abuse was what the army expected of them to "soften up" detainees. Some soldiers at dinner said they thought that the army was killing two birds with one stone by prosecuting Harman—the lesbian soldier would get a dishonorable discharge even though her sexual preference would never be raised as an issue, and blame would be shifted onto her as a rotten apple.

Harman was a nurturer and seemed out of place in the poisoned climate at Abu Ghraib. The army could have used her as an excellent ambassador of goodwill toward the Iraqis.

Takemura phoned me and said Spinner would see me at 11 p.m. that night in their makeshift office. I asked for directions, which involved a long drive down Tank Destroyer Boulevard. Looking at the map, I was struck by the names of the other streets on Fort Hood: Warrior Way, Hell on Wheels Avenue, Old Ironsides Avenue, Tank Battalion Avenue, and so forth. And then I recalled that the soldiers had told me that the army used some of the same techniques and tactics on them during basic training that were labeled as "abuse" at Abu Ghraib: yelling, shouting, nudity, humiliation, PT (physical training), and so on. The cultural ambiance of the army, as I experienced it at Fort Hood, was one of intensely machismo values. I came to believe the soldiers who told me that they simply could not make out the difference between appropriate versus inappropriate behavior.

When I arrived, I found Harman sobbing and her partner trying to comfort her. Takemura was preparing portfolios of Harman's childhood and young adulthood that included photographs that showed her to be an ordinary American woman, not a monster. She would show those photographs to the jury the next day to plead for a light sentence. Spinner arrived late, and we spoke for ten minutes at most. We did not go over my testimony or prepare for it in the usual way. He said that he and I would have a conversation in the courtroom while I was on the stand.

The Mitigation Phase

It was now May 17. Wisdom was recalled to the stand and told the jury that the morale of his unit fell when the investigation began, positives were forgotten, families were worried, and he could no longer pursue a career as an MP. His overall plans for his life were destroyed at Abu Ghraib. Under cross-examination, Wisdom said that Harman was a great individual, helpful to both Iraqis and soldiers, and a good person all-around.

DiNenna testified for the defense and gave testimony similar to what he said at Davis's court-martial. Conditions at Abu Ghraib were deplorable with trash, wild dogs, looting, disarray, sickness, bad hygiene, and many medical problems. There were not enough guards, and they had to work twelve to sixteen hours per day. At times, there was absolutely no illumination at night. He said, "Prisoners had nothing to do all day but come up with ways to make weapons." He attributed the uprisings among the prisoners to deplorable conditions: bad food, overcrowding, indefinite detention, constant danger. He mentioned that there were women and children in the prison, and they were brought in if the male was arrested, but no offense was listed on the capture tag. There was insufficient water: two liters of water all day per soldier. The portable toilets were overflowing, and Abu Ghraib was in the middle of a combat zone. There were not enough blankets and clothing for the prisoners. The Iraqi corrections officers were corrupt. He became emotional when he said that the soldiers at Abu Ghraib felt abandoned and that they were on a forgotten mission. (One can imagine that the prisoners also felt abandoned.) He sent out daily e-mails for help, but it did little good.

Under cross-examination, the prosecutor got DiNenna to talk about how prisoners were "handled" and their daily routines in the morning and at night: moving the prisoners, attacks, no illumination, feeding, cleaning, and more moving.

1SG Bryan Lepinski testified that Sabrina made a positive impact on the community at Al-Hillah: people knew her by name and called out her name with delight. She gave candy to children. She had a positive impact on soldiers and Iraqi families. She filled gaps in a country that was in need. Under cross-examination, the prosecutor made the point that Harman's good actions do not detract from her bad actions.

Ambuhl testified again that Harman was good with kids; that she brought families food, clothing, and even a refrigerator. Families and kids flocked to her. Her impact was positive, and she made a great impression. Iraqis brought her presents, and none of the other soldiers got gifts.

Harman's partner took the stand again and said Harman was a generous, gentle, caring, loyal person. Harman's main flaw is that she is too trusting of people, naive, young, and innocent. She described Harman as an open-hearted person who takes in strays and gives love, money, and time to those who need it. She also said her partner cannot handle conflict and standing up to authority.

The defense presented written depositions from prisoners concerning Harman. One prisoner described her as a "peaceful woman" who gave aid with meals and medicines; who treated them like a sister or a brother after they were tortured by other soldiers; who called medics for emergency services; who did not shout or hit prisoners. Harman is a "good woman," and "there is no cruelty in her." Another detainee wrote that Harman did not abuse the detainees; that she treated the prisoners "peacefully" and "kindly;" that she laughed and made jokes to make the prisoners laugh. She was "the only good woman, the only good guard" at Abu Ghraib.

The judge asked the jury to leave the courtroom twice during my testimony: once when I mentioned Afghanistan and again when I said that Harman was not a sadist. This drama made the jury sit up and pay more attention to my testimony than usual when they were allowed to reenter the courtroom.

The exchange between the judge and Spinner presented here takes up several pages, but it shows how explosive the issues of Guantánamo and Afghanistan were at the trials. The reader will recall from chapters 1 through 3 that the government reports admit that unlawful techniques were imported from Gitmo and Afghanistan. It took a legal battle of words to state these documented facts in open court. Here I quote from the transcript of my testimony.[2] Spinner asked me:

Q. Well, as you look at the Abu Ghraib situation and what happened there, weren't there safeguards in place to keep this deviance from coming about?

A. No, I mean, the Taguba Report especially is crystal clear. Geneva Conventions were not posted. The Schlesinger Report is even more critical and says that there was confusion about whether Geneva Conventions applied. In principle they were supposed to apply in Iraq, but they did not apply in Afghanistan and some of the people who were at Abu Ghraib, the MI, were coming from the—

TC: Objection—

MJ: —that—

TC: —to relevance as to Afghanistan.

MJ: What's the relevance?

CDC: Your Honor, he's tying it in, some of the people who were at Abu Ghraib came from Afghanistan and they brought some of these practices—

MJ: —members, I ask you to return to the deliberation for a second please.

BAILIFF: All rise.

[All persons in the courtroom did as directed, and the members withdrew from the courtroom as directed.]

[The court-martial recessed at 1308 hours, 17 May 2005.]

[END OF PAGE]

[The Article 39a Session was called to order at 1308 hours, 17 May 2005.]

MJ: Please be seated.

[All persons in the courtroom did as directed.]

This Article 39a Session is called to order. The members are absent, all other people are present. Mr. Spinner, I know it's a sentencing case and you have broad latitude but there is still a little relevance here. And my question becomes is that we're talking—we want to talk about impact on Sabrina Harman—or Specialist Harman, I understand that, but if we're going to get into what happened at Afghanistan, there's no evidence that anybody involved in Afghanistan was involved in this case, true?

CDC: Well it may have been in some of the reports, Your Honor—

MJ: —okay—

CDC: —and as an expert he can rely on hearsay—

MJ: —yes—

CDC: —when it's—

MJ: —no, I understand that but the problem is that he's talking about, and know we're talking about two doctors, but he's talking about what is in all of these reports. I am not disputing the stuff is in all of these reports—

CDC: —right—

MJ: —that doesn't make it relevant in this sentencing inquiry. For example, we're talking about the dysfunctional of the interrogation techniques, you've already talked about that. Is there any evidence whatsoever before this court that what she was convicted of somehow was tied into some type of interrogation?

CDC: Yes, Your Honor.

MJ: What?

CDC: There's the evidence that Special Agent ___ told Frederick to do things to Gilligan to prepare him for interrogation.

MJ: But is there any evidence that your client heard that?

CDC: But my inference, there is, Your Honor, I think there is a clear inference that she may have been aware of that or heard that.

MJ: Well, there's no direct evidence whatsoever of that—

CDC: —right, from—

MJ: —he said—

CDC: —for—

MJ: —she didn't hear it.

CDC: Right, but, Your Honor, well yeah he said other things and he may or may not—

MJ: —what I'm saying-so the absence of the evidence is there's some evidence that she heard.

CDC: Well circumstantial evidence and it's a fair inference, Your Honor. Otherwise why would you have given the instruction regarding obeying a lawful order. I mean I thought that was the basis for why you even gave the instruction on obedience to a lawful order as a defense.

MJ: Okay, but of course the members rejected that. If such—if even such order was given.

CDC: Right, but you said that the—the question you just asked me is there some evidence and, Your Honor, you gave an instruction because you said there's some evidence that raises the issue—

MJ: —well just go back to the issue though of, we're going—well what I'm saying is I'll give you some leeway—

CDC: —right—

MJ: —but we got to tie it into this case. What I'm saying is I don't want to hear about what happened—because does it make any difference what happened at the macro level for example in your—when you offered this witness in an earlier hearing you gave me a 50 page—about a 50 page paper of what he has said.

CDC: Right.

MJ: Now, a lot of this has to do with things at a very high level of what happened at Afghanistan, Guantanamo Bay, and I'm not saying they're not connected—

CDC: —right—

MJ: —but if they're connected to this—you just got to connect it to this case, that's all I'm saying.

CDC: Forgive me, Your Honor, I just feel like you pulled the trigger too soon. All he said—

MJ: —I haven't pulled anything yet, but I'm just trying—

CDC: —all he said was there was some people who came to Abu Ghraib from Afghanistan and he was just going to talk about how some things came over. I don't intend to go into what happened in Afghanistan and talking in those general terms, but he has read all this material, he has formed an opinion. This information supports the basis for his opinion. I don't intend to go into all of those things that are in his report—

MJ: —okay—

CDC: —just because they're in his report—

MJ: —but we're not giving an opinion, what we're doing again is the representation of all these reports.

CDC: He—but he considered those reports to form his opinion.

MJ: I didn't say that, we haven't—what—and it's partly—I understand that you're—but are we hearing opinions or are we hearing what is in these reports?

CDC: We're hearing his opinions, but, anticipating cross-examination he has a right to explain how he formed his opinion and we're not going to—I'm not going in—I'm not asking him any more questions about Afghanistan. I think he just said there were people at Abu Ghraib engaging in certain practices. They brought those with them from Afghanistan.

MJ: And of course there's no showing that your client knew about any of this?

CDC: I don't think there has to be a showing of knowledge. We're explaining how the abuses came about and why safeguards didn't work. So that—that doesn't have anything to do with—my client doesn't have to know about that for it to not be a mitigating factor. For it to be a mitigating factor—

MJ: —that was a mitigation of your case here, your client has nothing, doesn't know about it.

CDC: Well, Your Honor, I mean I can explain it very simply, the deviance developed over time based on things that happened in other places and that were brought to Abu Ghraib. And she was caught up in this environment of obedience and all we're explaining is how did this deviance develop at

Abu Ghraib. So she doesn't have—she's not a sociologist, she doesn't know the deviance was going on without her based on these other things. That's why we have the expert come testify because she doesn't understand that. She's not capable of understanding that. She just knows she lived in it.

MJ: But the deviance you're talking about may apply and I would tend to agree with you that there may be, on the issue with the Gilligan situation, but is there any evidence that it applies at all to the 7 November?

CDC: No, I'm not saying that it—I will say, here's where we're going to go, I'll give you a preview. At some point, you know, she ends up in a picture with a pyramid of naked bodies and in her statement to CID she says, you know, I didn't think that was wrong. And I'm going to ask this expert witness why would Sabrina Harman say that that wasn't wrong and he's going to explain because this deviance that developed over time in Abu Ghraib changed her mindset in thinking and would cause her to say that and so I think that's what we're going to lead to ultimately, Your Honor. And if there's a problem with that I'm sure that trial—Captain Graveline is perfectly well-qualified on cross-examination—

MJ: —again, Mr. Spinner, since it is sentencing I'll give you some leeway, but I'm just asking—I'm just telling you based on the proffer I saw before is we're talking about a lot of things of—the proffer you gave when you asked to employ an assistant indicates this witness has got a lot of opinions about a lot of things and I'm not disputing that they're well held opinions, I'm just saying is we need to tie it into this case and this accused. Now, I'm giving you leeway on this, but as to what happens at other places like Guantánamo Bay or the fact that some people say that the Geneva Convention didn't apply or did apply. I mean if it's tied into this case go right ahead but—

CDC: —well that's what I guess, Your Honor, sometimes I feel you and I are talking past each other. I gave you a proffer a long time ago just because I was trying to get funding for an expert.

MJ: Okay.

CDC: I'm not tied to that proffer, I'm not looking at the specific case and now he's a witness—

MJ: —okay—

CDC: —and he said people at Abu Ghraib that came from Afghanistan at one time—

MJ: —well that sort of—

CDC: —I don't intend to do that.

MJ: That was only just based on what you gave me earlier, but you tell me that was based solely to get—to see whether you needed them this is—?

WIT: —right.

MJ: So, again, the only reason I sent the members out is that I just wanted to—because of the—you know, I'm going to give you some leeway, but

again, and doctor don't take this the wrong way [laughter in courtroom].
Sometimes experts have a tendency to be very expansive—

CDC: —right—

MJ: —and again I'm not saying that this is one, but if they go into things
that have nothing to do with this case—

CDC: —right—

MJ: —and rather than interrupt the flow, I'm just saying bring it into this
case, that's all.

CDC: And I'm—just to inform the court, I discussed this with my witness
beforehand and I gave the government a 100, that initial report of 50 pages
to over 100 pages, and I gave that to the government, but I also explained to
Captain Graveline, I don't intend to go into all of that stuff. I'm just giving
you this because this is what he gave me and I'm obligated to give it to you,
but don't worry we're not going to make it that extensive—

MJ: —okay—

CDC: —so if that's your concern, Your Honor, I have instructed my witness—

MJ: —well just, my first objection and I thought since this had the potential
let's talk about it one time and you don't have to talk about it again.

CDC: Yes, sir. And I think the witness understands what you're saying, and
what I'm saying—

WIT: —Your Honor, if you ever want me to be specific all you know—you
know, you have to just ask me and I will give you the very specific answer.

MJ: Doctor, I understand that, but that's really not how the system
works.

[Laughter throughout the courtroom.]

WIT: Okay.

MJ: Let me rephrase that, our system whether it's dysfunctional or not,
doesn't work that way, so—

[Laughter throughout the courtroom.]

TC: We're good, sir.

MJ: Okay, bailiff please recall the members.

[The bailiff did as directed.]

[The Article 39a Session terminated at 1317 hours, 17 May 2005.]

[END OF PAGE]

[The members entered the courtroom and the court-martial was called to
order at 1317 hours, 17 May 2005.]

MJ: Please be seated.

[All persons in the courtroom did as directed.]

Court is called to order. All parties, including the members, are again present and the witness is still on the stand. Mr. Spinner?

Questions by the civilian defense counsel continued:

Q. Sir, do you remember where you were when the members left?

A. No, that I don't.

Q. Okay [laughter throughout the courtroom]. I think you were saying that there was some practices that were brought from Afghanistan into Abu Ghraib—

A. —the Schlesinger—

Q. —that led to deviance and the—created the environment at Abu Ghraib.

A. The Schlesinger Report says very explicitly and there was a long section to the fact that there was a 1987 version of FM 34-52 which had a provision in it that there was some—

MJ: —doctor, I don't mean to interrupt, but the question is not that. The question was, was there evidence that practices from Afghanistan were brought to Abu Ghraib? That's the question—

WIT: —yes—

MJ: —we don't need to know about the 1987 FM.

Questions by the civilian defense counsel continued:

Q. —yes, without going into what was brought—

A. —okay, I'm sorry—

Q. —yes—

A. —the Schlesinger Report explicitly states just that, that practices which were called folk or unofficial practices were brought into Abu Ghraib from Afghanistan.

Q. And did you see evidence of these practices at Abu Ghraib based on the reports that you have seen?

A. Yes.

Q. Now, can you identify what some of those things were that were—are these violations of the norms that existed in the Army?

A. Yes, and here I have to go in to FM 34-52, which is the Authoritative Normative Standard still for the Army—

Q. —Okay—

A. —that's the thing that's interesting about this?

Q. Please explain?

A. Well, FM 34-52, the Geneva Conventions apply. It tries to establish rapport between the interrogator and the detainee. And it works on willing cooperation. Practices were put in place in Afghanistan where the Geneva Conventions did not apply and the Schlesinger Report says the problem—the confusion stemmed from the fact that these practices migrated, that's exactly what they used, into Iraq, and therefore caused confusion for the soldiers. The other source of confusion was the merging of the MI and the MP functions. This created this climate, this poison atmosphere, which led to further abuse.

So many words and so much effort spent just to allow me to state a documented fact: some of the abusive techniques migrated from Afghanistan. Note that Spinner had to promise to the judge that he would not go into any further details about Afghanistan or Guantánamo Bay or the government's own reports. However, I will say that I appreciated the judge's sense of humor—there was laughter in the courtroom during this serious legal battle.

The second time that the judge cleared the courtroom, I was asked to leave the courtroom as well so that I did not hear all the arguments. The occasion for the judge's reaction was that the prosecutor objected to my conclusion that Harman was not sadistic. Spinner again argued effectively, and I was brought back into the courtroom, not knowing what had been discussed. When the jury returned to the courtroom, they seemed to be more puzzled than I was. But they certainly seemed attentive. So much drama, again, for me to testify that Harman's psychiatric tests proved that she was not a sadist, so that the motives for her smile were most likely something else, ranging from depression to anxiety to other unknown factors—but not cruelty.

During cross-examination, the prosecutor asked me, referring to Harman, "So she could have walked out the door that night?" I answered that she could have walked out physically, just like I could walk out of the courtroom physically. But, in reality, I could not walk out the courtroom door until the judge dismissed me, and she could not walk out the door because of the poisoned climate that kept her there through fear, depression, learned helplessness, and other negative factors. When the judge dismissed me from the stand, I asked him if that meant I was allowed to walk out the door, and he laughed and said that I may. Some members of the jury also laughed.

Reflecting back on the drama, I realized that the laughing and smiling during the drama in the courtroom illuminated the meaning of the laughing and smiling at Abu Ghraib. Most of the people in the courtroom were good people, but most of us—including the judge—laughed nervously in response to a very tense and stressful legal exchange. I could sincerely understand why some good soldiers at Abu Ghraib had laughed and smiled at Abu Ghraib because their level of stress and tension were much higher.

Closing Arguments

The closing arguments were brief. The prosecution repeated the charges against Harman, for which the jury had found her guilty. The prosecution sought a bad conduct discharge and three years of confinement instead of the five years that she faced. Takemura said that nineteen months in Iraq was punishment enough and that Harman had already been punished emotionally. She asked the jury to consider the stigma of a court-martial as sufficient punishment and boldly asked for no confinement.

The jury returned a sentence of bad conduct discharge and a sentence of six months' confinement, which effectively became three months because she was given credit for three months' confinement.

Notes

1. The psychological use of the term *gaslighting* is typically attributed to the 1944 film *Gaslight,* in which the actress Ingrid Bergman starred as the wife of a man who tried to make her question her sanity.

2. The transcript of this fast-paced exchange is presented exactly as it was prepared, including the comments in brackets, interruptions (indicated by dashes), and so forth. Abbreviations used are as follows: TC, trial counsel, or the prosecutor; MJ, military judge; CDC, chief defense counsel, or Spinner; WIT, witness, or, in this case, me.

CHAPTER SIX

THE TRIAL OF LYNNDIE ENGLAND: THE STORY OF "LEASH GIRL" IN LOVE WITH THE RINGLEADER OF THE NIGHT SHIFT

It seemed like a bad omen that PFC Lynndie England's court-martial began amid preparations by the rest of Texas for the impact of Hurricane Rita. The trial began on September 22, 2005, and Rita hit the following the day. On my drive to Fort Hood, I had to join temporarily the hundreds of thousands of Texans on the crowded highways who were evacuating Houston and the surrounding area. They were heading north to escape the hurricane, and I was heading north to get to Fort Hood. The real hurricane hit Texas, and a metaphorical hurricane slammed into England: she was sentenced to three years.

But there is more to the hurricane metaphor. My mind wandered on the wet Texas highways, stuck in slow traffic, sharing the fate of others trying to escape catastrophe. The evacuation was a mild form of chaos. I could see instances of tempers flaring. It was difficult to get a motel room. Some gas stations were already out of fuel. I reflected that it really seemed true that social chaos leads to stress and negative consequences. If it was evident in Texas because of a hurricane, it seemed even more evident regarding Abu Ghraib. I realized that the government exhibits a consistent pattern in response to catastrophes: it downplays their impact and then shifts the blame for the consequences of being unprepared. After Hurricane Katrina hit New Orleans, the federal government shifted all the blame for being unprepared and unresponsive onto state and local officials. After the metaphorical hurricane of 9/11 happened, the federal government shifted most of the blame onto everyone except itself. In both cases, there were plenty of warning signs of an impending disaster.

And something similar is true with regard to the metaphorical hurricane that is Abu Ghraib: there were plenty of signs that Abu Ghraib was a disaster waiting to happen. Its effects have been nothing less than catastrophic for the U.S. mission in Iraq. Yet the dominant response by the federal government has been to shift all the blame onto the lowest-ranking soldiers. England was one of them, and she was forced to absorb the brunt of the blame for the effects of the photographs from Abu Ghraib. It is true that she took some photos and posed in others. It is not true that she is the personification of evil, sin, poison, pollution, and other bad things that some persons wish to project onto her.

But this court-martial was not about deep issues. Both the prosecution and the defense framed this trial in particular as an abusive love story between Charles Graner, the ringleader of the night shift, and Lynndie England, the naive "hillbilly" from West Virginia. The central argument by the defense was that England was following Graner's (not the army's) orders because she loved him. The counterargument by the prosecution was that England's compliant personality and personal life are no excuse for the shame and other devastation she allegedly heaped on the U.S. Army via the photographs.

Graner had inadvertently destroyed England's chances to avoid a full trial in August 2005, when she had pleaded guilty and was hoping for a light sentence from a jury. Graner testified that she was following his orders, and the judge had declared a mistrial. The judge ruled in August 2005 that she could not plead guilty and have the defense argue that she was following orders. Her defense attorney, CPT Jonathan Crisp, took the calculated risk of pleading not guilty on her behalf in September 2005, and thereby invited a full trial.

But this decision meant that her love for and affair with Graner would have to—and did—come out in trial. The defense gambled again by arguing that England's posing in the photographs was mainly the result of her love for and obedience to Graner. It seemed that England's trial was mostly about Graner and far less about her and her actions. Apparently, the jury had little sympathy for Graner and even less for a soap opera love affair as the main explanation for what England had done. More media showed up to cover England's trial than all of the other trials combined. There were so many journalists that they had to watch the proceedings from the nearby Officers Club via closed-circuit television. There was not enough room for them in the courtroom. It seemed that England could no more escape her fate than Texas could escape the forecast path of Rita.

Opening Statements

The prosecutor listed the charges against England, which were basically the same as the charges leveled at Davis and Harman. Some of the same incidents were invoked, especially the infamous naked pyramid. The additional event involved the detainee nicknamed "Gus," who was pulled out of his cell on a leash (later renamed a tether). The prosecutor anticipated the defense argument that England could not understand that she was the subject of an investigation when she signed her sworn statement. But, he added, she was able to reflect on it the day after she signed it. He asked the jury to ask themselves, "Why?" regarding the photographs. He also posed the question "Why did she do it?"

Like his predecessors on the previous defense teams, Crisp challenged the conspiracy charge, which carries the most severe sentence. He conceded that maltreatment occurred and soldiers agreed to it at the time it occurred. But he argued that for conspiracy, there had to have been a previous agreement to commit the abuse. There had to have been a previous agreement for moral responsibility regarding conspiracy. And there had to have been agreement prior to the overt acts of abuse that were committed. This was a difficult, complex legal and philosophical argument for anyone to grasp.

The Prosecution's Case: Charles Graner Steals the Show

Jeremy Sivits was the first soldier to testify for the prosecution. He had already testified in both the Davis and Harman courts-martial. As one of the convicted seven rotten apples, he had already served a year's sentence but was obligated to testify against the others.

He looked sad but composed on the witness stand. He described the infamous incident of November 7, 2003, in a monotone voice as involving "pyramid stacking, masturbation." Wisdom helped escort the detainees, and Ambuhl was put in charge of the females and teenagers. England was present, and she and Davis were both stepping on the hands and toes of detainees. The detainees had their hands tied behind their backs, had sandbags over their heads, and posed no threat. Snyder yelled at Davis to stop stepping on the toes of the prisoners, and Davis complied. This was a rerun of previous testimony with a few new additions. As Sivits was speaking, the defense team was struggling to see the photos of this incident on the monitor.

In previous trials, the prosecution had displayed selected, poster-sized photographs for everyone in the courtroom to see. In the England trial, jurors viewed the photos on TV monitors, but the photos could not be seen by journalists or the public.

Sivits said that Graner was also present and that he was known by his green gloves, which he always wore when he abused detainees. There was a lot of "laughing, jerking around." He, Frederick, Harman, and England all took photos. Graner used his fist to hit a detainee in the head. The prosecutor had Sivits repeat that the injured detainee had a sandbag on his head and was handcuffed. After Graner hit him, the detainee "was lying on the floor as still as he could be." Sivits said that this assault was followed by another from Frederick toward a different detainee. Sivits quoted Frederick as saying, "Watch this," then he "drew an X on a detainee's chest, then hit him." Sivits said he tried to help the hurt detainee and thought that the detainee had gone into cardiac arrest. He told Ambuhl to bring an inhaler and to call a medic. "The detainee did not see the punch coming," Sivits added.

The prosecutor asked Sivits to describe the mood of the detainees. They were "quiet, scared, and did not know what was going on." What were the soldiers doing and saying? After hitting the detainee in the head, Graner said, "Ouch, damn that hurt," but he was referring to his hand, not the pain he caused to the detainee. The soldiers were laughing, and no one was objecting to the abuse. The detainees were hooded the entire time they were in the pyramid, which lasted two to three minutes. Soldiers were taking photos, "smiling, and having a good time." England posed in a photo with a thumbs-up next to a detainee who was forced to masturbate. "Was she reluctant?" the prosecutor asked. "Yes Sir" Sivits answered. But the prosecutor got Sivits to agree that no one actually ordered her to pose.

Sivits said he felt disgusted when the masturbation began and was looking for an excuse to leave. He, Ambuhl, and Harman left before Graner put the detainees into sexual positions. England stayed. Sivits testified that as he was leaving the scene, Frederick turned to him and said, "You did not see shit." "What did he mean?" the prosecutor asked. "If anyone asks, that I did not know anything." Why didn't Sivits report this incident? Sivits replied, "I was trying to be friends with everyone and I did not want to get anyone in trouble." Could Sivits have left the scene? "Yes." Did he receive any orders to stay? "No." Did anyone give an order to do these things? "No." The prosecutor asked Sivits the terms of his sentence for his role in the abuse, and Sivits answered that he signed an "agreement to testify against everyone."

CPT Catherine Krull cross-examined Sivits. Sivits told her that he did not know who initiated the stepping on the toes of detainees, but that when Snyder said "Stop," it stopped. Then Snyder left, and Graner took over, even though he was outranked by Frederick. Sivits established that Graner did all the ordering, and England gave no orders. Sivits also said that other soldiers were similar to England in their compliance and that even Frederick—who was one of the supervisors—did not challenge Graner's authority. Davis had left long before the physical and sexual abuse began. The jury had one question for Sivits: Who were the prisoners? Sivits answered that he did not know. Sivits was dismissed.

The judge ordered a brief recess.

Wisdom took the stand. The prosecutor asked him to describe what happened on the night of November 7. Wisdom said that he was working in tier 4 and was asked to help escort some prisoners who had done something "along the lines of a riot." The detainees were supposed to go to tier 1–B for a "ten day cooling-off period." MPs were pushing the hooded, handcuffed detainees into the walls, and the detainees could not see. The judge interjected: Why did they have sandbags on their heads? "Security," Wisdom answered. Wisdom said that the detainees were "entangled" in the pile of bodies. He recounted that Graner posed and hit a detainee. After Frederick hit a detainee in the chest, he turned to Wisdom and asked, "Are you going to get some of this?" The prosecutor asked him to explain what he thought Frederick meant, and Wisdom replied, "Do I want to hit a detainee?"

Wisdom said he did not remember Sivits being there. Wisdom left after Snyder yelled at Davis. England stayed on the tier and Harman was taking photographs. "Did that strike you as odd?" "Yes," Wisdom replied, because there was a standing order that no photos were to be taken. Wisdom returned to the tier later that night, witnessed forced masturbation, and testified that Frederick said to him, "Look what these animals do when you leave them alone for two seconds." Wisdom heard England say about a detainee, "Look, he's getting hard," and he left for the second time. He said he reported the incident to his supervisor, who told him to do his job.

During cross-examination, Krull had Wisdom establish that England was not engaging in any assault or punching. Wisdom agreed. She asked Wisdom what happened after he reported this incident to his supervisor. "Nothing happened," Wisdom replied.

The jury asked Wisdom how long he worked at Abu Ghraib, and he answered that it was from November 2003 to April 2004. Did he see prisoners treated in this way before or after November 7? He saw such abuse only on November 7. Krull then established that he did not visit tier 1-A at any other time.

SGT Robert Jones, who had also testified at the Harman trial, took the witness stand to testify against England. He basically recounted the same narrative as before in slightly different words: Wisdom came to him and said something "absurd," that prisoners were being "beaten." "What did you do?" the prosecutor asked him. "I told him to go back to work. He's inexperienced." He went back to work but came back to Jones, saying that soldiers were making prisoners "jerk off." Jones confronted Frederick with the question "Was it true?" and said that "Frederick would not answer." Jones requested that Frederick reassign Wisdom to Jones.

Under cross-examination by Krull, Jones said that he did not take action the first time that Wisdom reported the abuse to him, and never reported it to anyone higher in rank than Frederick. "My job was to take care of my own soldiers," he explained. Jones also said that in general, "nothing was done until the pictures came out." Overall, this seems to be an accurate assessment. Jones also said that Graner had a "stronger personality than all the others" and that "Graner preyed on those who are weak." Jones elaborated that the other soldiers were "followers" who were susceptible to Graner's "charismatic personality." Jones added that Frederick outranked Graner and was supposed to be in charge of the tier, but "in reality, Graner was in charge."

Testimony Concerning England's Confession

Special Agent Warren D. Worth took the stand. He said that he had been in the army for eighteen years and worked for internal affairs for CID since October 1994. On January 15, 2004, he assisted another special agent in interviewing England. He explained how he went over the charges against her and asked whether she understood and whether she could read the English language. "Did she say she didn't understand?" the prosecutor asked. "No." He said he took her statement and mentioned that she had told him that "Graner had done something to his hand." Worth said that she never seemed confused and that she corrected the spelling of Graner's name.

During cross-examination, Crisp asked Worth, "Did she say anything that you left out?" Worth answered, "No, or I do not recall." Crisp then asked him whether January 15 was the first time he had met her. The judge interrupted and said to Crisp, "If you ask questions, you will open doors." Crisp seemed frustrated but continued with rapid-fire questions: Did Worth go over her education? No. Her training? No. Did he show her his credentials? Yes. Did he describe the basis for the charges of cruelty and maltreatment? No, he merely read the charges to her. Was this common practice? Worth said he did not know. How did Worth know that she understood? He asked her to initial each charge, adding, "It's just the way I do it." "Why?" Crisp asked. Worth said this is the way he was taught to do it. Does the person who initials understand what they read? The judge interrupted and told Crisp this was irrelevant. Crisp kept hammering away with similar questions. Would Worth want to correct an unclear statement? Would he correct mistakes? Would he clarify what she read? Was there a methodology in the interview? Worth kept giving yes and no answers but basically stayed with his position that he just did things the way he usually did things.

The prosecution had no further questions—but the jury had several. Was there an audio recording of the interview? No. Was there a video recording? No. Did Worth type the interview on a computer as they went along? Yes. Could England see the screen as he was typing? No. Worth then admitted that there was a power outage that interrupted the interview such that there was a three-hour time lag between interviewing her and reading back to her what he had typed. Worth was dismissed.

Excitement over a Juror's Remark

Excitement filled the courtroom as the judge dismissed the jury save for one juror. The judge said he had learned that the *New York Times* had quoted this particular officer by name as saying, during the jury selection process: "I would say there was definitely a failure of leadership" at Abu Ghraib. The judge wanted to know whether the prosecution or the defense wanted to remove this officer from the jury because someone had tried to contact him on his cell phone about his statement to the *New York Times*. Neither side wanted to strike him. The judge ruled that the trial would go on and that the officer would remain on the jury.

Additional Testimony

When the trial resumed again, Joyner took the stand. He was Graner's counterpart on the day shift. He described the "walk-through" he received from the 72nd Military Police Battalion that was in charge of Abu Ghraib before his arrival. Joyner said that he was told, "Here's the prisoners; this is how we feed them; good luck." Joyner testified that there were no standard operating procedures (SOPs) on how prisoners should be treated. He said that he relied on common sense. The prosecutor asked him about the leash incident with Gus, and Joyner replied "It just ain't right."

During cross-examination, Joyner used the word *nasty* repeatedly to describe the social milieu at Abu Ghraib: it "stunk," it was "nasty," and it was "the nastiest place on earth, for both soldiers and detainees." The prisoner-to-guard ratio was 75:1, which was "ridiculously, dangerously high." Did detainees complain to him? No. Joyner said he did not know anything about the night shift but that during the day shift, the detainee nicknamed Gus (who is in the leash photo) refused to wear clothes. "Gus left a lasting impression," Joyner added. Joyner explained that Gus was put on tier 1–A because he was disruptive at Camp Ganci (another area at Abu Ghraib) and that he weighed eighty to ninety-five pounds at most. Gus was a short, frail, and psychotic prisoner. (No one posed the question whether Gus was psychotic before he arrived at Abu Ghraib.)

Frederick's Testimony—More about Graner's "Charisma"

Frederick took the stand. He walked in confidently and explained his background in corrections at a civilian prison. The prosecutor took Frederick through a long discussion of a poster-sized, aerial view photo of Abu Ghraib prison. The prosecutor used multicolored sticky notes to mark various areas at Abu Ghraib. Apparently the prosecutor was trying to make the point, visually, that England was not assigned to the Hard Site, so she had to walk a considerable distance in order to be with Graner.

Frederick said that tier 1–A was for "high-value prisoners" and 1–B was for "females and juveniles." Although the judge said nothing about this in the Harman trial, this time, he interrupted and asked Frederick, "Why were there women and children?" Frederick answered, "Because that's where they put them." "Why?" the judge asked. "I don't know," Frederick replied. The prosecutor then moved to a discussion of the naked pyramid incident. Frederick said that Snyder stopped Davis from stomping on the toes of detainees, but "no one stopped Graner." Frederick added, "He hit a detainee pretty hard." "On a scale of 1 to 10, how hard?" the prosecutor asked. "Eight," Frederick answered. Frederick admitted that he hit a detainee also, whom he regarded as the "ringleader" who "threw a rock at one of my female guards."

Up to this point, there was nothing in his testimony about England but plenty of information about the ambiance of the night of November 7. I found it interesting that soldiers consistently rationalized their assaults on detainees as punishment for real or imagined wrongdoing.

Frederick described how Graner had ordered that the prisoners be strip-searched and England "to get into the photographs." There was "laughing, goofing off, lots of people, and lots of photos." The prosecutor tried to make Frederick admit that because of his rank, the other soldiers during this incident were subject to his orders. Frederick was evasive on this point. Finally, the prosecutor asked, "Did anyone in the chain of command order the abuse?" "No."

During cross-examination, Crisp asked, "Is this how detainees should be treated?" This was "a different mission," Frederick replied. Did Frederick ever see England step on the toes and fingers of the prisoners? "No." Crisp tried to establish that MPs had authority that night and England had no authority. He said that during the human pyramid incident, Frederick was not the senior noncommissioned officer (NCO) on the tier because Snyder was there, too. "He was within earshot," Frederick answered. "You were the next highest NCOIC [NCO in charge]" Frederick agreed. "You never corrected Graner or Davis." Frederick answered that both were "hard-headed." "Were you afraid of conflict?" Crisp asked him. Frederick said, "I didn't want to die that way." Apparently, Frederick was afraid Graner would kill him over any confrontation. He elaborated that Graner some-times had a weapon on him or nearby, even though this was forbidden in the tier. "So you're normally not compliant," Crisp said, and Frederick agreed. I thought that here was still more evidence of intense fear and intimidation among the soldiers of each other. Rank did not matter.

When asked to describe England, Frederick said that she had "blind faith" in Graner and "trust," such that she would do "pretty much whatever he asked." He also said that she sometimes slept in tier 1–B.

Frederick also told Crisp that from his experience, there was no confusion in the civilian world as to how a prison should be run. But Abu Ghraib was confusing, and no one would offer clarification. For example, Frederick said he had approached Phillabaum about the nudity and panties on the heads of detainees and was told "That's the way MI does it." Crisp asked him to explain the forced masturbation, and Frederick said he was curious to see whether they would masturbate and surprised that they did. He denied that the masturbation was sexually arousing to him or the other soldiers. Instead, he said there was a "sense of frustration and anger" among the soldiers.

The jury posed questions to Frederick: Why did he punch a detainee? Was he angry? Frederick said he hit detainees because of stress and com-mented that there was no support from his supervisors. Did Frederick ever say, "You didn't see shit?" Frederick answered evasively that when Jones approached him about Wisdom's complaints, they were talking mostly about Davis's behavior, not Frederick's. Frederick said that he told Jones, "I would take care of it."

The Forensic Photography Expert's Testimony

Brent Pack, a former special agent, took the stand in his role as an expert witness in computer forensics. The gist of his testimony was that he examined approximately 16,000 photographs taken by the rotten apples at Abu Ghraib, of which 281 were photos of abuse. In other regards, he basically repeated his testimony from the Harman trial about which cameras were used and when.

No Terrorists among the Abused

Special Agent Bill Higgison took the stand and testified that based on his examination of the magistrate numbers of the detainees who were abused in incidents pertaining to the charges leveled at England, none were terrorists, and none posed a threat to the United States or to soldiers. No one asked whether England or any of the other rotten apples knew this fact about these or any other prisoners while abusing them or whether this knowledge would have made a difference.

The prosecution rested its case. The judge ordered a recess.

Charles Graner: Star Witness for the Defense

The defense called Charles Graner as its first and chief witness. He was unshackled in the hallway and entered the courtroom at 2:21 p.m. on September 22, while we were all thinking about Hurricane Rita in the backs of our minds. He answered curtly about his "dating relationship" with England following their deployment in November 2002. But he did not make eye contact with her even though she was sitting directly in front of him.

Crisp asked him about the leash incident with Gus. Graner stated that on October 24, 2003, he was instructed by MI to move Gus from isolation to another cell. England and Ambuhl were in his office, so he asked them for their help in moving Gus. "I pulled Gus out of his cell. I dealt with Gus three times prior to moving him." Graner referred to this process as "extraction." He approached Gus in his windowless cell and found him laying in feces and urine. Graner put a "sling" around his own shoulders, which slid onto his neck, and Gus began to crawl. When his head was out of his cell, Graner said he handed the "tether" to England and took three photos. Did England ask why Graner handed her the tether? "No, she just did it." Was she compliant? "Yes." Did Graner show the pictures to anyone? "Yes." Graner said he was not reprimanded. Was Graner interested in demeaning Gus? "No." "Did England trust you?" Crisp asked. "Yes."

Crisp turned to the pyramid incident. Graner said that he "placed" the detainees "in a pile." "Why?" Crisp asked. "I had no idea" Graner replied. Then he added that "it was an ad hoc SOP." Graner went on to say that he was "in processing" the detainees. "They were yelling and disruptive. I told them in Arabic to be quiet. I slapped them in the face when they disobeyed." Graner went on to say that he processed them one by one and strip-searched them.

"We had no other restraints at the time" Graner said, so that he made them "face the wall on their knees." Why did he make them "sit" on top of each other? Graner answered that he had no choice in that he had to control them in case "one attempted something." He said that he had worked in a civilian prison environment where he learned that he would have to "exercise some sort of control." "Why?" Crisp asked. Because the detainees had been "extracted from a riot." "They were dangerous," Graner added. "I was on my fifth one, and they began to talk." "Why were you concerned about their talking?" Crisp asked. "We soldiers had no weapons." Graner said they were getting louder, so he began to "stack" them and "finish the process." "Did you tell England it was illegal or inappropriate?" ""No." "Were there similar incidents?" "Yes." "Was England present?" "Yes."

It is consistent testimony that there were similar incidents of abuse at Abu Ghraib, but no one pursued this line of inquiry at the trial. Yet, when the news story broke on February 15, 2006, that additional photos of additional abuse at Abu Ghraib were discovered and broadcast, journalists, the government, and the public seemed to react with surprise.[1]

Graner was asked to describe the living conditions at Abu Ghraib. He said the toilets were "hit or miss," water was "hit or miss," there was no heat, and "we slept in the other prison from the old regime." He said Abu Ghraib was "Bizarro World." I thought this was yet another interesting allusion by a soldier to Abu Ghraib as a crazy, disordered place. It is in tandem with other testimony and descriptions by other soldiers that Abu Ghraib was nothing like a normal social space or even a normal prison.

Graner went on to describe tier 1–A as composed mostly of "foreign fighters, extremists" and the "B-side" as composed of "females and juveniles and problems." He said that when he arrived at Abu Ghraib, he was told to follow the instructions of the MI. He said that he was told, "If they talk, chain the prisoners to a wall." Graner elaborated that in the civilian world, "You can restrain a prisoner but not to an object," that this was one of "the biggest no-no's in corrections." "I had corrections experience, so I worked there," he added. Apparently Graner had had thirteen years of corrections experience. This is consistent with Reese's testimony in the Harman trial as to why Graner was chosen to work the night shift on 1-A.

Crisp switched to a few questions about England. Was she quiet and submissive? Yes. Did her aunt become ill from cancer? Yes. What was the effect on her? She was "distraught." Crisp then focused attention back to Abu Ghraib. At this late point in the questioning, he asked Graner to explain why he used the phrase "Bizarro World." Graner said people were often screaming, prisoners were often "restrained in stress positions," and this was "painful." "Did interrogations occur in the showers?" Yes. The prosecutor objected to this line of questioning, but the judge said he would allow the defense attorney some leeway. Crisp continued by asking Graner to elaborate on the yelling on the tier. Graner said the yelling was "from MIs and the detainees." Crisp also brought out the fact that from 1988 to 1994, Graner was in the U.S. Marine Corps. Finally, Crisp asked whether England had ever stomped on the fingers and toes of prisoners in the pyramid incident. "No," Graner replied.

In the cross-examination, the prosecutor began by asking how tall he was and how much Graner weighed in 2003. Graner said he was 5'11" and weighed between 195 to 200 pounds. The prosecutor established that Gus weighed no more than one hundred pounds. He then asked Graner why he wanted Gus out of the cell. Graner answered that MI wanted the cell but did not want Gus. Graner added that in his experience in civilian prison, "you get a number of backup" to extract a prisoner, three to four, maybe five, up to seven guards. The prosecutor asked him to describe the extraction process, and Graner said the object was to grab a limb, control the prisoner, secure him, and move him. "So this was a dangerous situation with Gus?" the prosecutor asked. "Yes." And that is why he got two other guards to help him? Yes. Did he wear a flak jacket? No. Did he call for other backup? No. Did he wear any special gear? No. Did he wear any protective equipment? No. Graner added that he only used a six- to eight-foot-long "sling" that "slid down to his neck." Was this dangerous? Yes. Was he concerned about England? Yes. "And you immediately handed the tether to England?" Graner replied that Gus "was not dangerous now." The prosecutor then stated, "You were concerned about England so you took a photo." Graner replied that he wanted to document the extraction. "Why?" the prosecutor asked. Graner said one always wants to document the use of force in these situations. The prosecutor asked him whether he wanted to take the picture in order to humiliate the detainee. "No," Grainer answered. How many photographs did he take? Three. But he was worried about England, the prosecutor repeated. Graner said that the small size of Gus did not matter. And the pictures were only to document the use of force? There was a long pause, but Graner did not answer. "You never took a photo to humiliate him?" the prosecutor repeated. "No, sir," Graner replied.

What was the purpose of the photos? "I had no purpose," Graner replied. Did Graner think it was funny? No. But there is a smile on his face in some of the photos, the prosecutor pointed out. "I usually have a smile on my face," Graner replied. The prosecutor pointed to a different photograph and asked, "Why was this picture taken?" Graner answered that he was waiting for the medic. "You have a big smile on your face," the prosecutor said. Yes. "Was the picture funny?" No. "Did you pose to humiliate?" "No, I didn't feel it was humiliating." The prosecutor pointed to another photograph and stated that the detainees were tied, had sandbags over their heads, but were dangerous because they were yelling. Graner said they were posing a threat. Did he hit a detainee? Graner said it was a slap, "a punch or a slap." What happened to the detainee? Graner blamed Frederick for hitting a detainee so hard a medic had to be called. Couldn't Graner have put the detainees in a cell to control them? Graner said there were no open cells, but the prosecutor pointed to an open cell in one of the photos.

The prosecutor stated that as the incident continued, "Now the detainees are loose, how is the pyramid controlling them?" Graner answered, "If one moves, they all do." Were the soldiers laughing? "I don't know if there was laughter." But you're always smiling, the prosecutor said. "I smile for pictures," Graner answered. What happened after the pyramid came to an end? "I believe there was masturbation," Graner said. At some point, according to the prosecutor, all the guards had left the scene except for Frederick and England. The prosecutor asked him to explain the masturbation scene, and Graner replied, "This is what MI wanted me to do." These were MI instructions? Yes. Why did he eventually move the detainees into cells? Graner said he placed them in "stress positions" in cells to control the situation. Did he do the correct thing? "I did nothing wrong," Graner replied, because "nobody got hurt, prisoners or otherwise."

It was remarkable that most of Graner's testimony as well as the cross-examination were about Graner, not about England. After all, this was supposed to be England's court-martial. Yet precious little was said about her role in the abuse except the suggestion that she was weak and compliant. Ironically, Graner had stolen the show, again. He absorbed most of the attention in the courtroom.

Crisp tried to rehabilitate his witness. He asked Graner whether photography was prohibited, and Graner answered, "Only at Camp Vigilant." What was England's job at Abu Ghraib? "In processing." Why was she doing MP duties? "She was there with me, and I utilized different people," Graner said. Did anyone in Graner's chain of command comment on England's presence in the hard site? No. "How did you happen to have a camera?" "I had asked everyone to document with a camera," Graner replied.

The issue of why soldiers were taking photographs cannot be resolved from the testimony. The reasons given by soldiers for taking pictures range from wanting to document the abuse to taking pictures of everything, including but not limited to the abuse, simply because they had cameras and they could. It may not be an either/or alternative in choosing which explanation is most accurate. The true answer may lie somewhere between the extreme explanations of being a whistle-blower and a tourist. It is true that soldiers at Abu Ghraib behaved like tourists with their cameras and photographed each other, dogs, cats, vehicles, cots, and just about everything in their environment. It is also true that some of them took pictures of some of the abuse. Some of their motives in photographing the abuse may have stemmed from sadism, trophy hunting, and seeking to further humiliate prisoners, and some soldiers may have wanted to document Bizarro World out of a frustration that no one would believe them.

The prosecutor rose to ask his final question: Did anyone in the chain of command take issue with the relationship between England and Graner? Yes, the platoon sergeant had prohibited England at some point from visiting the Hard Site. Graner was finally dismissed from the stand, and court was adjourned for the day.

England's School Psychologist's Testimony

It was September 23, 2005, and Hurricane Rita had already slammed into the Texas coast. Its strong winds could be felt at Fort Hood. Dr. Thomas Denne, England's school psychologist, took the stand. During the voir dire, the judge read to him the criteria that England's actions had to meet in order for her to be found guilty of conspiracy: she must have entered into an agreement to maltreat others. This agreement could have been diminished by partial mental responsibility such as a mental defect of some sort, which would have to be established.

Denne said that he had evaluated England for the first time when she was four years old, then again in 1996 and in 2003. He went on to say that England was suffering from a complex language dysfunction that caused her to comply in the presence of authority figures and caused her to be anxious in social settings. The judge said that those sounded like symptoms, but what label would he give her? Denne answered, "Language-based processing disorder." Denne elaborated: England was "electively mute" and did not speak at age four, and even as late as sixth grade, she was speaking to only one person in school. She had practically no social interaction or social skills in school. Denne said that statistically speaking, she had a rare dysfunction such that her language skills and her visual skills were diametrically opposed. The result was that she felt confused in life most of the time. He gave the concrete example that when she saw fruit such as a pear, she could not reason that the fruit could be eaten. He explained also that she suffered from an overly compliant personality. What did all this mean in layperson's terms? "She would seek an authority to follow," Denne said.

The prosecutor had Denne repeat that on the Wechsler IQ test, England scored high on visual and low on verbal intelligence. But she had no behavioral problems in school? "No misbehavior," Denne replied. The prosecutor noted, she had a GPA of 3.0 in school, so that she was ranked in the middle of her class. Yes, Denne confirmed. The prosecutor stated that England performed well enough in school, basic training, and the army despite her cognitive and personal deficiencies. Crisp tried to recover his witness by asking him to explain the discrepancies that the prosecutor had pointed out: Denne said that he felt "humiliated" when he saw photographs of the abuse, and he had to reconcile those photos with the little girl he knew. He said that she compensated for her deficiencies with compliance and that he never taught her to question authority. "Did you feel responsible?" Crisp asked him. Denne almost broke down and cried but held back the tears. Then the prosecutor stood up and had the distraught psychologist agree with him that despite her problems, "she can lead a somewhat normal life." Denne agreed.

The jurors asked Denne whether England had a disorder, disease, or dysfunction. Denne gave a complicated reply about a listening, speaking, and reading problem. Another question from a juror had to do with the boundaries of compliance. Would she jump off a cliff if ordered by an authority? What was her boundary? Denne said this was hard to determine. The judge then interpreted yet another juror's question as to whether

England knew what she was doing was wrong. Denne said she did not know that her actions were wrong, but the judge disagreed with him. The judge said all this testimony amounted to "word games," and he ordered a recess for one and a half hours.

Following recess, the judge said he was required by law to instruct both the prosecution and the defense "regardless of the defense theory." The interaction between the judge and Crisp became heated. The judge said Crisp was wrong to argue that England was compliant and listened to Graner because she did not know the difference between right and wrong. Crisp retaliated that she knew the difference between right and wrong, but her defect precluded her ability to conspire. The judge wanted the defense attorney to agree that he was making an argument for partial mental responsibility on the agreement aspect of conspiracy, but Crisp would not comply. The judge asked Crisp, "She did not know it was wrong?" Crisp replied, "She did not believe it was wrong with Graner." The judge asked, "Because of her mental condition, and Graner, she did not know it was wrong?" Crisp said that "as a result of her compliant trait, she did not know what Graner asked was wrong." "So whatever Graner said was right?" the judge said. Crisp said she did not know it was wrong. The judge responded, "How can a trait take away one's ability to tell right from wrong?" And so it went. It was a painful discussion.

A Clinical Psychologist's Testimony for the Defense

Crisp asked another expert witness to the stand, Dr. Xavier Amador, who is a clinical psychologist. Now the three of them debated the intricate, academic difference between personality "traits" and "disorders." Amador said at one point that England did have the ability to tell the difference between right and wrong (which rules out the insanity plea) but because of the abusive relationship with Graner, she did not know the difference between right and wrong. The judge asked whether England's depression would have prevented her from knowing the difference between right and wrong, and Amador said it would not.

On and on it went like this. The judge finally concluded that according to the defense, England's disorder did not preclude her knowing the difference between right and wrong, but her traits did. The prosecutor stood up and said that the defense wants to have its cake and eat it, too: they want to make England seem insane yet not insane. He said the defense had two options: door 1, partial responsibility; or door 2, insanity. The judge quipped that the defense wants door 3, and there is no door 3.

Amador added that because of England's defect and a compliant trait, she did whatever Graner told her to do. The prosecutor said this was a word game. The judge agreed with the prosecutor and instructed Amador that when the jury returned, he would not be allowed to state that because of any trait in England's personality, she did not know the difference between right and wrong.

The jury was finally called back into the courtroom, and Amador began his testimony. He said that mentally ill people don't know that they are mentally ill; that because of England's overly compliant personality, she did not agree with Graner to commit acts, and her agreement was based solely on her traits. The judge stopped the proceedings and ordered the jury out of the courtroom. The judge reminded Amador that he was not allowed to say what he had just said. The judge and Crisp got into another heated exchange. When the jury returned, Amador restated in a different fashion that England was not capable of knowing the difference between right and wrong when it came to Graner.

A major portion of the defense seemed to be centered on the proposition that England did bad things out of obedience to Graner. The defense argued less about obedience to authority in general or to a poisoned authority structure at Abu Ghraib and more about obedience to one person, Graner, whom England loved.

During cross-examination, the prosecutor had Amador admit that he was involved in the defense of the Ted Kaczynski, Paul Reid, Andrea Yates, and other high-profile cases. The prosecutor also linked Amador to Jerry Spence and accused Amador of giving links on his Web site to sites for purchasing books he had written. Amador replied, "Name recognition won't help book sales." The prosecutor asked Amador whether he gave England any psychiatric tests or just interviewed her. Amador replied that there was no need for paper–and-pencil tests. The prosecutor asked about England's work at a chicken-processing plant prior to being deployed to Iraq. The apparent connection was that England had quit her job in West Virginia but stayed on the tier at Abu Ghraib—so she was not compliant. Amador replied that she had quit her job because of peer pressure from coworkers, so she was compliant. The prosecutor asked, "Would she have killed a detainee?" if Graner had given such an order. Amador said such an order would have been beyond the limits of her compliant personality.

Crisp asked why Amador did not give England any objective tests. "It wasn't relevant." He asked Amador to explain England's smile, and he replied that she enjoyed being with Graner but did not enjoy the abuse. Amador went on to say that Graner changed her normative standards of what is normative versus sadistic because of the abusive relationship he established with her. She could not tell what was abusive and what was not.

The jurors asked whether someone sane but angry could be abusive? Yes. Could someone without mental problems be abusive? Yes. Suppose that she posed in photos without being asked to do so. Amador answered that she was always told to pose. Would she realize afterward that she had done something wrong? Amador replied that being overly compliant would lead her to *not* see her behavior as bad later.

The Government's Rebuttal in the Battle of the Experts

MAJ Jennifer Laing, one of the U.S. Army psychiatrists who had examined Lynndie England, sat in the courtroom during the testimonies of Denne and Amador. She was knitting from a conspicuous spot in the courtroom, the end seat in the prosecution section. She took the stand. She said that she had interviewed England on February 11, 2005, for a total of one and a half to two hours (in contrast to thirty hours of interviews that Amador had with England). The army psychiatrist said that she did not diagnose what England had while at Abu Ghraib but does not believe she was depressed at Abu Ghraib. What about England's weight loss while at Abu Ghraib? "Everyone loses weight," the psychiatrist said. She explained that what the defense was calling a "compliant personality" means "follower" and agreed that England was a follower. The psychiatrist declared England sane and as knowing the difference between right and wrong.

During cross-examination, the defense got the psychiatrist to admit that England was prescribed an antidepressant medication since June 2004. When she was asked to comment on Amador's diagnoses, the major said that Amador was extreme in some of his assessments.

The judge ordered a recess until Monday morning, September 26, due in part to the impact of Hurricane Rita.

Closing Arguments

By Monday morning, the hurricane had passed, and it was a typically hot, sunny day in Texas. The prosecutor showed photographs of the abuse to the jury and said, "We have seen shit," apparently an indirect reference to Frederick's line, "You didn't see shit." He said that England participated in the abusive events and photos by mocking detainees. There was no other reason for the abuse except fun. The abuser knew what she was doing and entered into an agreement by virtue of her actions in concert with others. Graner took three photos of her with Gus. Harman wrote the word *rapeist* on a detainee's leg in order to make fun of the prisoners. They were all enjoying and participating in "sick humor." Did Graner order England to do these things? There is a difference between an order and a suggestion, the prosecutor said. She had a duty not to obey illegal orders. Could she agree? Yes. Did she know it was illegal? Yes. "This is a crime," the prosecutor said, and he asked the jury to find her "guilty as charged."

In the defense's closing statement, Crisp said, "This whole case is about authority." Did England agree to commit these acts? The army psychiatrist said that she did, but she had only two or three years of experience as a psychiatrist. Amador had over seventeen years of experience in family history interviews and says that she did not. Crisp said that how prisoners were treated around England established her norms. Who was in control? Frederick and Graner. Graner was putting the prisoners into these situations. England is not in all these pictures. Graner was England's social compass. Crisp alluded to Denne's testimony that he gave her skills for an academic environment but not for living in the rest of the world. How could she process the bizarre world of Abu Ghraib? Graner was in charge, and he was her boyfriend. She thought that he would not be in charge if he was so bad. Could she subjectively know that these orders were illegal? She was a nonentity with regard to authority. The evidence does not meet the standard for conspiracy.

The prosecutor had the last word. He said that being a follower does not get you off moral culpability or criminal responsibility. The mood at Abu Ghraib was one of joking around. Frederick told people they "did not see shit." Was England subject to orders? Yes, U.S. soldier orders. She engaged in indecent acts that incited the lust of people. There is evidence that she said of a detainee, "He's getting hard." She did it because it was funny. She did not have blind compliance to authority. This is because at the chicken plant in West Virginia, she was not compliant and quit. The prosecutor concluded that she was an active participant, laughing, and did not blindly follow orders.

The judge gave closing instructions to the jury, which he read from a list in front of him. The jury went off to deliberate and returned a guilty verdict on all counts later that evening.

Mitigation

It was now Tuesday morning, September 27. The prosecution introduced a dramatic piece of testimony: a letter from BG Mark Kimmitt, who was the public relations spokesperson for the U.S. Army in Iraq. The gist of the letter was that the photographs from Abu Ghraib were spread world-wide and had a negative impact on the U.S. mission in Iraq in terms of security, economic recovery, the restoration of essential services, and the establishment of a new government. The publication of the photos made conditions in Iraq worse, caused a negative turn in how American soldiers were perceived by Iraqis, and tarnished the reputation of the American military. Krull objected that there is no way to know with 100 percent certainty the effects the photographs had in Iraq, but the judge overruled her.

The prosecutor continued reading the letter: Iraq is such a large country that some Iraqis never saw an American soldier except on TV, and what they saw due to the pictures from Abu Ghraib set the negative view of the American army.

The Medical Component

The defense opened mitigation by reading a letter from the chief physician at Abu Ghraib, MAJ David Auch. This medical doctor wrote in his letter that medical supplies were minimal; that everyone was confused about mission goals; that the Geneva Conventions were not posted; that detainees were not distinguished as being "security detainees" versus prisoners of war; that slow "mission and morale creep" led to a breakdown in the medical treatment he was able to offer; that his medics focused on the detainees and not the soldiers; that in his estimation, 40 percent of the soldiers had PTSD; and that both the command structure and the environment failed the soldiers at Abu Ghraib.

All the points raised by this doctor are corroborated by other reports. The more important point is that the doctor's letter was read at the end of the report during mitigation, not during the trial phase in this or any other court-martial. His letter opens the door to questions that should be raised: What are the roles of physicians, medics, and the medical establishment in general vis-à-vis the abuse at Abu Ghraib and elsewhere? The medics and doctors were routinely treating some injured prisoners (this much is evident from testimony)—why didn't the doctors and medics report the abuse? In the government's case, *all* the blame for failure to report abuse was shifted onto soldiers, when, in fact, doctors and medics are obligated to report abuse. What shall one say of the Hippocratic Oath and the norms of the American Medical Association regarding the abuse? These are important sources of moral boundaries on par with the

Geneva Conventions and other national as well as international human rights standards. These important issues were treated as peripheral, at best, to the trials of Abu Ghraib. But they are key issues for any intelligent, fair, and objective assessment of the abuse at Abu Ghraib and elsewhere. The jury had no questions. The trial was moving rapidly.

Note that Auch did not testify in person. His testimony and that of the medic at Davis's trial were the only testimonies from medical personnel at the trials. M. Gregg Bloche and Jonathan H. Marks write the following concerning Auch and the medical conditions at Abu Ghraib:

> During an inquiry we conducted for *The New England Journal of Medicine,* the doctor, Maj. David Auch, told us that some of the prisoners at Abu Ghraib were psychotic and out of control. One, he said, would repeatedly strip off his clothes and smash his head against the wall. After handcuffs and a helmet failed to stop him and with straitjackets unavailable, some soldiers suggested the leash. Major Auch granted their request. "My concern was whatever it took to keep him from getting hurt," he said. It is easy to criticize Major Auch for allowing MPs to use a leash, but it is difficult to say what he should have done instead.... The atmosphere at Abu Ghraib hardly promoted sanity. Mortar shells landed almost daily, according to military personnel we interviewed, and prisoners often rioted, sometimes using smuggled weapons, with deadly effect....
>
> Through their nerve and initiative under fire, Abu Ghraib's clinicians saved lives. To try to do so, they broke rules: dentists aren't supposed to operate on hearts, and physician's assistants don't take off arms or legs. Nor do doctors manage mental patients by putting them on leashes. We don't condone this practice, and there can be no excuse for the torture and other abuse that many detainees endured at Abu Ghraib. But we are not inclined to blame Major Auch. The men and women who risked their lives to care for Iraqis and Americans alike were put in impossible circumstances by indifference or worse from above.... The catastrophic failings of medical care at Abu Ghraib put American lives at risk and violated the United States' obligations to care decently for detainees.[2]

DiNenna's Testimony

DiNenna, the major who was the supply officer at Abu Ghraib, testified at this court-martial as he had in the courts-martial of Davis and Harman. He described the general conditions at Abu Ghraib with the words *stench, filth, trash, urine, feces,* and *looting.* Most soldiers and prisoners were sick most of the time from the unsanitary conditions. There was a shortage of water, and the food was contaminated. There wasn't enough light because of power disruptions, and there were not enough generators. The toilets were dysfunctional. There were medical problems such that there was more illness and injury than the medical staff could handle. Small-arms fire was constant. The prison experienced internal and external threats. The ratio of 150 prisoners per guard was dangerous. There was a shortage in personnel and resources.

During cross-examination, the prosecutor made DiNenna admit that, officially, abuse of detainees was not tolerated and that soldiers received some training. The prosecutor also had the supply officer say on the stand that Abu Ghraib was a tough mission, but the army is used to dealing with challenges.

Graner Back on the Witness Stand

Graner testified during the mitigation phase of the trial as well. He said that the serial numbers of the prisoners were sometimes lost so the soldiers were never quite certain of the head count. In response to a question, Graner said that soldiers at Abu Ghraib were in contact with soldiers from the 82nd Airborne Division. There were two sets of "bosses" such that MPs had one set and MIs had another set of bosses. There were also MI rules for dealing with people, which were different from MP rules. Finally, Graner said that Frederick told him that he had been told that MI allowed masturbation as a "technique."

My Testimony

I will quote portions from an article by Matt Taibbi[3] regarding my testimony because this journalist captures the negative climate in the courtroom at England's court-martial:

> Why was Lynndie England smiling in those pictures? Ask her expert witness! "American culture places a great emphasis on smiling," pronounced Dr. Stjepan Mestrovic, one of the experts the defense called to the stand. The renowned sociologist is a gloomy-looking foreigner.... The doctor folds his arms, thinking he has said something significant about Lynndie England's famous grin. He has, of course, but what he's mistaken about is in thinking anyone here gives a damn. The court-martial of Lynndie England early on evolved into a kind of low-rent comic allegory about the American political scene, and Mestrovic played the role of the pointy-headed liberal who is too busy being right to see what a pain in the ass he is.... The judge, an impatient blockhead named Col. James Pohl, took an especial dislike to Mestrovic. His Honor looked like

a man who takes his wife on dates to the Elks Club and yells at his children at barbecues; he winced visibly every time the effete foreigner opens his mouth.... Mestrovic described Abu Ghraib as a "state of anomie." "A what?" Pohl snapped, frowning. "A state of anomie" the doctor repeated. Pohl shuddered and sipped his coffee seeming to wonder whether such a word was even legal in Texas.... Sure, one of Lynndie's lawyer's tried to call a certain Capt. Ian Fishback to testify to other similar abuses in Iraq ... but Pohl was having none of that crap .... Who needs that? We have hurricanes to worry about. Thanks for nothing, Lynndie. Leave the camera home next time.

For the record, I should clarify that I am not a foreigner and am a U.S. citizen. *Anomie* is a formal sociological word that means social chaos. Otherwise, the author captures the mood in the courtroom quite well.

The Clinical Psychologist Again

The defense called Amador back to the stand for the mitigation phase. Amador spoke about normative breakdown at Abu Ghraib, the confusion of norms, the lack of training for the soldiers, and the lack of supervision. He referred to the famous Stanley Milgram experiment that had demonstrated that people exhibit blind obedience and loyalty to authority. Interestingly, he steered this connection to the relationship between Graner and England: Graner was the surrogate for Milgram and was running an experiment on obedience with England as the subject. England was compliant, loyal, and looked up to Graner as a father figure, lover, and supervisor. The psychologist explained that because of her sexual relationship with Graner, she had to defensively rationalize experiences she perceived as wrong, but she needed him as a social compass and guide. Her relationship to Graner was psychologically and physically abusive for her.

My feeling about Amador's testimony is that Graner, England, and the other soldiers at Abu Ghraib were all in a hellish "experiment" on obedience to authority. I am less concerned with her relationship to Graner and more concerned with the effects of the poisoned social climate at Abu Ghraib on all the soldiers. But this difference between us probably comes down to the fact that Amador is a psychologist and I am primarily a sociologist.

England Takes the Stand

Finally, England took the stand and gave unsworn testimony so that she could not be cross-examined by the prosecution. Basically, she was pleading for mercy from the jury. She struggled and strained to speak: it was obvious that she did have a language deficit problem, as Denne had testified that she did. England said that school was always difficult for her, that she was scared to ask questions in class, and that it was very stressful for her. People made fun of her in school for how she dressed and acted, for her short hair, and for how she ate her lunch. She could not play sports and felt inadequate overall.

She said that Graner made her feel good about herself, and she liked the fact that he was older and more experienced than she was. She believed that he would lead her to do the right thing. She would dress up for him, put on makeup, and met his family. Before meeting him, she never wanted to go out on dates or socialize. But he wanted her to drink and socialize and go out to dinner. The only place to which she had ever traveled was Iraq, and "that's it."

She had never been in a prison before. She thought that Abu Ghraib held more prisoners than she expected, and there were not as many guards as she expected. She "hung out" on tier 1–A because she felt safer around Graner.

She went on to describe that her baby is something good, a "new life" for her. Initially, Graner was happy about the baby and showed concern for her pregnancy. It made her feel good because he was taking care of her again, but this didn't change anything between them. He broke up with her in January 2004, when the investigations into the abuse at Abu Ghraib began. Her son was born on October 11, 2004. At first, Graner's family was supportive. She said that her child had changed her, that she realized she can care for him, that he gives her courage and is a happy baby.

The public scares her, because she cannot tell who hates her and who does not. She receives hate mail. Fifty to a hundred reporters show up at her house. It had been stressful for her waiting for the trial. She said she feels scared at the thought that her baby might be taken away from her, and she is scared to have to leave her son because he will not know her.

She said that she let the army down by being in the photos and is embarrassed that she was used by Graner. She said she was sorry for what she did and apologized to the Army, to the detainees, their families, and to America. She heard that attacks were made on U.S. forces because of the photos, and she apologized for that, too.

She said she was sad that she could not stop the abuse.

Closing Arguments and Sentencing

The judge instructed the jury that she could be confined to a maximum of nine years. In his closing argument, the prosecutor emphasized that masturbation in Islamic culture is the worst sin. He said there were extenuating factors for England's crimes: poor training, poor conditions, confusion as to MI and MP roles, and the division of soldiers into leaders versus followers. "But being a follower does not make one not culpable," he added. And he said there are mitigating factors, such as her language processing deficit and her son. But the aggravating factor is that she tarnished the reputation of the army and that she had a negative effect on "mission impact." "We are at a war of ideas," the prosecutor said. He asked the jury to consider the men in the army, the victims, and the soldiers in Iraq. He asked that she be sentenced to four to six years as punishment and general deterrence. As in the other trials, the closing argument was primarily about the emotions of shame and humiliation for the army.

In the defense's statement, Crisp said that England was put in the worst possible situation: surrounded by authority figures doing bad things, and she was unable to articulate her objections. Abu Ghraib was an incubator for bad things. Even Army Command was convinced to put Graner into a position of leadership. So how strange is it that she looked up to him? Abu Ghraib was social chaos. It could not self-correct. Then Crisp said, "Think of the testimony of the officers in here," and added, "Oh right, there wasn't any." (It is true that there wasn't any in the first part of the trial, but there was testimony from three officers in the mitigation phase.) The abuse at Abu Ghraib was self-encouraging instead of self-correcting, he said. There were influences at Abu Ghraib which were out of her control.

The jury deliberated for two hours. England walked into the courtroom holding her baby, but the judge ordered that the baby be removed from the courtroom. The all-male jury composed entirely of high-ranking officers (colonels and majors) sentenced her to three years.

Notes

1. See Michael Perry, "New Abu Ghraib Abuse Photos Anger Arabs," Reuters, February 15, 2006.

2. M. Gregg Bloche and Jonathan H. Marks, "Triage at Abu Ghraib," *New York Times,* February 4, 2005, A19.

3. Matt Taibbi, "Ms. America," *Rolling Stone,* October 20, 2005, 48.

PART THREE

DETOX FOR THE ORCHARD

CHAPTER SEVEN

WHAT THE TRIALS REVEALED:
ABU GHRAIB AS HELL ON EARTH

Robert Louis Stevenson's story about the transformation of a kindly Dr. Jekyll into an evil Mr. Hyde comes to mind in trying to make sense of the trials, testimony, and my personal encounters with the so-called rotten apples, and the others who played their roles in the courts-martial.

Starting with the allegedly rotten apples, it seems to be the case that most of them came to Abu Ghraib as ordinary persons with no histories of crime, delinquency, or sadism. For example, I agree with the soldiers who said that Harman would have made a great social worker. I agree with the soldiers who expressed the opinion that Davis was someone they felt they could trust with their lives and who snapped for ten seconds. There is no way for me to escape the impression of England, conveyed by experts as well as other soldiers, that she was the ultimate follower or overly compliant personality. Sivits struck me as a loving, kind husband and father, and a loyal friend to his comrades. Reese seemed like the proverbial "nice guy." DiNenna seemed dedicated to his job of getting supplies for the mission. Fishback came across as admirable in his idealism. I could go down the list of the other soldiers and officers in the Abu Ghraib "orchard" who testified or whom I met, witnesses as well as the accused—they did *not* come across as monsters, sadists, or rotten apples. All of them came across as real people who got trapped in a place that was consistently described by them as unreal in a terrible sort of way: hell on Earth, a Mad Max movie come to life, Bizarro World, a crazy place, and so on. Their phrases are in line with the phrase "poisoned atmosphere," used in the Fay report. A consistent picture emerges from the trials of ordinary people who were mostly "good" being transformed into persons who committed, condoned, watched or otherwise went along with evil.

Soldiers testified consistently that MI were in charge. It is as if the monstrous transformation from Jekyll to Hyde took place at Abu Ghraib for most soldiers in the fall of 2003. The abusive methods truly seem to have "migrated" from Guantánamo and Afghanistan, as the government reports suggest. Karpinski, at the time the general who was theoretically supposed to be in charge of all the MPs and of Abu Ghraib, makes it clear that she felt powerless against MI: "In the fuzzy organization chart at Abu Ghraib, the intelligence people were really in charge."[1]

This point must be emphasized as one of the cardinal findings that emerged from the testimony at the courts-martial: MI was in charge of Abu Ghraib. The standard explanations given to MPs who questioned unlawful practices were along the lines of "It's an MI thing," "This is the way MI wants things done," "MI is in charge," and so on. This point is obvious from the testimony, and it was obvious to the lawyers, soldiers, and journalists with whom I spoke at the trials who followed them as I did. But it is not obvious from the way that the government framed and continues to frame the problem of Abu Ghraib as mainly the result of "rogue soldiers" in the MP.

Dr. Jekyll and Mr. Hyde at Abu Ghraib

In his immortal tale of Dr. Jekyll and Mr. Hyde, Robert Louis Stevenson invents two potions: one is a poison that transforms the good Dr. Jekyll into the monstrous Mr. Hyde, and the other is a medicine that transforms Hyde back to his ordinary self. Applied to the story of Abu Ghraib, Stevenson's powerful metaphor suggests the following: The poison that contaminated Abu Ghraib had been concocted at Guantánamo Bay. It was "imported" from Gitmo to Abu Ghraib in the summer of 2003. The abuse began in earnest in October 2003, and by December 2003, the atmosphere at Abu Ghraib had been thoroughly poisoned. It is not yet known how many people concocted the poisonous brew labeled "Gitmoization," nor who they are, nor all of its ingredients.

Some of the ingredients in the poisoned potion include disregard for the Geneva Conventions, the merging of MI and MP roles, making the MIs act omnipotent and the MPs act as gofers and helpers in carrying out unlawful orders, the use of dogs as weapons, humiliation, the unlawful policy of "softening up" prisoners, and wanton violence in the duplicitous guise of "interrogation techniques." Other ingredients may be isolated and discovered in the future. Real life is not supposed to read like fiction, but we have seen that at Abu Ghraib, real life became a horror movie and even resembles Stevenson's epic tale. In the story of Dr. Jekyll and Mr. Hyde, the poison is more powerful than the antidote, and over the course of time, Jekyll becomes unable to control the evil Mr. Hyde. Similarly, there seems to be some evidence that the poison from Guantánamo Bay seeped into Afghanistan and other places in Iraq and, in general, has contaminated a good portion of the "orchard" in Iraq. It seems to be an urgent task to apply the antidote to the poison as soon as possible. The antidote consists of a renewed commitment to the Geneva Conventions, the maintenance of the distinct roles of MI and MP, a clear policy that no one is above the law, a policy of establishing rapport with and respect for the human rights of prisoners, and strict adherence to the army's rules of conduct.

In summary, the trials of Abu Ghraib are a prelude to further inquiry, an invitation for more criticism, and a cry for real justice. The trials raised far more questions than they answered: Why were women and children imprisoned? Why were DiNenna's pleas for help ignored and by whom? Why was the company commander made to feel helpless to stop strange practices? Where was the platoon leader of the night shift? Why was MI allowed to run Abu Ghraib? Why were the physicians and medics at Abu Ghraib powerless to report and stop the abuse? And so on. Anyone who engages emotionally with the story of Abu Ghraib is bound to conclude in accord with Stevenson's line: "If there is a Mr. Hyde, I shall be Mr. Seek."

The Pathos of Abu Ghraib

If one reflects on the details of what was said at the courts-martial, one realizes that some witnesses made statements and expressed emotions that were not emphasized in media or government reports and that have not made their way into the general discourse concerning Abu Ghraib. The reader will most likely have his or her own choices for what was most striking and important in the trials. The following expressions of emotion struck me as being the most significant, because they touch on the Jekyll-Hyde dilemma and poisoned atmosphere at Abu Ghraib:

- Graner said that the Hard Site was constantly filled with the *screams of pain* coming from the prisoners who were shackled into torturous "stress positions."
- DiNenna said that the U.S. Army did not respond to his desperate pleas for food, water, medicine, and other essentials necessary not only to accomplish a mission, but necessary for human survival and safety.

- Rivera said that he felt helpless to protest the abuse against prisoners because *he felt afraid of his fellow soldiers.*
- Reese said that he felt it was strange that prisoners were forced to wear panties on their heads and was told that this was a "supply issue" or an "MI thing." It seems that Reese was *emotionally invalidated* by the response his superiors gave him.
- Several soldiers observed that if prisoners were "good guys" before they came to Abu Ghraib, they left the prison as "bad guys" who would become future terrorists.

Constant Screams of Pain

Graner was the only person in the courts-martial that I witnessed who stated that soldiers could always hear the screams of prisoners at Abu Ghraib. He added that at night, there was often total darkness. He made it seem as if the cries of pain were something like the constant background noise of traffic in large cities—urbanites get used to it and, after a while, cease to notice it. Similarly, it seems that the soldier at Abu Ghraib became blasé to the tangible consequences of torture—namely, pain and suffering.

Graner's observation reminds us that the prisoners at Abu Ghraib were in great pain from actions taken by soldiers that are described by euphemisms such as "interrogation techniques," "stress positions, " "physical training," and so on. The pain and sadism inflicted on the prisoners became "background noise" not only at Abu Ghraib but also in the trials, media coverage, and overall discourse on Abu Ghraib. Most of the discourse pertaining to Abu Ghraib is about the need for intelligence, the shame that the photographs heaped upon the U.S. Army, the fine legal and academic distinctions of what constitutes torture and other abstractions that fail to get at the reality of being at Abu Ghraib—namely, that any human being who is shackled in contorted positions will be in agonizing pain. When many individuals are tortured daily in this as well as in other ways—when torture becomes "business as usual," to quote Frank Spinner—the environment can no longer be considered as "normal" or "normative." Perhaps it is for this reason that Graner labeled Abu Ghraib as "Bizarro World." This observation may seem so obvious that it does not need to be stated, yet it needs to be emphasized precisely because it gets lost in all the thousands of pages of reports, transcripts, and media accounts. Emotionally speaking, Abu Ghraib seems to have been a crazy place that involved extreme suffering for soldiers and prisoners alike.

One of many pieces of evidence that corroborates Graner's poignant observation came from the court-martial of one of the dog handlers at Abu Ghraib, SGT Michael Smith, on March 15, 2006. Another dog handler testified at his trial that his working dog became so disoriented and upset from the screaming at Abu Ghraib, the dog bit an interrogator. If an animal went "crazy" at Abu Ghraib from the screams of pain and other noise pertaining to abuse (shouting, yelling), there is no good reason to suppose that the humans at Abu Ghraib—soldiers and prisoners alike—could remain immune to the craziness.

Emotional and Physical Abandonment

DiNenna, the supply officer, said the army failed to provide its soldiers as well as its prisoners with the most basic resources of food, water, clothing, medicine, training, and clear moral boundaries. The major's observation is corroborated by other testimony as well as the U.S. government reports. More important, he gave a human face to the realities of this neglect. It is as if the soldiers at Abu Ghraib were emotionally and physically abandoned. The prosecution tried to rationalize away and invalidate this emotion by claiming that Abu Ghraib was a "difficult mission." It seems inconceivable that of the many billions of dollars that were spent on the war against Iraq, a tiny fraction of that amount could not have been found to meet the most basic human needs of soldiers and prisoners alike—including safe food and water.

The major made it clear that lack of food, water, and lighting led to terrible consequences: frequent riots among and by the prisoners, vomiting and illness for soldiers and prisoners alike, a terrifying atmosphere in which everyone feared for their lives in the dark, because the army would not send generators and other equipment necessary for adequate lighting, and so on. Bergrin remarked that when people are treated like animals, they come to behave like animals. When basic human needs are not met, people resort to aggression, frustration, and all sorts of other negative symptoms.

The discourse on Abu Ghraib needs to be expanded to include the issues of abandonment and caring in formal organizations such as the U.S. Army. The negative consequences of the emotional abandonment of the mission at Abu Ghraib are clear to anyone who reflects on what was disclosed in the trials: they range from low morale, abuse, and symptoms of PTSD among soldiers to depression, rioting, and hatred for the United States among the prisoners.

The Climate of Fear and Intimidation among Soldiers

Socrates remarks in one of his dialogues that even a band of thieves needs to possess some sense of justice and trust among themselves in order for the thieves to achieve their unjust, evil goals. If one accepts the government's basic premise, for the sake of argument, that the evils at Abu Ghraib are the result of a few bad apples, one has to accept the implicit assumption that the rotten apples had to trust each other in carrying out their unlawful deeds. Indeed, this assumption may lie behind the prosecutor's insistence that the rotten apples were all involved in a "conspiracy" of some sort in all the incidents chosen for trial. Putting the legal definition of *conspiracy* aside for the moment, it is clear that the soldiers did not really trust each other. Furthermore, Rivera's remark shows that the government's assumptions are fundamentally flawed: the allegedly rogue soldiers were *not* unified in carrying out the abuse. MIs knew what was going on, but MPs did not. Rivera feared that his fellow soldiers would abuse him in the same way that they abused prisoners had he protested the abuse. Frederick said he feared for his life with regard to Graner. Sivits testified that the soldiers were all afraid of each other. Darby feared retribution.

Again, the fact that the prisoners as well as soldiers at Abu Ghraib lived in constant, chronic fear has become background noise in the entire discourse. The important point is that an emotional climate of fear was established at Abu Ghraib that was based on unpredictable, arbitrary, and capricious directives, orders, and behaviors. Again, the closest analogue to this state of affairs is the dysfunctional family. Over the course of time, chronic chaos always leads to abuse.

The normal and normative functioning of army units is based upon trust and a sense of camaraderie among soldiers. Samuel Stouffer demonstrates this in a book entitled *The American Soldier,*[2] and it has been corroborated in many other studies. Soldiers bond with each other emotionally in smoothly functioning units, and when they fail to bond emotionally, the result is that the unit performs poorly. An important area for future research, investigation, as well as reflection is the issue of fear and its opposite, the sense of trust, in the U.S. Army. What were the mistakes made by the U.S. Army that led to the extreme climate of fear and intimidation at Abu Ghraib—even for its own soldiers? What are the consequences of a climate of fear for soldiers and prisoners alike? What steps can the Army take to instill a normative sense of trust among its soldiers? What steps can the Army take to create a safe environment for soldiers and prisoners alike so that a prison is run in the way that structural-functionalists describe the smooth functioning of any social institution? The consequences of the unpredictable, arbitrary, and capricious social environment at Abu Ghraib have been disastrous. One of the lessons learned might be that a predictable, orderly, and morally bounded prison might have yielded the very intelligence that was sought, fostered a better image for the U.S. Army, and contributed to democracy in Iraq—the very goals that the government expressed at the beginning of the war.

Lack of Emotional Validation

The prosecutor hammered away at the point that soldiers have a duty to prevent and report abuse. But consider again the testimony of Reese, the company commander at Abu Ghraib. The captain said that he was upset and concerned at the sight of naked male prisoners wearing panties on their heads and that he did raise the issue with his superiors. He said that he was told that it was a supply issue or an MI matter. In human terms, his appropriate and normal response to the abuse was invalidated by his superiors. The importance of this observation is that it highlights the role of emotional invalidation in the layers of authority above as well as below Reese. The International Committee of the Red Cross had raised issues of abuse early in the fall of 2003, but its observations were invalidated by officers high in the chain of command. Similarly, doctors and medics at Abu Ghraib had an obligation to report abuse—but to whom could they turn? There is the example of Harman reporting an incident in which a prisoner's hands were turning blue from lack of blood circulation due to the fact that he was handcuffed to a jail cell and abandoned. In the words of several witnesses, "nothing was done" as a result of her reporting. Testimony from the trials of Abu Ghraib reveal numerous similar incidents of invalidation as the response to the reporting of abuse. The U.S. government reports also cite many other incidents in which MIs discounted concern at and reporting of abuse. The general response seems to have been "This is the way MI does things."

In general, the dialogue in the testimony at the trials went something like this: "Did you report the abuse?" "Yes, sir." "What happened?" "Nothing happened."

Clearly, the army needs to establish policies for protecting whistleblowers and responding to them by validating their reports of abuse. Otherwise, the charge of "dereliction of duty" for failing to report abuse rings hollow.

The Issue of Women and Children at Abu Ghraib

A highly charged emotional issue that was mentioned at the trials—but never pursued—is that of the imprisonment of women and children at Abu Ghraib. The prosecution was forced to admit the fact that this occurred, but did not go through that door. The judge asked Frederick why women and children were kept at the Hard Site, and Frederick answered to the effect that it was because that was where the soldiers put them—this was an evasive answer. The judge accepted it. But what is the correct answer? It is impossible to tell because the judge's important question has not been pursued in the discourse pertaining to Abu Ghraib. One needs to ask related questions: Who dreamed up the tactic of imprisoning women and children at Abu Ghraib and why? How were these orders conveyed and by whom? Why were women and children imprisoned at places in Iraq other than Abu Ghraib? How many women and children were imprisoned? The fact that women and children are imprisoned in places other than Abu Ghraib is evidenced by occasional media reports of rioting and reprisals by Iraqis over precisely this issue.[3]

The informal, private answers given by soldiers whom I met are that the women and children were kept as hostages of sorts and that the presence of women on the Hard Site among men who were stripped naked added to the sense of humiliation for both sexes. It seems certain that the seven rotten apples could not have dreamed up or enforced this "technique" at breaking down Iraqi prisoners on their own. The women and children were arrested along with the men by different soldiers, so the orders to arrest them must have come from orchard keepers who have not yet been identified.

One should note the larger pattern that female U.S. Army soldiers as well as Iraqi females were forced to witness the sexual humiliation of the Iraqi men at Abu Ghraib via forced nudity. There is an unmistakable link in this regard with the documented, deliberate use of female soldiers and interrogators to sexually humiliate prisoners at Gitmo (documented by James Yee and others).[4] Furthermore, it seems that some of the Iraqi women at Abu Ghraib were sexually abused. For example, there is a photograph of a female Iraqi prisoner who was told to expose her breasts. There are references to voyeurism and sexual abuse in the showers. There are also statements by soldiers that several soldiers and officers competed for the sexual favors of some of the female prisoners.

In summary, the sexual abuse and humiliation of female Iraqi prisoners, the use of female American soldiers to humiliate male prisoners, and the use of female Iraqi prisoners to humiliate male prisoners—all are part of the untold story of Abu Ghraib.

No Aims Other Than Amusement

The prosecution went out of its way to establish that interrogation was *not* a motive in any of the incidents that were invoked in the courts-martial. It argued that soldiers abused prisoners for the sake of amusement. This begs the question: What was the role of sadistic amusement in seemingly bona fide interrogations and police functions at Abu Ghraib and elsewhere? In his book, James Yee reports that soldiers at Guantánamo used seemingly legitimate "extraction" techniques as a form of amusement to torment prisoners:

> When it [extraction] was over, there was a certain excitement in the air. The guards were pumped, as if the center had broken through the defense to score the winning goal. They high-fived each other and slammed their chests together, like professional basketball players. I found it an odd victory celebration for eight men who took down one prisoner ... although these practices were not necessarily uncommon in high-security prisons, here it was being used against prisoners locked in cells and, as I quickly learned, with extraordinary frequency. (74)

Similarly, Human Rights Watch has documented abuse at FOB Mercury that was done for amusement and stress relief. The prosecution unwittingly opened the door to many questions which ought to be pursued: Is there a pattern of sadistic abuse as amusement across detention facilities at Guantánamo, Afghanistan, and Iraq? How many interrogations were legitimate and nonabusive? What good (actionable, useful information) came from all these interrogations and detentions across the globe? How can one tell the difference between unauthorized abuse and legitimate interrogation, given that MP and MI roles were merged such that MPs were "softening up" prisoners twenty-four hours a day, seven days a week, purportedly for the sake of interrogation?

Intolerable Stress for Prisoners and Soldiers Alike

The prosecution established beyond any reasonable doubt that Abu Ghraib was a "difficult mission." But it discounted, repressed, or otherwise tried to avoid many facts that were exposed during the trials which suggest that the "difficulties" were unreasonable and extreme. What the prosecutor called a "difficult mission," some soldiers called "hell" or other words to that effect. Several of the rotten apples as well as witnesses were diagnosed with PTSD. How many other soldiers at Abu Ghraib had PTSD or other symptoms of extreme stress? The trial exposed the fact that the prisoner nicknamed "Gus" was psychotic and that psychotic prisoners were routinely held at the Hard Site. How many of the prisoners were psychotic? Yee reports that at Gitmo, depression, suicide attempts, rioting, and other symptoms of extreme stress were common and frequent among the prisoners. One needs a similar accounting of depression, suicide attempts, riots, and other symptoms of stress at Abu Ghraib regarding both soldiers and prisoners. Many witnesses referred to the social environment as "hell on Earth," "the nastiest place on Earth," "Bizarro World," "not like a normal prison," and other emotionally laden phrases. One of the lessons to be learned from Abu Ghraib is that the army should have prepared for and tried to minimize the stressors on both soldiers and prisoners in order to accomplish its mission. Examples of minimizing stress include adequate supplies of food, water, and shelter; standard operating procedures in place; an adequate medical staff and medical supplies in place; making sure that toilets, water, and electricity were available; minimizing the capricious and arbitrary aspects of staying at Abu Ghraib for both prisoners and soldiers; and so on.

Duplicitous Logic

Soldiers conveyed the following "logic" concerning abuse at Abu Ghraib: everybody was doing it, so it must have been OK. Officers and other people in charge witnessed the abuse daily and did not stop it, so the abuse must have been authorized. There were no guidelines, and everything was really on-the-job training. The few soldiers who reported the abuse were immediately invalidated, so there was no good reason to suppose that one could stop the abuse. The factual evidence presented during testimony and in the government reports seems to explain how soldiers might have arrived at these desperate conclusions. One does not have to agree with the soldiers, but one can understand how they arrived at these views. When one considers the facts that Ken Davis and Fishback reported the abuse as far up the chain of command as Congress, one is tempted to conclude that the soldiers who used this disturbing logic were being realistic.

On the other hand, the prosecution argued the following "logic": Everybody knows the difference between right and wrong. The soldiers had a duty to report the abuse. The soldiers had a duty to protect the prisoners. One does not need the Geneva Conventions or written guidelines to know that punching, humiliating, and otherwise victimizing prisoners is wrong. The subtly duplicitous aspect of this reasoning is that it assumes a normal, smoothly functioning, and stable social environment. Functional and healthy families and workplaces will validate and support the correct perception of the difference between right and wrong. Dysfunctional, poisoned families and social settings such as Abu Ghraib reward wrong behavior and invalidate morally correct behavior. The reader may find numerous instances in the testimony of each of these crazy responses to the difference between right and wrong.

Genuine moral indignation is typically directed at those who choose to commit evil in a stable social setting that gave the evildoer viable choices to do good. The soldier's choices at Abu Ghraib were extremely limited: short of desertion or some other dramatic, dysfunctional exit from the situation, the soldier had little choice but to go along with abuse that was treated as if it were authorized.

Lack of Ethics

Under normal circumstances, moral boundaries and ethical principles are in place in social settings and precede moral judgments. Had the Geneva Conventions been incorporated into policies and procedures in Iraq and at Abu Ghraib, officers would have been in a position to insist that soldiers comply with them. Similar reasoning applies to the many other moral boundaries that routinely guide human behavior: the AMA's moral code for the medical staff; the international prohibitions against torture for the interrogators; the army *Field Manual* for all the soldiers; the normal rules for saluting and respect that apply to all soldiers; the *U.S. Code of Military Justice* (UCMJ) for performing one's duty as clearly specified, and so on.

Testimony at the trials of Abu Ghraib suggests the opposite: these and other moral boundaries were not in place prior to the soldier's deployment to Abu Ghraib. The Geneva Conventions were not posted and, more important, were not incorporated into army rules, techniques, and procedures at Abu Ghraib and Iraq. Some soldiers had some minimal training in the Geneva Conventions, and others had none. The judge said that the Geneva Conventions were irrelevant at the courts-martial. Testimony revealed that SOPs did not exist and were replaced by on-the-job training. The medics pretended that abuse was not happening. The army *Field*

Manual was superseded by unlawful memorandums. Respect among soldiers was replaced by fear and intimidation. What was the meaning of "dereliction of duty" in a social setting in which no one was sure what their duties were?

Under such circumstances, ethical principles literally did not exist. It was as if soldiers were performing a mission without a moral compass or moral gyroscope. A soldier thrust into such a situation would experience the harrowing feeling of being sane in an insane place. Eventually, as evidenced by Harman's letter to her partner, the soldier begins to doubt his or her own sanity. The poisoned atmosphere does not validate normative responses, emotions, and behaviors, but it does reward going along with unethical, unlawful, and otherwise questionable responses, emotions, and behaviors.

The Themes of Shame and Honor

Major divisions exist as to how the themes of shame and honor were allocated at the trials and are treated implicitly in the larger discourse pertaining to Abu Ghraib. The first division has to do with army versus prisoner shame and honor. The prosecutor literally said, "Shame on you," to Harman during one of the trials. A defense attorney retorted with "Shame on the army!" In general, the prosecution emphasized that the photos of the abuse embarrassed the army and the United States, caused insurgents to further despise U.S. soldiers, and disgraced army values. Soldiers and officers alike testified that they felt their needs were neglected by the army at Abu Ghraib. Soldiers testified that they sometimes encountered contempt, derision, and disdain from each other when they tried to report or stop the abuse. There was a scornful tone in the phrase sometimes used by soldiers to cover up abuse—namely, "You didn't see shit"—as well as the phrase used by a prosecutor in saying to the jury, "We did see shit." The convicted soldiers received dishonorable discharges and were shackled before they left the courthouse following their convictions. The news media waited patiently outside the courthouse in order to capture these sensational moments of degradation on film. The careers of other soldiers and officers affiliated with Abu Ghraib seem also to have been ruined in many cases. Defense attorneys complained that it was dishonorable for high-ranking soldiers to evade responsibility for the abuse. In these and other ways that emerged during the trials, it becomes apparent that shame to the army emerged as the dominant theme of the Abu Ghraib trials.

On the other hand, shame to the prisoners was a more implicit theme, even though it was sometimes made explicit. The prosecution pointed out that prisoners were deliberately humiliated through the use of sexual positions. The obvious humiliation of being forced to be naked in front of other male as well as female prisoners was not emphasized at the trials. Similarly, the deeply humiliating fact that women and children were imprisoned at Abu Ghraib was frequently mentioned at the trials but not pursued in depth. Aspects of the abuse that pertain to specifically Arab and Islamic culture, such as exploiting the alleged "Arab fear of dogs," disrespect for the Koran, and being forced to eat food that violates religious rules, were issues that tended to be avoided at the trials, although they are mentioned in the government reports.[5] No experts in Islamic culture were called to the stand in order to explain the cultural insensitivity and humiliation that was heaped on the Iraqi prisoners.

In general, there can be little doubt that the trials came across as America-centric: the shame and humiliation to the army and to Americans stemming from the abuse and the photos of the abuse were a much more dominant theme than the shame and humiliation experienced by the Iraqi prisoners. This difference in emphasis is all the more pronounced when one considers that the prosecution established that the prisoners who were abused in the incidents invoked at the trials were not terrorists and did not pose any harm to Americans. In addition, the government reports make it clear that most of the prisoners at Abu Ghraib were not terrorists and were not dangerous to Americans.

Honor, as the opposite of shame, also emerged through the testimony at the trials. The two officers who testified as well as several soldiers made it clear that they were dedicated to the army mission and to army values. Some soldiers testified that they would trust some other soldiers with their lives. I gained the distinct impression that most of the soldiers were honest on the stand, as evidenced by the strong corroboration from other testimony as well as the government reports. Some soldiers were described as humane, thoughtful, and kindhearted. The patriotism of the soldiers is unquestionable. The whistle-blowers I have described all risked retribution from their fellow soldiers and, sadly, invalidation from the army as well. Without a doubt, disobeying and reporting unlawful orders at Abu Ghraib came across as heroic.

The government reports come across as remarkably honest assessments of what went wrong at Abu Ghraib in order to restore army values and honor. The only exception to this rule is the relentless effort to shift all (not even most) culpability from the top brass onto low-ranking soldiers. This effort, in itself, was labeled as dishonorable by most of the soldiers and officers I met at Fort Hood. I was told repeatedly that, according to army values, officers are accountable for the actions of their soldiers. We have seen that during the trials, a high-ranking officer on one of the juries was quoted by the *New York Times* as saying that the abuse at Abu Ghraib signified a failure in leadership. Arguably, most army officers would agree with him in principle and on the basis of army codes of honor.

As for the Iraqi prisoners, honor and courage were exhibited by those who testified on behalf of accused American soldiers. Those prisoners were not obligated to rise in defense of their captors. The news media tended to ignore the testimonials of these particular prisoners, but, indeed, their testimony is a noteworthy event. In general, precious little is known about the Iraqi prisoners. It seems that no rational system was in place to give them fair trials, punish the guilty, and release the innocent.

Throughout this book, I have argued that one must consider the many layers of authority that the abuse at Abu Ghraib violated. This applies to the layers of shame and honor as well. The military judge at Fort Hood focused on violations of the UCMJ but not the Geneva Conventions. By contrast, the United States Supreme Court ruled on June 29, 2006, that regarding U.S. policy to establish military commissions at Guantánamo Bay, "its structure and procedures violate both the UCMJ and the four Geneva Conventions signed in 1949."[6] It is particularly noteworthy that the Court cited the Geneva Conventions in addition to United States military laws because the government had declared that the Geneva Conventions do not apply to the prisoners at Gitmo. Similar to the approach taken by the Supreme Court, the government reports describe the abuse at Abu Ghraib as violations of both the Geneva Conventions and the UCMJ. Without wishing to reenter this complex legal discussion, the important point is that both the UCMJ and the Geneva Conventions represent different layers of a vast, interlocking, code of honor. We have seen in the testimony that other codes of honor in this interlocking, layered system of values were violated as well, including the ethical code of the AMA and the ethical code of the International Red Cross.

In general, a meticulous reading of the testimony at Fort Hood suggests an interlocking and vast layering of shame as well as honor from the soldier on the ground through the orchard keepers to international institutions and treaties. The trials were not just about the shame of a handful of soldiers or just the U.S. Army. Similarly, any serious effort to restore the codes of honor must go beyond the handful of soldiers and the army to include the honor and prestige of the Geneva Conventions and other international treaties.

Conclusion

The courts-martial humanized the rotten apples and all the other witnesses and participants in the trials—except the prisoners. The supposedly corrupt soldiers did not come across as monsters. Instead, they came across as ordinary people who were caught up in hellish circumstances that they did not choose or create, that they could not change, and that they could not escape. All the soldiers who testified consistently described Abu Ghraib as a weird, crazy, hellish, abnormal, nasty, bizarre place. The great irony is that the government sought to describe the defendants in negative terms but its own soldiers ended up describing the environment that the army created for them in negative terms. The army took the position of "Shame on you" with regard to the defendants. The defense literally said, "Shame on the army," in Spinner's words. Bergrin tried to put the army on trial. In the end, the soldiers who testified described the poisonous, fear-inducing, filthy, abandoned, crazy environment that the army created and failed to repair.

Notes

1. Janis Karpinski, *One Woman's Army: The Commanding General of Abu Ghraib Tells Her Story* (New York: Hyperion, 2005), 15.

2. Samuel Stouffer, *The American Soldier,* 2 vols. (Princeton, N.J.: Princeton University Press, 1949).

3. See, for example, Charles J. Hanley, "Documents Show Army Seized Wives as Tactic," Associated Press, January 27, 2006. Hanley writes, "The U.S. Army in Iraq has at least twice seized and jailed the wives of suspected insurgents in hopes of leveraging their husbands into surrender, U.S. military documents show. In one case, a secretive task force locked up the young mother of a nursing baby, a U.S. intelligence officer reported. . . . Iraqi human rights activist Hind al-Salehi contends that U.S. anti-insurgent units, coming up empty-handed in raids on suspects' houses, have at times detained wives to pressure men into turning themselves in." American journalist Jill Carroll seems to have been kidnapped partly as a way to pressure the army to release some of the Iraqi women. See Sameer N. Yaccoub, "U.S. Military to Release Five Iraqi Women." Associated Press, January 26, 2006.

4. See, for example, James Yee, with Aimee Molloy, *For God and Country: Faith and Patriotism under Fire* (New York: Public Affairs, 2005).

5. The alleged fear of dogs is in reality a Muslim cultural belief that holds that dogs should not be present during prayers.

6. *Hamdan v. Rumsfeld, Secretary of Defense, et al.,* decided June 29, 2006, No. 05-184.2006(3).

CHAPTER EIGHT

RECOGNIZING AND OVERCOMING DYSFUNCTIONAL RESPONSES TO ABU GHRAIB

The abuse at Abu Ghraib was part of a widespread pattern of abuse that includes Guantánamo Bay, Afghanistan, and other sites in Iraq. Government reports describe a poisoned or otherwise toxic social climate, atmosphere, and environment at Abu Ghraib that can be traced to unlawful techniques and attitudes imported from Guantánamo Bay and Afghanistan. During testimony, soldiers described Abu Ghraib as hell on Earth or used other words to that effect. The Geneva Conventions and other international treaties were violated at all of these sites of abuse. Soldiers consistently expressed the view that that they were confused as to the difference between right and wrong, and were not validated by their superiors in questioning, reporting, or trying to stop abuse.

A logical, rational response to these facts seems to be, Fix the problem by finding a way to detox Abu Ghraib and its consequences, and cut off the source of the poison. As of this writing, the source of the poison—Guantánamo Bay—is still operating without the protection of the Geneva Conventions. As of this writing, public policy regarding the meaning of the terms *torture, cruel, degrading,* and *dehumanizing treatment* is still confused and confusing. The United Nations has criticized the United States for its treatment of prisoners and "called for shutting down the detention camp at Guantanamo Bay, Cuba."[1] As mentioned in chapter 7, in a landmark decision, the U.S. Supreme Court ruled on June 29, 2006, that government policies at Guantánamo Bay violate both the *U.S. Code of Military Justice* and the Geneva Conventions.

By way of analogy, suppose that one had a relationship with a person who espoused the following attitudes and behaviors: I'm allowed to have affairs, but my partner is not. I'm not an addict, but others who do drugs are addicts. I'm a devout Christian, and nothing I do contradicts this. According to most psychologists, such a relationship would be dysfunctional, chaotic, and toxic. The person who espoused such contradictory attitudes could be accused of hypocrisy, betrayal, denial of reality, and other negative characteristics. Sometimes the healthier person or persons in such a toxic relationship become angry, violent, and dysfunctional in response to such obnoxious attitudes.

Let us extend this analogy to nations and international relationships. The discussion thus far suggests the following: If the government were a person, and it was explaining itself regarding Abu Ghraib and similar sites of torture, its words and behavior would seem to convey the following to the rest of the world: I am allowed to break the Geneva Conventions and other international human rights standards I have agreed to uphold, but the rest of the world must not break those standards. I do not support torture, but others who behave as I do are torturers. I am devoted to democracy and freedom, and nothing I do contradicts this. The rest of the world—and especially the Islamic world—reacts to these attitudes, words, and behaviors in the same way that most people would respond to a person who espoused similar attitudes, words, and behaviors: they are put off, repelled, and try to confront the contradictions in order to resolve them and make logical sense. Many Muslims throughout the world who have no connection to Iraq or the war on terrorism also turned to violence, exhibiting an attitude that is captured in the title of Akbar Ahmed's book, *Islam under Siege.*[2] It is counterproductive when both sides in any conflict see themselves as being under siege, when both sides perceive that their honor can be maintained by humiliating the other, and when each side sees the other in mainly negative terms.

I have no wish here to engage in "gaslighting" or the contest often found in dysfunctional relationships that can be characterized as "Who is really the bad guy here?" Throughout this book, I have sought the middle ground at all levels of analysis: the soldiers who have been labeled as rotten apples definitely possess good characteristics, *and* they did bad things that most of them regret; the army holds laudable standards that include duty, honor, and country, *and* it created a poisoned atmosphere for soldiers and prisoners alike that resulted in abuse and negative consequences for all concerned at Abu Ghraib and elsewhere; the United States had noble goals of bringing democracy to Iraq, *and* it disregarded the Geneva Conventions and other international treaties, which led to negative consequences; the U.S. government reports convey truths, facts, and honest assessments, *and* it scapegoats low-ranking soldiers so as to spare commanders from facing their responsibility; and so on. In practice, the war in Iraq was not treated as a separate war from Afghanistan but as part of the global war on terror. It is not clear whether the Geneva Conventions apply fully in the global war on terror, but it is clear that they were and are supposed to apply in Iraq.

As a result of the fact that, in practice, the Geneva Conventions were not applied in any of the wars that the United States has fought since 2001, "gaslighting" has emerged on an international scale as a result of the unsafe global environment created by the negative, dysfunctional attitudes uncovered thus far in this discussion. Through the sliding of meanings in the words and concepts it uses, the United States has cast a wide net in depicting any resistance as insurgency and terrorism. On the other hand, the Islamic world has cast a wide net in depicting all intentions by the United States as negative. For example, in February 2006, several events occurred in close proximity to one another that triggered widespread violence by Muslims throughout much of the world. Danish cartoonists re-issued "cartoons" of Mohamed that had already offended many Muslims in the winter of 2005. The Danish government defended the publication of these cartoons as an example of the right to free speech. Many Muslims linked the Danish problem to U.S. intentions in general as being anti-Muslim.

At about the same time, the UN issued a report that recommended that the United States shut down the detention facility at Guantánamo Bay and either release the prisoners or put them on trial. The U.S. government flatly rejected the UN's credibility and recommendation. In addition, in February 2006, Australian media broadcast about a thousand images from Abu Ghraib that had not been previously seen. Many of these photos and video clips depicted blood-stained cells at Abu Ghraib, new scenes of torture, soldiers engaged in sex and pornography, and other images that clearly revived the initial outrage at the first, relatively small batch of photos that were leaked to the media in the spring of 2004. The "new" images of abuse from Abu Ghraib were quickly broadcast throughout Muslim countries. Human rights organizations such as the ICRC, Amnesty International, the ACLU, and others quickly issued statements that the newly released images suggest systematic violations of the Geneva Conventions. Western media and governments could no longer tell whether the resulting demonstrations and violence from Nigeria through the Middle East to Indonesia were a response to the Danish "cartoons" or the fresh reminders of abuse at Abu Ghraib or the flagrant disregard for the UN and the Geneva Conventions or continued torture at Gitmo—or all these events, on top of other, long-accumulated events that many Muslims find humiliating and frustrating. What little is clear is that America is blamed, and its image as a beacon of democracy in the world has been tarnished to an extreme degree.

Chaos and confusion reign at seemingly every point in the long chain of events that led from 9/11 to Abu Ghraib. If Osama bin Laden was responsible for the terrorist attack that constitutes 9/11, why did the United States go to war against Iraq, which was not linked to 9/11 in any way? It almost seems as if the understandable desire for revenge concerning 9/11 was not focused on the perpetrators but was displaced onto those who were not responsible for 9/11. A widespread sliding of meanings occurred such that anyone who opposed the United States in any manner was labeled as a potential terrorist, insurgent, or sympathizer to terrorists and insurgents. You're either for us or against us. Black-or-white thinking took hold on a collective scale.

According to the Geneva Conventions, those who are captured during wartime are prisoners of war, and are entitled to specific rights. But in the sliding of meanings that occurred during the Iraq war, the term *prisoners of war* was replaced with the euphemisms *detainees* and *"PUCs"* (persons under control). Some journalists, human rights groups, and others engaged in this discourse also sometimes refer incorrectly to the prisoners in Iraq as "detainees."

Let me be clear that the critical issue here is not whether the Geneva Conventions applied or not, and consequently, whether the prisoners in Iraq were prisoners of war or detainees, PUCs, or some other euphemism. The Geneva Conventions apply because the United States is a signatory to them, thereby making persons who are imprisoned during war into prisoners of war. The same is true for other international conventions and treaties pertaining to torture and human rights. The critical issue is that the United States exempted itself from strict adherence to the Geneva Conventions at the same time that it continues to demand strict adherence to the Geneva Conventions as well as other human rights standards for its soldiers and from other nations. This is the rub in international relations at the present time—an attitude that seems to convey, "One law for me, but another law for everybody else."

In this and the last chapter, I propose specific public policy shifts that need to be implemented on many social layers, from the international through the national to the local levels of analysis, if constructive change is going to occur. One might think of this chapter as an application of psychological self-help principles to international relations and politics. It is cynical to disparage attitudes that promote respect, understanding, and efforts to find a middle ground in social interactions, including international relations. These positive attitudes are the building blocks of all successful relationships, between individuals, among families, and up to and including relationships among nations. In the words of Emile Durkheim, the first professor of sociology, "Family, nation, and humanity represent different phases of our social and moral evolution, stages that prepare for, and build upon, one another. Consequently, these groups may be superimposed without excluding one another."[3] The unwelcome alternative is to watch helplessly as the hatred and poisoned atmosphere represented by Abu Ghraib spills, spreads, and further corrodes wholesome values. The toxic social spill from Guantanamo through Afghanistan to Abu Ghraib is still injecting poison into international relations.

Respect for Moral Boundaries

The U.S. attitude toward the Geneva Conventions and other international treaties as moral boundaries for how warfare should be conducted at the present time may be characterized as a lack of respect. This negative change in attitude was signaled by White House memorandums about four years ago, against the objections of many officers, legal experts, and human rights organizations. The Geneva Conventions are deemed to apply and also not apply to some aspects of the war on terror. Torture has been distinguished from cruel, degrading, and inhumane treatment such that—at least in some memorandums—the government condones cruelty so long as it does not cross the line into torture, which is defined as permanent physical or mental injury. None of these terms are defined in practical terms that would set realistic moral boundaries for the soldier. Does breaking a detainee's bones constitute a permanent bodily injury if it is short of death? Does breaking a detainee's spirit so that he or she develops psychosis constitute a permanent mental injury? What about posttraumatic stress disorder? It is estimated that 20 percent of U.S. soldiers returning from Afghanistan and Iraq have developed PTSD, but no one, to my knowledge, has studied the rates of PTSD among prisoners. In any event, there is something ghastly about such legalistic calculations as to how much pain is permissible yet falls short of torture.

In particular, Article 17 of the Geneva Conventions forbids all physical or mental torture or any other form of coercion on prisoners of war to obtain any kind of information whatsoever. The pragmatic rule is that prisoners who refuse to answer may not be threatened, insulted, or maltreated in any way. The United States has contravened this article in at least two ways: by changing the definition of torture and changing the status of POWs to PUCs. Even when permanent physical damage and homicide has occurred in the treatment of detainees, courts-martial for such abuse have resulted mostly in reprimands. At the Abu Ghraib courts-martial at Fort Hood, the issue of psychological torture and mental damage to detainees who were put in isolation, handcuffed and abandoned in the dark, and otherwise driven to the point of psychosis was simply never raised. As I have indicated previously, the focus was on the titillating sexual and violent abuse as well as watching the abuse passively or posing in photographs or taking photographs. The government is not respecting the Geneva Conventions or its own expanded definition of torture. Mental and psychological torture is as real and devastating as physical torture.

Article 3, section 1b, of the Geneva Conventions forbids the taking of hostages. But as we have seen from the government reports as well as testimony at Fort Hood, it is common practice to arrest members of a suspect's family in the disorganized raids that U.S. soldiers perform on Iraqi homes. Abu Ghraib and other prisons hold women and family members as leverage for information or for a suspect to turn himself in. This openly admitted fact was ignored at the courts-martial and is largely ignored in the public discourse pertaining to the treatment of prisoners.

Article 3, section 1c, forbids humiliating and degrading treatment. Again, the commonplace nudity at Abu Ghraib and the fact that prisoners are routinely stripped, though evident from the courts-martial, photographs, government reports, and other evidence, is ignored. It does not register as a violation of human dignity or the Geneva Conventions. So much attention has been focused on sexual and physical violence that the ordinary, daily degradation of prisoners is scarcely noticed.

Many different articles and protocols to the Geneva Conventions exist, dating from 1864 through 1949. These were followed by additional statutes up to and including responses to war crimes in Yugoslavia and Rwanda. It is beyond the scope of the present discussion to delve into all or even most of these conventions from a legal point of view. The important points are that the Geneva Conventions operate in tandem with a host of other international conventions and treaties, and that all these statutes are supposed to regulate the conduct of war, including the treatment of civilians as well as prisoners. Thus, international treaties prohibit the destruction of civilian property, the targeting of civilians, the targeting of hospitals, the sieges of towns, and in general the wanton treatment of civilians during war.[4] For example, the very existence of a prison at Abu Ghraib violated the Geneva Conventions because it was in the middle of a war zone.[5]

For these reasons, it is not sufficient that the Geneva Conventions be merely posted or that soldiers are trained in them, although these are necessary steps to ensure their application. It is crucial that the Geneva Conventions, in tandem with other international treaties and conventions, are incorporated into strategies, policies, procedures, and other operational aspects of the conduct of warfare. For example, it would come across as a mockery of the Geneva Conventions if they were posted at prisons at the same time that civilians were unjustly arrested. The very fact that Abu Ghraib was in the middle of a war zone is a violation of the Geneva Conventions, which require that prisoners of war are kept in safe areas away from fighting.

Constant Chaos and Confusion

Taken together, and in tandem with other dysfunctional attitudes, the attitudes that have been discussed thus far perpetuate the state of chaos that has been cited as one of the factors that set the stage for abuse. Chaos and confusion are the primary words that jump out of the testimony and reports concerning Abu Ghraib. Psychologists have found that chronic chaos and confusion are among the primary characteristics of dysfunctional families and relationships. It may seem obvious that the antidote to chaos is long-term stability. Practically speaking, this would mean that the Geneva Conventions and other international treaties would have provided some predictability, stability, and order for soldiers and prisoners alike. However, in practice and in fact, the chronic chaos has not been confronted, and it continues at all levels of analysis, from the soldier on the ground who is confused as to the difference between lawful versus unlawful techniques to the government's debate as to the precise meaning of the word *torture.*

For example, in a statement released on November 4, 2005, Senator John McCain described the amendment he offered regarding detainees held by the United States: "Mr. President, I rise to offer an amendment that would (1) establish the Army Field Manual as the uniform standard for the interrogation of Department of Defense detainees and (2) prohibit cruel, inhuman, and degrading treatment of persons in the detention of the U.S. government."[6] The amendment passed ninety to nine in the U.S. Senate. (In an episode of *The Daily Show*, the comedian Jon Stewart wondered out loud as to who were the nine senators who voted for torture.) As I have shown in chapter 3, the *U.S. Army Field Manual on Interrogation,* or FM 34–52, is not a long-lasting or fixed normative standard because of the many confusing ways it was interpreted in Iraq, because it can be changed at any time by the executive branch, and because there exists confusion at the present time as to whether the 1987 or the 1992 versions (which differ greatly on the issue of how detainees should be treated) apply or are in sync with the Geneva Conventions and other treaties. Indeed, the senator seems to be aware of the tentative nature of FM 34-52 when he writes in his statement, "My amendment would not set the Field Manual in stone—it could be changed at any time." A standard or moral boundary that can be changed at any time is not a satisfactory standard or boundary in the long-term. Such a temporary standard can only promote further chaos.

Moreover, as I have shown, the Fay and Schlesinger reports cite the *Field Manual*—in its two contradictory versions—as contributing to the overall "confusion" at Abu Ghraib and elsewhere that led to abuse. The senator does *not* mention or imply the Geneva Conventions in his statement, although he does cite the Convention against Torture. The 1992 version of the *Field Manual* was supposed to have been in line with the Geneva Conventions, but because of the many memorandums that have watered-down the applicability of the Geneva Conventions, the connection between the two documents has become problematic. Indeed, as of this writing, the Geneva Conventions seem to have been dropped from discourse offered by the government pertaining to abuse.

The second part of the amendment is equally problematic because the terms *cruel, inhuman* and *degrading* hold divergent meanings for different human actors, groups and cultures. The amendment that was passed by the U.S. Senate does *not* address the practical and fundamental problems raised by Fishback and others concerning the confusion regarding the terms *cruel, inhuman,* and *degrading.* The Geneva Conventions offer a more fixed and stable normative standard than the army *Field Manual* in that they have remained unchanged for many years, would require a consensus of many nations to be changed, and prohibit specific actions and behaviors that leave little room for interpretations (e.g., nudity is flatly prohibited, so that no soldier has to decide whether forcing detainees to be nude is cruel, inhuman, or degrading).

And what about the issue of torture? As we have seen in chapter 3, some White House lawyers do not equate torture with cruel, inhumane, or degrading treatment. Does the McCain amendment prohibit torture? There is no easy answer to this question because of the context of the many conflicting memorandums concerning these issues. The prohibition against cruel, inhuman, or degrading treatment is in line with the Universal Declaration of Human Rights, the International Covenant on Civil and Political Rights, and the Convention against Torture. But it still does not offer practical guidance to the soldier in the midst of war; it does not distinguish these treatments from torture; and it does not resolve efforts by some lawyers to circumvent international standards through confusing definitions of the terms: *torture, cruel, inhumane,* and *degrading.*

In sum, McCain's amendment unwittingly adds to the present state of chaos and confusion, and it does not offer a real remedy.

I do not intend to delve into McCain's personal or political motives in framing the amendment in the way that it was worded. As a victim of torture during the Vietnam War, his personal motives are most likely noble. To his credit, he seems to take seriously the facts uncovered in the reports and testimony that soldiers were sincerely confused at Abu Ghraib and elsewhere as to the difference between right and wrong. But his amendment stops short of referring to a fixed moral standard that might eventually put an end to the chaos and confusion symbolized by Abu Ghraib. Indeed, as I write this book, the media reports that "the Pentagon is pushing for its new policy on prisoner detention to omit a key tenet of the Geneva Conventions that bans 'humiliating and degrading treatment' . . . and intends to issue a new *Army Field Manual*"[7]

Image versus Reality

McCain's amendment and other government reactions to Abu Ghraib seem to be more concerned with U.S. image than the reality of torture and its consequences. For example, he writes in his statement: "Prisoner abuses exact on us a terrible toll in the war of ideas, because inevitably these abuses become public. When they do, the cruel actions of a few darken the reputation of our country in the eyes of millions." At England's trial, the prosecutor also referred to the "war of ideas." It is true that the abuse at Abu Ghraib has darkened the reputation of the United States in the eyes of millions. It is not true that they were the cruel actions "of a few." They were the concerted actions of many. When one adds the abuse that has been documented at places other than Abu Ghraib, such as Guantánamo, it seems even less true that one is discussing the cruel actions of a few. One is discussing a pervasive and widespread pattern of abuse. Furthermore, the amendment addresses only the abuses that became public. Human Rights Watch reported in September 2005 that abuse in Iraq occurs in the backs of trucks, storage containers, hallways, and other places that are out of sight. The release in February 2006 of additional photographs from Abu Ghraib suggests that much of the abuse there had never become public. In addition, this amendment seems to imply the government's few bad apples theory: in reality, the problem is not limited to a few bad soldiers, but to a widespread, systemic pattern of abuse, as admitted in the government's own reports.

It seems that throughout the courts-martial, in the reports, and in this amendment, the dominant reaction to abuse by the U.S. government has been and continues to be about protecting its image. Karpinski reports in her book that the dominant reaction by her superiors to the release of the photos of abuse at Abu Ghraib was that the army had a public relations problem on its hands. Even the prosecutor at Fort Hood addressed the jury in terms of what the defendants did to stain the reputation of "his" army and the jury's army. Karpinski writes in this regard:

> "And I think about the impact this is going to have on my Army," Taguba said. Hearing the echo of Sanchez's rude formulation, I didn't have to wonder where he got that one from.
> "You know, sir," I said, "it's my Army, too."[8]

In reality, the U.S. Army is the army of the United States and does not belong to any individual. In reality, the United States has a formal obligation to follow the Geneva Conventions in tandem with other treaties because it is a signatory to them. The consequences to the United States for acting as if it were above international law and for being concerned with image more than substance have been severe and continue to mount: anti-American sentiment continues to grow among Muslims and America's allies as well. Concern with the image problems that stem from breaking internationally respected rules suggests a concern with simulacra commitment to international norms. In addition, the amendment does not raise concerns about the human rights of the Iraqi prisoners. The jurisdiction for this amendment is not specified. Does it apply to prisoners at Guantánamo and prisoners who are "rendered" to overseas "black sites" for torture?

The amendment seeks to establish the *Field Manual* as the basis for interrogation techniques while it admits that this standard can be changed at any time. This ambiguity suggests a greater concern for image than the reality of what the *Field Manual* represents vis-à-vis the Geneva Conventions. It is as if the amendment is an other-directed document that seeks to appeal to the "jury of one's peers"—namely, domestic public opinion. But public opinion shifts constantly in the galaxy of confusing choices and interpretations.[9] What seems to be cruel or degrading behavior today may not seem to be cruel or degrading behavior yesterday or tomorrow. The amendment comes across as an other-directed copy of inner-directed gyroscopic standards. The Geneva Conventions were written in an in-ner-directed era and were meant to last for at least a lifetime. Instead of referring to the Geneva Conventions, this amendment refers to a standard that could change in a month, a year, or at any other time.

McCain writes, "The enemy we fight has no respect for human life or human rights. They don't deserve our sympathy. But this isn't about who they are. This is about who we are. These are the values that distinguish us from our enemies, and we can never, never allow our enemies to take those values away." Elsewhere he adds, "We can't let prisoner abuse tarnish our image." But abuse is a problem that involves both U.S. policies and their impact on the Islamic world, including the rise in insurgency that resulted from the Abu Ghraib abuse. Yet the amendment focuses on the image and self-image of Americans. Outside the United States, many countries and governments regard the United States as not respecting human rights because of the abuse at Abu Ghraib and elsewhere, and also because of the inadequate responses to the abuse.

Scripted Responses and Magical Thinking

Psychologists typically look for signs of scripted emotional responses as one of many signs of dysfunctional responses to emotionally traumatic events. The Abu Ghraib saga holds many such scripted responses.

Had the photographs of abuse from Abu Ghraib not been leaked, American society might have succeeded in convincing itself—at least for a while—and others that the war on terror was like a movie: the "good guys" (Americans) won effortlessly against the "bad guys" (terrorists). In this script, the liberators were supposed to be greeted with flowers. Alas, the leaked photographs interrupted the script and the "magical thinking" about delivering liberation and instant democracy to Iraq. The good guys looked like bad guys in the photos. Instead of engaging in genuine soul-searching and reforms that would prevent such abuse in the future, Americans turned to yet another, scripted, performance to fix the problem in a magical way—the courts-martial at Fort Hood. Of course, magic is a fantasy. In reality, the courts-martial did not fix the problem.

Conclusion

One can try to imagine a genuinely emotional response to Abu Ghraib that psychologists might deem healthy and that would be an alternative to the shallow, dysfunctional, and mostly counterproductive responses described above. Shallow emotional responses are a defensive reaction that may work in the short run, but they are dysfunctional in the long run. The horrible reality of what happened at Abu Ghraib is not like a TV show. The response to the My Lai massacre in Vietnam was to strengthen U.S. commitment to international norms regarding war crimes, including the Geneva Conventions, and to rewrite the *Field Manual* such that it was more in line with international human rights standards. The response to Philip Zimbardo's famous Stanford Prison Experiment in the 1970s was that the U.S. Navy used films of his experiment as part of a rigorous course that was mandatory for its prison guards. The goal was to lessen the sorts of abuse that he and other social scientists characterized in terms of blind obedience to authority. Fixing the consequences of Abu Ghraib in the long term would require a realistic program with clear goals to improve America's long-term international relations, not just its short-term image.

Notes

1. Tim Golden, "U.S. Should Close Prison in Cuba, U.N. Panel Says," *New York Times,* May 20, 2006, A1

2. Akbar Ahmed, *Islam under Siege: Living Dangerously in a Post-honor World* (Cambridge: Polity, 2003).

3. Emile Durkheim, *Moral Education* (New York: Free Press, [1902] 1961), 74.

4. See, for example, Roy Gutman and David Rieff, *Crimes of War* (New York: Norton, 1999).

5. The following book offers a fine analysis of which specific conventions and treaties were violated in the war against Iraq: Richard Falk, Irene Gendzier, and Robert Jay Lifton, *Crimes of War: Iraq* (New York: Nation Books, 2006).

6. "Statement of Senator John McCain: Statement on Detainee Amendments on (1) the Army Field Manual and (2) Cruel, Inhumane, Degrading Treatment," November 4, 2005.

7. Julian Barnes, "Pentagon Set to Drop Geneva Convention," *Los Angeles Times,* June 6, 2006.

8. Janis Karpinski, *One Woman's Army: The Commanding General of Abu Ghraib Tells Her Story* (New York: Hyperion, 2005), 226.

9. See David Riesman, *The Lonely Crowd* (New Haven, Conn.: Yale University Press, [1950] 1992).

CHAPTER NINE

DETOX FOR THE CONTAMINATED APPLE ORCHARD

Based on the preceding analysis, I make the following general recommendations that may help to avoid future Abu Ghraibs and may help to ameliorate some of the negative consequences of the abuse at Abu Ghraib and elsewhere:

- Restore the military's traditional understanding of the doctrine of command responsibility to balance the trend shown in the Abu Ghraib trials to shift all blame onto low-ranking soldiers. In general, follow the principle that civilian and military leaders knew or *should have known* of the abuse committed below them in the chain of command, and are responsible for it.
- Restore, respect, and apply the Geneva Conventions in conjunction with other international treaties and conventions pertaining to human rights. The Geneva Conventions should not only be posted at U.S. military detention facilities but should be incorporated into all standard operating procedures, techniques, and variations of mission statements in general that pertain to warfare.
- Take steps to humanize both soldiers and prisoners in all conflicts that involve the use of military force. At the same time, take active, systematic, and long-term steps to prevent the dehumanization of soldiers and prisoners alike.
- Closely related, ensure that the most basic human needs are met for soldiers and prisoners alike in future military conflicts: food, water, access to medical care, toilet facilities, clothing, and shelter. In the current millennium, no military post or prison should resemble the cruel physical environments exemplified by Andersonville Prison during the Civil War.

- Take steps to treat PTSD in soldiers and prisoners alike, and take steps to minimize PTSD in future military conflicts as well as peacekeeping, detention, and other postcombat activities through the deliberate construction of healthy social environments. PTSD is the current version of "shell shock" or "combat fatigue," but it can be caused by factors other than and in addition to combat, such as the witnessing of and participation in chronic abuse. No army can function effectively when 20 percent of its combat troops suffer from PTSD. Democratization of conquered peoples cannot occur effectively when the majority of them have been traumatized and continue to be traumatized by dysfunctional social climates.
- Respect commitments to and advice from other international conventions, organizations, and treaties to which the United States is a signatory, including but not limited to the International Committee of the Red Cross, United Nations, the Convention against Torture, and others. Ideally, national and international standards should be synchronized as far as possible.
- Implement national and international codes of ethics in all professions that intersect with the military profession. Military doctors should follow the codes of the AMA and the World Medical Association. Military psychologists and psychiatrists should follow the ethics codes of the American Psychological Association and other respected professional organizations. Similar adherence to professional ethics should be followed with regard to military chaplains, lawyers, and other professionals. This would ensure a *layering* and sharing of responsibility to report and prevent abuse, especially in combat situations and at detention facilities.
- Make intelligent use of social scientists for constructive, positive contributions in understanding the enemy, maintaining the mental health of soldiers and prisoners alike, fostering cultural awareness, creating nontoxic social environments within the military, and so on. This would be in sharp contrast to the dubious use of psychologists and other behavioral scientists to break prisoners and to create the hostile, toxic social environments and ineffective interrogation "techniques" that led to abuse at Abu Ghraib, Guantánamo, and elsewhere. The social scientists should always work within the boundaries of their professional ethics—even with regard to interrogation.
- Create a policy whereby whistle-blowing in the military is validated, protected, and encouraged. Along these lines, the military should eliminate fear and intimidation as "methods" of obtaining information from its own soldiers regarding abuse. One alternative approach

might be to gain a soldier's "willing cooperation"—which is the same principle that the *U.S. Army Field Manual on Interrogation* advocates for interrogations.

- Promote cultural sensitivity and understanding among soldiers and prisoners alike. The purpose is not to "coddle" prisoners. Rather, the pragmatic goal should be to create and maintain a healthy social environment in which a mission can be accomplished in accordance with international human rights standards. The negative, long-term consequences of abuse outweigh perceived, short-term benefits. These long-term negative consequences affect the physical safety and mental health of soldiers, the image of the United States, morale within the military, and a host of other factors.

These recommendations are based on the facts that were uncovered in testimony and reports and upon the most fundamental assumptions in psychology and sociology about fixing dysfunctional social relationships. For example, the major problems at Abu Ghraib were chronic chaos, confusion and lack of validation, absence of fixed normative standards, severe supply issues, lack of responsibility and accountability, the disproportionate shifting of blame onto low-ranking soldiers, dehumanization and other negative factors, all of which contributed to abuse. But these are the universal problems of any dysfunctional social unit anywhere in the world, from the smallest (dysfunctional relationships and families) to the largest (dysfunctional workplaces and governments). The principles for fixing dysfunctional social units come from mountains of research and knowledge in both psychology and sociology. The basic principles that psychologists use to fix dysfunctional, toxic relationships are to establish firm boundaries, fixed and fair responsibility and accountability, fulfillment of basic human needs, an emotionally "safe" environment, and respect for other persons, among other positive conditions. Most therapists and most self-help books in psychology seem to rely on these principles. Similarly, structural-functionalism, which is the most dominant paradigm in sociology, is mostly about how healthy social systems are self-regulating and self-correcting when the proper norms, values, sanctions, and beliefs are in place and synchronized with each other.

Specifying the Poison and the Antidote at Abu Ghraib

The antidotes to the poisoned climate from Abu Ghraib—which continues to have negative consequences long after the incidents and the trials—must be very precise. It is clear from all the preceding facts and discussion that (1) the abuse at Abu Ghraib was part of a larger pattern of abuse at Guantánamo, in Afghanistan, and elsewhere in Iraq; and (2) the social system at Abu Ghraib did *not* self-correct. What was the nature of the "poison" at Abu Ghraib such that it not only led to abuse, but failed to trigger self-corrective mechanisms? The most important conclusion that can be drawn from the preceding analysis of the trials, reports, and other facts pertaining to Abu Ghraib, is the following: The social environment at Abu Ghraib was characterized by chronic and extreme social chaos and social disorganization at the same time that evidence suggests that unlawful directives and policies were issued by officers high in the chain of command to (1) Gitmoize Abu Ghraib and (2) "break" the detainees through a policy encoded in the phrase "We're taking off the gloves, gentlemen." In a sense, the gloves were already taken off in 2002 with the torture memorandums and the weakening of adherence to the Geneva Conventions, so that the order issued in 2003 was just one of several expressions of this policy.

I do not wish to get into a philosophical or academic argument here as to what constitutes lawful versus unlawful or secret versus open. Such discussions can become as tedious and impractical as the debate during Lynndie England's trial as to the meaning of the phrase "knows the difference between right and wrong." Whose standard of right and wrong is being invoked? Is it the standard of one soldier or one component of the Army or a nation or the international community? Typically, standards of right and wrong involve all of these simultaneously. Laws and norms always come in layers—ranging from local through national up to international—and abuse always violates several layers of laws and norms simultaneously. For the purposes of the present discussion, the important point is that such discussions bespeak the very conceptual chaos that has dogged the Abu Ghraib drama from the outset. The United States is a signatory to the Geneva Conventions; hence, any orders, policies, procedures, and so on that were out of sync with the Geneva Conventions were unlawful. Psychologists have already established that *toxic* families and relationships exhibit secrets and confusing standards as *symptoms* of dysfunction. The secrets and the unlawfulness can be rationalized and excused ad infinitum, but in the end, an unlawful order is just that—unlawful. A similar principle can be applied to national and international levels of analysis: the secrecy and lack of consensus on the difference between "right" and "wrong" bespeaks the poisoned atmosphere exhibited at Abu Ghraib, that has spilled over into a much wider context internationally.

Gitmoization is at best a contentious policy by international standards, while, at worst, it violates the Geneva Conventions. The most significant aspect of Gitmoization is that it turned Abu Ghraib—like its model, Guantánamo Bay—into a total interrogation unit involving all soldiers, twenty-four hours a day, seven days a week. It seems that there was no real distinction between "interrogation" and "detention." Rather, everything that was done at Abu Ghraib, from the forced nudity to the constant yelling and screaming was part of an illicit, imported "interrogation technique" designed to break the wills of prisoners. In Karpinski's words:

> The next day we greeted another visitor, who really would change our lives. Major Geoffrey Miller, commander of the terrorist detention center in Guantanamo Bay, Cuba, had been sent … to suggest improvements.… His prisoners, accused terrorists of many nationalities, were not regarded as prisoners of war, and thus were not subject to the restrictions of the Geneva Conventions. Ours were. It was hard to see how Miller could "Gitmo-ize" a chaotic hellhole like Abu Ghraib.[1]

The antidote to this poisoned state of affairs seems straightforward: Gitmoization is yet another euphemism for the reality of deliberately creating an unlawful social environment. The United Nations and international human rights groups have demanded that Guantánamo Bay be shut down and the prisoners be given access to legal due process. The Supreme Court decision handed down on June 29, 2006, declares that the current legal policies regarding Gitmo violate both the Geneva Conventions and the UCMJ. It seems that policies in Afghanistan were a variation of Gitmoization, although at this point in time, it is not clear which came first.

Bottom-Up versus Top-Down Explanations of Legal Responsibility

The U.S. government chose a bottom-up approach to legal responsibility that is out of sync with the top-down approach established by the International Tribunal at the Hague. Specifically, the least powerful and lowest-ranking soldiers who participated in the abuses at Abu Ghraib have been made into scapegoats who have absorbed *all* (not even most) of the criminal responsibility as of this writing. This bottom-up approach to legal responsibility is out of sync with the facts that were revealed, with the military doctrine of command responsibility, with international standards of command responsibility—and with common sense. Testimony revealed beyond any reasonable doubt that some officers were aware of and condoned the abuse, tacitly or overtly. To be sure, the military intelligence officers who were the most aware of the abuse were the least mentioned at the trials. Military protocol dictates that officers are responsible for the conduct of soldiers who are below them in the chain of command. International precedents for prosecuting war crimes focus on the responsibility of political and military leaders who hold the most power to influence events, including the power and obligation to prevent abuse. Common sense suggests that the lowest-ranking soldiers could not possibly be responsible for the creation of widespread policies that led to abuse.

However, the doctrine of command responsibility assumes that officers could have taken measures to report, prevent, or stop abuse. It is not immediately apparent that this is the case with regard to abuse from Abu Ghraib to Guantánamo. Overwhelming evidence emerges from reports and testimony that officers and soldiers alike were ignored, intimidated, invalidated, or otherwise rendered helpless when it came to efforts to exercise their duty in these regards. It seems to be the case that the doctrine of command responsibility presupposes a fairly normative, self-correcting structure in which some officers and soldiers *choose* to do unlawful things when they have the power to do lawful things. The poisoned climate at Abu Ghraib and elsewhere seems to have prevented such genuine powers of agency. Further prosecution is not likely to fix the systemic problems that have been uncovered. The poisoned climate has to be detoxified to the point that command responsibility can function.

It is evident from both testimony and reports that the main causes of the abuse at Abu Ghraib were chronic social chaos and a "poisoned" social atmosphere. Significantly, the poison was injected into Abu Ghraib with the toxin called Gitmoization. It did not arise spontaneously at Abu Ghraib. The solutions to the abuse—the abuse that is ongoing at Gitmo and other places in Iraq as of this writing, as well as preventing abuse in the future—involve the self-conscious creation and maintenance of a social climate with built-in safeguards and antidotes to the social toxins that produced the abuse. The detoxification process should be taken seriously, will require a long period of time to implement, and will require real commitment. I have demonstrated throughout this book that the evils of Abu Ghraib were not an aberration or some sort of unique event. The abuse at Abu Ghraib was inevitable given the poisoned social climate that the army created over a long period.

Antidotes to Dehumanization for Both Soldiers and Prisoners

Immediate and commonsense steps can be taken to humanize both the prisoners *and* the soldiers. Both the government and the information media engaged in stereotyping of the rotten apples as un-American and monstrous individuals, and in stereotyping of the prisoners as terrorists, insurgents, "bad guys," or by other labels that imply that they were something other than humans who were abused. Again, testimony revealed that a more realistic appraisal lies somewhere between these extremes. The soldiers at Abu Ghraib came across as fully human—good and bad—in the testimony, and it was clear that the soldiers suffered from the abusive environment and from committing abuse. Many had symptoms of PTSD. Similarly, the prosecution could scarcely have emphasized more than it did that most of the prisoners at Abu Ghraib were *not* terrorists or insurgents, and that most *were* ordinary Iraqi citizens or ordinary Iraqi criminals. The antidote to dehumanization must aim at the harmful and useless degradation of both soldiers *and* prisoners.

An obvious start is the use of real names. We have seen that the prisoners at Abu Ghraib were referred to by numbers or nicknames and not by their real names—not even at the trials at Fort Hood. The prisoners should be called by their names and should be given name tags that display their real names. Writing on prisoners should be forbidden. The soldiers, also, should be required to display their real names. We have seen that discipline was so lax at Abu Ghraib that many soldiers did not recognize each other because many soldiers as well as civilian contractors and OGA representatives did not wear uniforms or identification markers. This issue may become heated between those who insist that the interrogators should be anonymous for the sake of security versus those who insist that prisoners have a right to know who is interrogating them and for what purpose. Arguments of this sort may be little more than a red herring. Security may have been an excuse, but not a real reason for dehumanizing practices. Why weren't the real names of prisoners used at the court-martials after the prosecution demonstrated beyond any doubt that the abused prisoners posed no security threat to the United States? The most reasonable answer seems to be: the dehumanization of prisoners had become so routinized that it carried over into the courtroom. It seems that prisoners were dehumanized out of *habit*. It is difficult to break any habits.

It has become a truism in law enforcement that when a victim is abducted by a dangerous criminal, appeals are sent to the criminal that include the victim's name. It is more difficult for any person to abuse another person who is seen as fully human versus a situation in which the victim is perceived as anonymous or less than human. A person's name, possessions, face, and idiosyncrasies make them seem fully human in the eyes of others. Conversely, mountains of social research have shown that crime and abuse are more frequent in settings that foster anonymity—ranging from urban centers to dysfunctional families. The anonymous victimizer does not fully experience his or her accountability. The anonymous victim is perceived as less than human.

Furthermore, nudity should be strictly forbidden. It is highly dehumanizing to be forced to strip naked, literally like an animal. Along these lines, hooding, shackling, needless strip searches, lack of privacy while using toilets and showers, and other practices that humiliate and dehumanize a person should be forbidden. If any of these intrusive practices *must* be performed, in the name of security or some legitimate goal, then they should be performed with the same safeguards and respect for human dignity that are required of doctors giving physical examinations or performing other intrusive acts. In other words, hooding, shackling, strip searches, and lack of privacy should not be business as usual or a policy without a rational purpose, as they were at Abu Ghraib. The policy should be one of respect for the privacy, dignity, and regard of the human person.

This is a tall order, given that some of these dehumanizing practices persist in U.S. civilian prisons. Indeed, they persist to some extent in "total institutions"[2] of all sorts (military academies, prisons, mental hospitals, etc.). Nevertheless, mountains of social research and theory suggest that dehumanization sets the stage for abuse. In the case of Abu Ghraib (and Guantánamo), the consequences of the policy of abuse have been grievous. If abuse is to be prevented, prisoners and soldiers alike have to be humanized.

Similarly, there was no reason to shackle the convicted soldiers at Fort Hood, just as there was no good reason to handcuff prisoners within the prison of Abu Ghraib. It seems that in both cases, the shackling was done mostly for the sake of humiliation—as part of what Erving Goffman calls a degradation ceremony. Shame and humiliation are an integral aspect of this story, from Abu Ghraib to Fort Hood. Where could a soldier on the premises of Fort Hood escape? Foucault may have been premature in his book, *Discipline and Punish*,[3] to argue that modern, civilized societies are moving away from punishing, humiliating, and controlling the body of the prisoner.

Some soldiers at Abu Ghraib were forced to live in jail cells, lacked adequate toilet facilities, did not have enough water, and in general, also lived "like animals." Testimony revealed that many of the soldiers were "grateful" for these improvements in contrast to the worse living conditions at Al-Hillah. The prison was under consistent attack from rockets, and was not protected adequately. I have already made the comparison of the living situation for soldiers at Abu Ghraib to the unsanitary, primitive living conditions of soldiers at the Civil War prison called Andersonville. It is also striking that at Guantánamo, like at Andersonville, a deliberate decision was made to detain prisoners under the hot sun, and *not* to build shelters for them. There can be no good or realistic excuse for failing to make progress in the course of over a century and a half with regard to how either prisoners or soldiers are treated by governments. Mistreatment of prisoners is counterproductive in the long run. There can be little doubt that the army has the funding and resources to provide tents, toilets, water, medicine, and other essentials that contribute to the human dignity of the soldiers as well as the prisoners. There can also be little doubt that the army could have and should have picked a site for a prison that would not be in a war zone (a decision that violates the Geneva Conventions), and could have and should have protected both the soldiers and prisoners from hostile attacks and the elements. We saw in chapter 2 that the Herrington report recommended that the army build a new facility instead of using Abu Ghraib—but these recommendations were ignored. To dismiss the extreme fight for survival at Abu Ghraib—for soldiers and prisoners alike—with the euphemism, "it was a difficult mission," is to evade reality as well as responsibility.

Again, mountains of psychological theory and research suggest that any individuals whose basic needs for survival are not met adequately (shelter, food, water, security) will and typically do revert to aggressive, "primitive," and antisocial behaviors. Prisoners will riot. Guards will become abusive. Everyone will develop symptoms of stress as the result of psychological trauma. As a rule, humans act fully human (responsible, kind, professional, etc.) only when their most fundamental needs are met. When people or animals are stressed, they resort to irrational fight-or-flight, aggressive behaviors. Testimony revealed that Abu Ghraib was perceived by the soldiers as something like the social setting in William Golding's novel, *The Lord of the Flies.* According to established international as well as U.S. military doctrines, orchard-keepers high in the chain of command were and remain responsible for establishing and failing to ameliorate the dehumanizing setting and policies at Abu Ghraib and elsewhere.

The Problem of PTSD

Another white elephant in the "room" that constitutes discussions of this sort is the topic of PTSD. According to estimates, as much as 20 percent of the American military force in Iraq suffers from PTSD. The three soldiers in the courts-martial that I followed suffered from this disorder, and none received treatment for it. Many of the soldiers who were witnesses also suffered from PTSD. It would be important for the military to accurately diagnose and actively treat PTSD among its soldiers.

PTSD is a serious disorder with severe consequences and impairments that prevent full functioning in any aspect of life, especially combat. The PTSD sufferer is prone to anxiety attacks, fits of crying, intrusive thoughts, depression, phobias, and other symptoms. PTSD is a general psychiatric diagnosis that pertains to the aftereffects of any event that is experienced as traumatic by an individual, *not* just combat. While PTSD has replaced the terms *shell shock* and *combat fatigue* in previous wars, a subtle difference from previous wars needs to be investigated. The soldiers at Abu Ghraib may have developed PTSD partly in response to the combat stress at Abu Ghraib, but they may have developed it also partly in response to the abusive, invalidating, disorienting, and in a word, "poisoned" social climate at Abu Ghraib. Witnessing and being forced to participate in abuse is itself a traumatic event that can lead to PTSD.

Independent, scholarly research is needed into the causes, extent, and prevalence of PTSD among soldiers who participated in recent wars. Particular attention should be paid to a soldier's exposure to abuse (witnessing or participating in abuse) in addition to exposure to combat. Recommendations should be made to create healthier social climates that ameliorate PTSD and how to avoid, repair, and correct toxic social climates that contribute to PTSD. The unwelcome and dysfunctional alternative is to wait for returning veterans to develop symptoms of PTSD once they are back in the United States, which is what happened following the Vietnam War. Rational plans to prevent or at least minimize PTSD among soldiers as well as civilians might be considered as an important component of planning for war in the future.

In general, abuse and the witnessing of abuse are among the several causes of PTSD. One more practical reason to avoid abuse is that abuse is detrimental to the mental health and fighting capacity of the military. We have seen that a working dog was traumatized by the social environment on tier 1–A. One can surmise that all the humans in that environment were likely to have been traumatized as well—prisoners and soldiers alike.

Despite the stigma associated with PTSD in the military, its consequences are serious: no military force can perform its missions effectively if a large portion of it is afflicted with this disorder. Soldiers should be screened for diagnosis with this disorder, and if they are diagnosed, they should be treated. Several soldiers with PTSD disclosed to me that they were afraid to seek treatment from Army physicians because the form that is handed to them at the clinics stated that anything they disclosed about the cause of their symptoms could be used against them. Soldiers should be able to seek treatment for PTSD without fear or intimidation.

Finally, PTSD and other symptoms of trauma among prisoners should also be addressed. We have seen throughout this analysis that Iraqi prisoners are "invisible" and anonymous in a discussion of abuse that tends to be America-centric. There were many sources of psychological trauma (some deliberate) for Iraqi prisoners: isolation, abuse, humiliation, uncertainty, witnessing abuse, and so on. One should consider not only prisoners who are locked up in American facilities but also large populations under siege, as in Fallujah. In general, the United States cannot expect to democratize easily a population that has been traumatized. Studies should be conducted on the prevalence, cure, and prevention of PTSD in the Iraqi population that has been traumatized by war and abuse.

Antidotes to Chaos

The theme of chronic chaos runs through both the testimony at Fort Hood and the U.S. government reports that were suppressed at the courts-martial. Most people follow rules that they can *respect* and understand. The norms and rules must be in sync with each other and with *layers* of authority on local, national, and international levels.

The Geneva Conventions Do Apply in Iraq and Should Be Enforced

We have seen that the Geneva Conventions are supposed to apply in Iraq. In practice, the Geneva Conventions have not been enforced in Iraq and testimony revealed that U.S. troops get incomplete or perfunctory training in the Geneva Conventions, if they get any training at all. Soldiers testified that they received no more than an hour and a half of training in the Geneva Conventions. Privately, some soldiers told me that the training "was a joke." It is recommended that the U.S. honors its obligation to the Geneva Conventions in the ongoing war in Iraq. There exist serious negative consequences for the United States of not honoring the Geneva Conventions. These consequences include but are not limited to the creation of Gitmoization as a legal no-man's land that then influences other sites; the perception that the U.S. acts as if it were above international law; a deterioration in international relations; a marked drop in prestige for the United States when it comes to enforcing human rights where they need to be enforced internationally; the real danger that U.S. soldiers who become prisoners of war may not be afforded the protections of the Geneva Conventions as retaliation; growing anti-American sentiment internationally; and the increased likelihood that U.S. soldiers will commit more abuse in the war against Iraq and elsewhere. Furthermore, I make the following recommendations:

- U.S. military soldiers should get extensive training in the Geneva Conventions that lasts for several weeks and in the case of sensitive assignments and missions such as interrogations and detentions, that the training last for several months. Testimony suggests that at the present time, training in the Geneva Conventions is half-hearted at best. The training should be rigorous, and be comparable to other educational programs the United States has undertaken domestically, such as No Child Left Behind, standardized academic testing, the establishment of minimal standards, and so on. It should be a rigorous course that includes lectures, reading material, written tests, audiovisual presentations and all the other things that go into taking a course in anything, from Spanish to history. Training in the Geneva Conventions should not be treated as a joke.
- The recommendations by the authors of the U.S. government reports that the Geneva Conventions should be posted whenever and wherever prisoners are held should be taken seriously. The Geneva Conventions should be printed in English as well as Arabic and any other languages that are appropriate to the prison population. In addition, it seems reasonable that the military should post the name of a person to contact in cases where soldiers as well as prisoners witness violations of the Geneva Conventions. The posting of the Geneva Conventions should be more than a dead letter or an empty gesture. Definite, clear, and functional mechanisms for whistle-blowing and reporting abuse should also be posted.
- The *Field Manual* should be in line with the Geneva Conventions. Senator McCain's and any other similar amendments in the future

regarding the use of the *Field Manual* should specify that no provision may be out of sync with the Geneva Conventions or other treaties signed by the United States, such as the Conventions against Torture. We have seen that this has been a problem with regard to the 1987 (which is out of sync) and 1992 (which is more in sync) versions of the *Field Manual,* and this problem should be resolved. If a particular version of the *Field Manual* is out of sync with the Geneva Conventions, what is the point of posting either standard? The standards will be in conflict with each other and will create still more confusion and chaos.

- All SOPs, memorandums, and other directives regarding interrogation and detention of prisoners of war should be required explicitly to comply with the Geneva Conventions. This compliance should be stated clearly and incorporated into the written SOP, memorandum, or other directive. Consider the analogy that most American universities require that the syllabi created by professors must include a statement that the professor will comply with the Americans with Disabilities Act. Similarly, the government should require that all documents pertaining to how prisoners are treated should incorporate a clear and written reference to compliance with the Geneva Conventions. Again, a contact person should be listed with a phone number, e-mail address, or other method of making contact if and when anyone wishes to report lack of compliance.

- The prisoners of war in Iraq are just that: prisoners of war. This fact should not be obscured with the misuse of euphemisms such as *detainees, PUCs,* or other terms. Prisoners of war are required to be protected by the Geneva Conventions. One must guard against the sliding of meanings which was evident even in the courtroom at Fort Hood, where prisoners were referred to as "detainees." According to the government's own reports, the fact remains that the Geneva Conventions were supposed to apply in Iraq so that the prisoners at Abu Ghraib were prisoners of war. Euphemisms ranging from *detainee* to *persons under control* were invented to refer to prisoners at Guantánamo and in Afghanistan, where the Geneva Conventions supposedly did not apply. Much is at stake in using the correct words to denote the appropriate meaning, because the attitudes of both soldiers and prisoners are affected by words. The status of being a POW automatically carries with it some prestige, rights, status, and accountability. A soldier might think twice about abusing a POW. But the words *detainee* and *PUC* connote a legal no man's land. What legal or moral boundary can prevent a soldier from abusing a PUC?

Other International Standards

In addition to being a signatory to the Geneva Conventions, the United States is a signatory to a plethora of other international treaties and standards pertaining to torture, human rights, and obligations to organizations such as the International Red Cross. All of these other international treaties and obligations should be honored and enforced. Again, these other conventions and human rights standards should not serve as empty gestures. Soldiers and officers should have access to a point of contact in order to report violations of any of these other international standards.

National and International Ethical and Professional Standards

We have seen that the roles of physicians, psychiatrists, medics, nurses, and others in the medical and helping professions have been compromised with regard to witnessing abuse and not reporting or preventing abuse in Guantánamo, Afghanistan, and Iraq.[4] The AMA should enforce its ethical standards among military personnel in the medical profession. The AMA is part of the World Medical Association, which strictly prohibits doctors from participating in abuse and torture. The same sanctions and enforcements that obligate domestic American doctors not to harm patients, not to condone abuse, and not to assist in abuse should be applied to U.S. military physicians anywhere in the world.[5] We have seen that the physicians and medics at Abu Ghraib were aware of the abuse, but they did not prevent or report it, as required by AMA as well as military norms of conduct. Instead, all the burden for reporting and preventing abuse was shifted onto low-ranking soldiers. The AMA shares some indirect culpability for the abuse of prisoners.

Reports indicate that psychiatrists, psychologists, and physicians were and are involved in the interrogations of detainees at Guantánamo Bay. It seems that the plan to Gitmoize Abu Ghraib also involved a plan to use psychiatrists, psychologists, and physicians in interrogations. If the "interrogations" are a euphemism for torture, then this plan has very disturbing implications. It brings to mind the roles of psychiatry in committing war crimes vis-à-vis the Serbian war criminals who were also psychiatrists, Dr. Jovan Raskovic and Dr. Radovan Karadzic. The American Psychiatric Association, the American Psychological Association, and international organizations in psychiatry and psychology have begun to take up this issue, debate it, and come up with clear standards for their professionals to follow. The use of psychiatrists and psychologists to devise normative methods of interrogation may be legitimate, but we have seen that the meaning of "interrogation" has often slid into psychological torture. Persons who work in the helping professions should not give tacit or explicit assistance in devising techniques of psychological torture.

Herein lies the rub. The "Report of the American Psychological Association Presidential Task Force on Psychological Ethics and National Security," issued in June 2005, asserts that "psychologists do not engage in, direct, support, facilitate, or offer training in torture or other cruel, inhuman, or degrading treatment and that psychologists have an ethical responsibility to be alert to and report any such acts to appropriate authorities" (1). However, we have seen that one of the major problems in comprehending torture as well as cruel, inhuman, or degrading treatment is that *these terms hold different meanings for different individuals and groups.* The "sliding of meanings" into chaotic interpretations afflicts this debate within the American Psychological Association. Moreover, the task force concluded that "it is consistent with the APA Ethics Code for psychologists to serve in consultative roles to interrogation and information gathering processes for national security related purposes." Again, the problem is that the term *interrogation* sometimes takes on ambiguous meanings that are tantamount to torture. To repeat: "interrogation" at Guantánamo and Abu Ghraib was not confined to specific acts, places, or times but blurred or "slid" into a 24/7 operation such that everyone was involved in "interrogation" at all times. The medical profession seems to be strong on ethics when it comes to one-to-one relationships with patients "but weak when applied to communities, and therefore open to distortion and misrepresentation."[6] U.S. medical and psychological professional organizations should take unambiguous and explicit stands regarding the moral boundaries established by the Geneva Conventions instead of relying on terms that can be interpreted and possibly misused in various ways.

Similarly, there exist national as well as international organizations and ethical standards for the conduct of lawyers, chaplains, and other professionals in the United States that should apply to U.S. military officers in these same professions. The professional ethical standards for the various professional groups should be enforced within the military in the same way that they are applied in civilian life. This applies to business corporations and private contractors which apparently did an unsatisfactory job of supplying water, food, interrogators, and other "commodities" to Abu

Ghraib. Such a layered strategy of professional ethics, proposed over a century ago by the sociologist Emile Durkheim,[7] would help to keep the various layers of ethical standards that emanate from the different professions in sync with each other and offer a powerful counterweight against the "poisoned atmosphere" that leads to abuse.

Other Organizations, Including Other Branches of the Military

The government reports, information media, and the courts-martial have framed the role of the U.S. Army as primary for discussing abuse at Abu Ghraib. However, and in fact, other branches of the U.S. military were and still are involved in the many adjunct activities, policies, and issues pertaining to Abu Ghraib. Some of the working dogs and their handlers were from the U.S. Navy. Some of the raids that arrested prisoners involved the U.S. Marine Corps. Abuse has been documented at Bagram Air Force Base in Afghanistan, which is run by the U.S. Air Force. Abuse has been documented among all the branches of the military at various sites ranging from Guantánamo and Afghanistan to Iraq. Civilian contractors and OGAs were involved from Guantánamo through Afghanistan to Iraq. The process of Gitmoization itself appears to be a joint military venture that involved the facilities of the navy and the techniques of the army, which were also influenced by civilian leadership as well as civilian contractors. The abuse is not limited to the U.S. Army or to Abu Ghraib but seems to be part of a pervasive and widespread pattern that involves elements of all branches of the military. In general, all the recommendations in this chapter for preventing abuse in the future apply to all the branches of the U.S. military as well as civilians who are involved in Department of Defense activities. It is misleading and incorrect to regard Abu Ghraib as an exclusively army problem.

The Intelligent Use of Social Scientists to Gather Intelligence and Maintain Social Order

Throughout the testimony and the U.S. government reports, one gathers ominous hints that learned treatises in psychology, sociology, and anthropology have been used in sinister ways as "how to manuals" for breaking down prisoners and abusing them. One such example is the deliberate effort to exploit the "Arab fear of dogs." In an article published in the *New Yorker,* Jane Mayer documents that Behavioral Science Consultation Teams, known as "Biscuits" in the military, do lend their professional knowledge and skills in devising interrogation techniques at Guantánamo and elsewhere.[8] Further inquiry should be conducted—by social scientists themselves—as to how the social sciences were misused to develop unlawful policies.

The bottom line is that these creepy misapplications of findings in the social sciences seem to have been largely ineffective. The *Field Manual* states that the goal of interrogation should be to obtain the prisoner's "willing cooperation." Willing cooperation yields desired information, if it exists, while torture and abuse do not yield useful information. The military should use findings from the social sciences to establish its already existing goals from the *Field Manual*: how to best establish "rapport" with prisoners, how to understand their culture so as to build positive emotions instead of hostility, and how to use tactics that will preserve the prisoner's human rights yet still obtain information.

Some philosophers, jurists, and social scientists have published opinions to the effect that torture is justified when the "good guys" need desperately to obtain information from "bad guys."[9] The most compelling retort to such reasoning was revealed by soldiers who served at Abu Ghraib and commented to the effect that "If the prisoners weren't bad guys before Abu Ghraib, they certainly will be bad guys afterwards." Those who support the use of torture for "good" causes seem to fail to consider the negative consequences of torture: Torture does not yield the desired information; torture dishonors the U.S. military; torture produces more people who will hate the United States. If one considers Abu Ghraib as a weird experiment of sorts in the social sciences, in which the hypothesis was that abuse and torture would yield information on insurgents, then one is compelled to conclude that the hypothesis was disproved. The government reports and testimony did not reveal any breakthrough in information as a result of the abuse that was committed. On the contrary, the insurgency increased since the torture season in the fall of 2003, and has been increasing in Iraq and some neighboring countries ever since.

Other Constructive and Ethical Usages of Behavioral Scientists

We have seen in chapter 2 that an internal psychological report on Abu Ghraib recommended that psychologists and other behavioral scientists should monitor social conditions and look for signs of stress, excessive anger and anxiety, and other symptoms of dysfunction. I agree with this recommendation and believe that it should be expanded: behavioral scientists should be used in numerous capacities to construct, maintain, and repair healthy social environments within the military, including prisons. Up to the present time, it seems that the main function of behavioral scientists has been with regard to interrogation. This has been a fruitful endeavor with regard to some versions of the *Field Manual* (the versions that are in sync with the Geneva Conventions) but a dismal failure with the interrogation methods and climate that came out of Guantánamo. In general, behavioral scientists should (1) restrict themselves to making ethical and effective recommendations with regard to interrogation, with the caveat that the boundaries between what constitutes lawful interrogation versus lawful detention should be spelled out clearly and followed; (2) lend their advice to tasks that go beyond interrogation and include treating and preventing PTSD in the military, minimizing trauma on civilian casualties of war, ensuring that self-correcting mechanisms are in place and function properly in the military, and other tasks that would lead to positive and constructive outcomes for the long-term goals of attaining peace and democracy.

Whistle-Blowing Should Be Validated and Protected

Government reports as well as testimony reveal a catastrophic breakdown in mechanisms for reporting abuse. Whistle-blowers were ignored or invalidated or intimidated or otherwise rendered ineffectual. This breakdown is evident in attempts that range from low-ranking soldiers trying to report abuse to officers such as Fishback, who was not allowed to testify in court.

The military should encourage and protect whistle-blowing, because it criminalizes the failure to report abuse as "dereliction of duty." Clear, specific, and nonintimidating mechanisms for reporting abuse should be established that go beyond the current and ineffectual mechanism of reporting abuse up the chain of command. One possible alternative is that abuse could be reported outside the chain of command, to a designated officer or point of contact whose job is to make sure that the reports travel up the chain of command. The military could make it clear and explicit that whistleblowers will not be punished or intimidated by anyone for reporting abuse. The purpose of this recommendation is to ensure that military units are capable of self-correction when unlawful behavior or climates are recognized.

The clear, and tragic lesson in the Abu Ghraib saga is that the chain of command did not function properly with regard to validating soldiers who reported unlawful behavior. Of course, one of several reasons for this is that part of the chain of command was apparently intent upon the unlawful implementation of Gitmoization. Whistle-blowing reform has to occur in tandem with other systemwide reform that ensures a healthy and self-correcting social system.

Cultural Sensitivity

The government reports as well as testimony revealed disturbing facts concerning cultural awareness of differences. In an effort to accomplish an important and complex mission for gathering intelligence, the army used untrained, inexperienced reservists, most of whom had never been outside the United States and had no skills for comprehending a foreign culture. The reports state that cultural insensitivity and racism were significant issues at Abu Ghraib. Implicitly, the reports suggest that long-term planning for constructive goals was also an issue.

Cultural sensitivity is not a luxury for university students who take courses in multiethnic studies. It is a necessity for accomplishing the most basic tasks in a contemporary, fast-paced, and globalized context. The soldier at Abu Ghraib had to confront fundamental cultural differences in everyday interaction with prisoners on occasions when prisoners required medicine, had to use toilets, needed to bathe, wanted to pray, and so on. Prisoners were sometimes abused simply for making ordinary requests, largely because soldiers did not understand them, but also because soldiers had dehumanized them. If soldiers could not communicate and exchange information regarding basic human needs, it is difficult to fathom how they could have recognized much less obtained valuable intelligence. The abuse itself impeded effective communication.

In line with the general approach taken in this book—namely, that a healthy, functioning social system, including a prison, is preferable to a dysfunctional one—for all the reasons already cited, cultural sensitivity training should be conducted with constructive goals in mind. One should not learn about Islamic culture in order to learn which "buttons" to push in order to degrade and humiliate prisoners. Such aims are counterproductive in the long run with regard to important goals such as gaining the cooperation of prisoners, promoting goodwill among Iraqi citizens, and promoting democracy.

Promoting Democracy

One can detect "magical thinking" in early predictions about the outcome of the wars that were fought against Afghanistan and Iraq. Democracy was going to blossom almost instantaneously, and the citizens would greet Americans with flowers. It is difficult to fathom how planners could have arrived at such unrealistic expectations given all the circumstances that have been reviewed in this book, from cultural insensitivity to outright abuse and torture.

In *Democracy in America,* Alexis de Tocqueville was right to observe that democracy spread throughout the United States (and not in Europe at the time he was writing) because of actions, behaviors, and what he called "habits of the heart"—not through ideological indoctrination.[10] In contrast to the aristocratic traditions in Europe, Americans tended to greet and interact with each other as equals, with less regard given to class and other indicators of social distance than that of their European counterparts. The important lesson to be learned from Tocqueville's apt conclusions, and applied to the postwar restructuring of Afghanistan and Iraq, is obvious: Americans might have been far more successful in spreading democracy among the peoples they conquered had they treated them with respect. Imagine how differently things might have turned out had the United States built and run a model, functional prison. Imagine how differently things might have turned out had the army's established interrogation techniques—which *are* in line with the Geneva Conventions—been applied at Guantánamo and elsewhere. Consider the multitude of interactions between Americans and Muslims as occasions in which Americans could have demonstrated, through example, how respect, equality, and the lessening of social distance between peoples promote goodwill and the spirit of democracy.

To be sure, Tocqueville also discussed the negative aspects of American democracy, including slavery and racism toward Native Americans. His assessment is objective. But, in the end, he believed that the symbol of America as a beacon of light set upon a hill would prevail and would influence other aspiring democracies in a positive manner. Arguably, a similar goal inspired Americans to support the war against Saddam Hussein in the first place. As of this writing, the goal has not been achieved because the negative aspects of American intervention have not been adequately confronted and repaired. One can only hope that Tocqueville's positive vision will prevail.

Peace with honor is always preferable to continued warfare, and military victory without honor is a hollow, short-lived achievement. The prosecution singled out the themes of U.S. Army honor and its opposite, shame to the army, as the central themes of the trials of Abu Ghraib. It does not seem to be the case that America's and the army's honor will be restored by scapegoating low-ranking soldiers and sending them to prison. Apparently, the dysfunctional social climates that led to the abuse are still in place. Honor to the victors can be restored by treating the vanquished with due respect in accordance with army, American, and international values regarding human rights.

Notes

1. Janis Karpinski, *One Woman's Army: The Commanding General of Abu Ghraib Tells Her Story* (New York: Hyperion, 2005), 197.

2. Erving Goffman, *Asylums* (New York: Anchor Books, 1967).

3. Michel Foucault, *Discipline and Punish: The Birth of the Prison* (New York: Vintage Books, 1977).

4. See M. Gregg Bloche and Jonathan H. Marks, "When Doctors Go to War," *New England Journal of Medicine,* January 6, 2005, 3–6.

5. See Jane Mayer, "The Experiment," *New Yorker,* July 11, 2005.

6. Michael Wilks, "A Stain on Medical Ethics," *The Lancet,* August 2005, 3.

7. See Emile Durkheim, *Professional Ethics and Civic Morals* (London: Routledge, [1902] 1993).

8. Mayer, "The Experiment."

9. See, for example, Jeffrey Tiel, "Rights Argument Invalid When It Comes to Matters of Evil Conduct," *Research News,* July/August 2005, 9.

10. Alexis de Tocqueville, *Democracy in America,* trans. Arthur Goldhammer (New York: Library of America, [1848] 2004).

INDEX

ABOUT THE AUTHOR

S.G. Mestrovic is professor of sociology at Texas A&M University. He has published extensively on social theory and war crimes pertaining to the war in the Balkans in the 1990s. His published books include *The Barbarian Temperament, Habits of the Balkan Heart,* and *Postemotional Society.*